$$\begin{bmatrix} \text{free speech} \\ \text{and} \\ \text{false profi}^t\text{s} \end{bmatrix}$$

free speech and false profits

ethics in the media

ted schwarz

The Pilgrim Press
Cleveland, Ohio

35792339

The Pilgrim Press, Cleveland, Ohio 44115

© 1996 by Ted Schwarz

All rights reserved. Published 1996

Printed in the United States of America on acid-free paper

01   99   98   97   96   5   4   3   2   1

LIBRARY OF CONGRESS CATALOGING-IN-PUBLICATION DATA

Schwarz, Ted, 1945–
    Free speech and false profits : ethics in the media / Ted Schwarz.
        p.   cm.
    Includes bibliographical references and index.
    ISBN 0-8298-1148-6 (alk. paper)
        1. Freedom of the press.   2. Freedom of speech.   3. Mass media—
Moral and ethical aspects.   I. Title.
PN4736.S38   1996
323.44'5—dc21   96-47386
                                                                                CIP

Congress shall make no law respecting an establishment of religion, or prohibiting the free exercise thereof; or abridging the freedom of speech, or of the press; or the right of the people peaceably to assemble, and to petition the Government for a redress of grievances.

—*The First Amendment to the United States Constitution*

Contents

Introduction: Whose Ethics Are They, Anyway?

The scandal had been building for years. Everyone knew that the politician was a womanizer, and the greater the power he accumulated, the more blatant he was about his romantic affairs. His security guards kept silent, of course, and journalists knew that their access to stories would be cut off if they revealed what, for them, was an open secret.

It was spring when the political leader went what most people considered too far. Trying to get a few minutes of peace in the midst of business meetings and ceremonial duties, he used a roof access to reach the one place where no one was likely to see him. Enjoying the morning air, he discovered that from his unusual vantage point he could see into surrounding homes. In one of them, a woman, perhaps the most beautiful he had ever seen, was bathing herself. She thought she was hidden from view, never suspecting that anyone might see her. But the man did see her, was fascinated by her beauty, carefully noted the location of her home, and then returned to his office and arranged an introduction.

The woman was married, and her husband, who was a soldier, was on active duty. She was undoubtedly surprised by the request to meet the politician, although she knew that to ask too many questions would not be wise. The politician was officially her husband's commander-in-chief. Although he could hold no higher office and was not in danger of losing his powerful position, he may have arranged to meet the families of some of the "little people" who served their country, as a way to impress those who would record the events. Certainly he was considered the most media-savvy of all those who had held his office, even doing some writing himself. But whatever the reason for the invitation, she knew she dared not refuse.

What happened next was never fully detailed by either of the two people involved. Some observers suspect that the woman had been raised to respect all male authority, no matter what was asked of her. Her parents were Orthodox Jews, and she and her husband followed the traditions of their faith. Far from being liberated, she was probably viewed as little more than her father's property until she came under the authority of her husband. Moreover, because her husband was a military man, where they lived, when they were together, and when they were apart were dictated by other powerful men who were to be obeyed at all costs. Thus she was probably accustomed to being passive and submissive, never thinking that such a background could have the consequences it had.

Later, when "inquiring minds" reviewed the scandal, public opinion was fairly evenly split. Some felt that the woman's marriage had been a bad one, that she had been so lonely that her judgment had been impaired, or that she had been afraid to say no to the man who was her husband's boss. Others agreed that she had had no intention of getting involved in such a predicament but still viewed her as calculating, a woman who understood how to turn a potentially bad situation into one that would bring her fame, fortune, and a life that she could never even have dreamed about had she refused his advances, raising a child alone. No matter what her motives, the woman let herself be seduced. And when the encounter was over, she was pregnant.

The politician knew that the soldier could cause him trouble. A scandal wouldn't force him from office, but it could make life difficult for him, especially because it would be easy to prove that the soldier was not the father of his girlfriend's baby. He decided that the simplest way to avoid trouble was to have the man murdered.

The incident occurred during a brief, bloody skirmish in a Middle East area where trouble was constantly flaring up. When the fighting began, the soldier was placed in a lead position facing the enemy's strongest troops. Normally there would have been troops supporting him on all sides. This time, however, the support unit was pulled back, so that no matter how lucky he was, no matter how valiantly he fought, the soldier's death was certain.

The adulterous widow did not know that her lover had killed her husband. As the wife of a military man frequently sent to trouble zones, she had always known that he might be killed in battle. She probably assumed that his death had been unavoidable, and when she grieved, she made no connection between her loss and her illicit love affair.

Eventually the widow returned to the concerns of daily living. She had no job prospects, a child on the way, and a rich, powerful lover who was willing to marry her. He apparently wanted to do the right thing, and so, for whatever reason, she agreed to spend the rest of her life with him.

The scandal was bad. Worse were the stories that the politician had other wives he had not divorced. But the twist of fate that caused all the media hype, led to inclusion of the story in a runaway best-selling book, and provided the subject of numerous sermons by outraged religious leaders, had to do with the man's children.

The politician's daughter was as beautiful as her mother. He knew that his lusting after female beauty was not unique. There would be many a man who would do literally anything to have the girl as his wife. What the politician did not expect was the tabloid-type story that unfolded.

One of his sons had quietly desired his sister from the time he had reached puberty. However, the politician was rich, and the family was large, so there were always people around to witness any attempt at incest.

Eventually the teenage boy could no longer restrain himself. He was going to have sex with his sister whether she wanted it or not.

The sister was close to her brother, loving him in an appropriate manner and being totally unaware of his immoral feelings toward her. When he became ill and asked to be left alone except for meals, no one questioned his wishes as being unusual. And when he asked to have his sister bring his meals to him, again no one was surprised or alarmed. The siblings seemed to be best friends, and the sister was happy to comfort her ailing brother.

Finally alone with his sister, the boy told her of his desires. She was shocked and angry, and started to flee, thinking him too weak to follow. Instead he overpowered her, removed her clothing, and raped her.

The politician, undoubtedly shocked, was amoral enough to look upon the incident as a case of "boys being boys." It was wrong, of course, but there would be no punishment.

Ultimately the sister was avenged. There were other children in the family, and one of the brothers felt that the disgrace to his sister could not be tolerated. He left home, took a job in another city, and marked time until he could arrange for a reunion of all his father's sons. When the reunion finally came, with no one suspecting any problems, his employees murdered his rapist brother.[1]

The politician's story represents the worst aspects of the media, at least according to contemporary critics of media ethics. First there was the fixation on the salacious. The politician was a brilliant man, well educated, fearless, and a born leader who had been honored for his bravery from the time he was a very young man. He was a poet, a songwriter, a musician, a gentle soul, and an often wise leader. His private life was an abomination, but was there a need to degrade him by telling the story in graphic detail, as occurred at least twice, the second time as part of a best-selling book?

Could the media have used more self-restraint? After all, critics may argue, the United States was not hurt by the questionable behavior of George Washington, whose collected letters recount a love affair with Sally Fairfax, or Abraham Lincoln's roving eye before his marriage, or Franklin Roosevelt's infidelities—or, for that matter, by John Kennedy, who cheated on his wife inside the White House itself. The public felt very different about the leadership roles and good works of these men than they did about their private lives, which hurt only the women they had married.

Martin Luther King Jr. had trouble with alcohol and at least once succumbed to extramarital temptation. But Dr. King had prepared himself for a life of scholarly contemplation, of teaching and preaching, of pastoring the members of a single church. He was not prepared to be thrust into the national spotlight, to be made the de facto leader of the Civil Rights movement and harshly criticized on all sides. He was damned for being too passive in his nonviolent philosophy. He was damned for being too active for his lunch-counter sit-ins, bus boycotts, and protest marches. He was accused of pushing too hard to bring change to long-established areas of racism, and he was challenged for not pushing hard enough. Tape recordings of his famous "I Have a Dream" speech during the 1967 March On Washington reveal the occasional angry cry of "F— you, Martin, we want it now!" Yet, because King did battle during an era when the media seemed to have more self-control, the focus was on his public works. By the time his private demons were revealed, most people had come to see his personal failings as proof of his greatness. He was a normal man, a man who could give in to stress and temptation, yet he still rose to heroic greatness when fate so demanded.

Today, King might be vilified for his weakness and overlooked for his enormous contributions. It seems that sleaze is an integral component of the business of the media, important even in selling advertising in broadcasting and print. The attitude of publishers and other media executives appears to be that if you can't be critical, if you can't find good sex scandals or catch politicians with their hand in the till, you will have a boring newspaper, magazine, or radio or television news show.

As cynical as this seems, the reality of much of the media is that tales of sex and violence are the stories of choice. They are shocking. They get attention. They sell. More important, this has long been the case, even in what is now studied as great literature, such as Shakespeare's plays, which tell of violent vengeance, incest, murder, teen suicide, and other horrors.

At the same time, it is possible to find much in the media that is good. From educational children's television programming to opportunities for even the poorest of individuals to enjoy great music, dance, and theatrical performances, much that is uplifting is available. There are also stories of ordinary citizens engaged in compassionate and at times heroic actions that show the triumph and glory of the human spirit. Thus, in spite of the less noble side of the popular media, the selective user has access to resources that can enhance the quality of life. The media industry is not the personification of Satan. It is a troublesome field, though—one in which ethical concerns are currently being raised almost exclusively outside the circle of professionals who control broadcasting, the print media, and the cyberspace world of online computer access services.

Media ethics is a difficult subject. When do the press, the movies, and radio and television go too far, and when does society tolerate too much? Should the electronic communication made possible by the Internet make available materials that contain pornographic sex and graphic violence to anyone with a computer and a modem? How dare the reporters think that we want sleaze, such as the story of the politician that begins this book? Why should there be "chat lines" on the Internet in which anyone can read descriptions of sexual acts best left within the privacy of the bedrooms of consenting adults? Why, say critics of the media, can't we get back to basic virtues, family values, perhaps even the uplifting words of Holy Scripture, which seemingly are appropriate for a country that prides itself on having been founded on Judeo-Christian principles?

One problem in addressing the question of media ethics is that one person's sleaze is another's moral inspiration. Some people are titillated by stories of adultery and murder in high office. They like their heroes to have feet of clay, to know that despite their prestige, big salaries, and great power, these guys are really no better than they are. If anything, the biggest difference between the two groups is that most of the readers or viewers of these stories would never commit such misdeeds themselves, although they might get a vicarious thrill by fantasizing about them.

Others feel that the press needs to tell these kinds of stories so that we can be outraged, for with outrage may come a return to conventional "family values" such as monogamy and children being born in wedlock. And still others feel that the press should let the private lives of public figures stay private. If such a person is doing wrong, it is up to someone else—the voters, the criminal justice system, or God—to correct matters.

Yet these divergent attitudes are the reasons I chose to begin this book with the story of a politician and his children. I wanted to shock, to titillate, and to remind readers that human behavior has not changed very much in well over two thousand years. The politician in question was King David. His girlfriend/wife was Bathsheba. Her murdered husband was Uriah. It was David's son, Amnon, who raped his sister, Tamar. And ultimately it was another of David's sons, Absalom, who avenged Tamar by having Amnon murdered. This drama, originally written on scrolls, was collected into the book we now call the Bible in approximately 90 C.E. This particular story, found in Second Samuel, is meant to teach morality, and is sometimes preached from the pulpit of a wide variety of denominations. At other times it goes unmentioned because it so severely undermines the image of the house of King David. Yet the truth is that if the politician had been a contemporary politician in power, society would be debating whether or not it was right to expose and capitalize on such scandals. The Internet would carry the debate worldwide, with chat lines being established to discuss the intimate details and titillating rumors concerning the incest, the cover-up, and the illicit love affair of David and Bathsheba before their marriage.

The family members would receive requests to appear on tabloid television and talk shows. Tamar might be a guest on *Geraldo*, as well as *Inside Edition* and *Hard Copy*. The murder trial of Absalom would make the cover of *People* magazine. An unauthorized biography of Bathsheba, a best-seller hot off the presses, would be produced as a television miniseries, and the surviving members of Uriah's family would sue to stop her from earning any proceeds. David would make the covers of *Time* and *Newsweek*. The *National Enquirer* would offer fees starting in the six figures to any of King David's present or former staff members who could provide eyewitness accounts of the love affair. The *National Examiner* would produce a photo re-creation of the murder of Amnon as part of its coverage of what would become the "Absalom Murder Case." Naturally, Court TV would be involved in the coverage of Absalom's trial, and *Life* magazine would do a retrospective on the tragic lives of the family of David.

Am I being facetious? How can I compare the stories in the Bible with contemporary journalism? After all, the Bible is filled with morality tales, stories of the lives of the very human individuals whose triumphs, failures, and occasional redemptions teach us about God, about right and wrong, about ethics and righteousness.

At the same time, it could be argued that present-day journalism frequently offers morality plays of its own. The O. J. Simpson murder trial involved a man who was a gifted athlete, a business success, surrounded by adoring women, and an individual of growing wealth. His public success could have defined him as one of "God's favored." Yet there was also an underside. Simpson was a man who admittedly was brutal during his marriage, who committed adultery, who pursued fame and fortune to the exclusion of other concerns. The murder of his ex-wife and a male friend of hers who chanced to come by at the wrong moment brought into focus this underside of Simpson even as the jury was hearing evidence. Based on the stories of his past told by those who knew him, Simpson was revealed to be good and bad, to have moral weaknesses and strengths, perhaps to be a vehicle for both God and Satan—or so it could be argued.

If we viewed the current state of the media in the context of a morality play, there are those who would argue that with the modern media we are writing a new Bible, this time an electronic messenger of good and evil. Television focuses our attention on moral issues just as the story of David is supposed to do.[2]

In the 1970s, technological breakthroughs resulted in Marshall McLuhan's discussing the idea of a "global village," a metaphor signifying that everyone on earth could share the same experiences the moment they occurred. The global village concept is meant to convey the idea of people having experiences throughout the world in a manner similar to that of the earliest human communities.

Ancient peoples were often isolated from one another. Travel was limited to a day's walk. Communities were established in areas where survival was fairly simple. If a source of water, wild food plants or soil that could be farmed, and fish, fowl, or other wild game were available, a settlement could sustain itself. In the simplest cultures, the people were hunters and gatherers, working together to meet the collective needs. They lived as extended families, a lifestyle that continues to exist in some isolated parts of the world.

In more advanced cultures, people bartered their skills in making needed objects for a share of food they neither hunted nor gathered. A shoemaker might barter a pair of shoes for a chicken. A clothing maker could trade warm garments for vegetables grown by someone else.

When small communities lived in isolation, the stories relating to the people in those communities were self-censored, never deviating from what was considered appropriate by the extended communal family. The stories they told, the language they used, the humor that was part of their culture might be obscene by the standards of a community a hundred miles away, but the two communities would never interact, so there was no conflict.

The introduction of the horse changed everything. Distances far too great to be covered on foot could be traveled routinely. For the first time in history, people could regularly encounter radically different ideas about interpersonal relationships, about language, about the stories that shaped their cultures. Along the way they needed something that would transcend the culture of barter, so they developed coins. It was from these coins that the first newspapers evolved.

The idea behind the development of coins is simple. Within a village, everyone had skills that were of some value to others in the group. The man who raised chickens could trade them to the man who made shoes. The woman who gathered fruit could exchange some of what she took from trees and bushes for clothing made by the person who sewed animal hides. An artist would create carvings of a design that pleased the others in the community. But once someone could mount a horse and travel for several days to a distant village, the horizon expanded, and what had been acceptable barter might no longer be desired. Thus, instead of trading actual labor, which might be difficult for those who were not neighbors to exchange, people began to use tokens, or coins, as a more universally valuable representation of quantities of work to exchange. These coins were frequently made from precious metals prized in several different villages. The chicken raiser could thus place some of these coins in a pouch, ride to a distant village where everyone hated chicken, and still trade profitably. Instead of having to barter for some work he wanted done, he could trade a coin of equal value. By the days of the Roman Empire, coins were used for exchanging information. The empire was so vast that people in one part of the Roman world had no idea what was being done in other parts. Coins were used to display architectural wonders, sporting events, and other important components of Roman culture. The various changes in the Circus Maximus, the massive arena where chariot races and other events were held, were all chronicled on Roman coins. In addition, power struggles were documented.

The emperor always appeared on the obverse, or "heads," side of the coin. If a second person's portrait appeared on the same side, he or she was considered a coruler. If the two heads were placed as equals, the power was shared; if one head was in front of the other, the person in front was in charge.

The most dramatic "soap opera" conveyed on the coin was the story of the emperor Nero and his mother, Agrippina, who maintained an incestuous relationship with her son in order to have power. This situation was confirmed in the eyes of Roman citizens by the coins, which depicted their heads together on the obverse side. When Nero began asserting his independence from Agrippina, he placed her portrait on the reverse side. This told the people that Agrippina no longer should be considered their ruler, but that she was still to be honored.

Finally, Nero decided to break with his mother entirely. He had her portrait removed from the coins, an act that suggested to all the people, including Agrippina herself, that she was to be killed. When Nero arranged for her to travel on a barge with her handmaiden and some guards, none of whom were familiar to her, Agrippina knew she was in danger. When the guards pulled out support poles and collapsed the barge while they moved onto an escape vessel, she knew this was to be the moment of her death. Fortunately, the guards did not recognize her, and when Agrippina's handmaiden began shouting to be saved, claiming to be Nero's mother, Agrippina remained silent. The guards clubbed the handmaiden to death and rescued Agrippina. She managed to foil the murder plots until 59 C.E., five years into her son's reign, although the coin designs made it clear that she would never reach old age.

The coins were the news medium of their day. They told stories of sex, violence, politics, business, and sports. And because of the way they circulated, they catered to what some people felt were the lowest of the peasant class.

In more contemporary times, the philosopher, statesman, businessman, inventor, and ladies' man Benjamin Franklin seemingly delighted in stories of sex and violence when he published the *Pennsylvania Gazette*. Among the items found in the weekly publication were this one:

> Friday Night last, a certain St-n-c-tt-r was, it seems, in a fair way of dying the Death of a Nobleman; for being caught Napping with another Man's Wife, the injur'd Husband took the Advantage of his being asleep, and with a Knife began very diligently to cut off his Head. But the instrument not being equal to the intended Operation, much struggling prevented Success; and he was oblig'd to content himself for the present with bestowing on the Aggressor a sound Drubbing. The gap made in the side of the St-n-c-tt-r's Neck, tho deep, is not thought dangerous, but some People admire, that when the Person offended had so fair and suitable an Opportunity, it did not enter into his Head to turn St-n-c-tt-r himself.

The following week he printed:

> We hear, that on Tuesday last, a certain C-n-table having made an Agreement with a Neighboring Female, to Watch with her

that Night; she promised to leave a Window open for him to come in at; but he going his Rounds in the dark, unluckily mistook the Window, and got into a Room where another Woman was in bed, and her Husband it seems lying on a Couch not far distant. The good Woman perceiving presently by the extraordinary Fondness of her Bedfellow that it could not possibly be her Husband, made so much Disturbance as to wake the good man; who finding somebody had got into his Place without his Leave, began to lay about him unmercifully; and 'twas thought, that had not our poor mistaken Galant, call'd out manfully for Help (as if he were commanding Assistance in the King's name) and thereby raised the Family, he would have stood no more Chance for his Life between the Wife and Husband, than a captive L— between the two Thumb Nails.

The issue of ethics in the media is obviously not a recent concern. The story of David was written well before the saga of Nero and his mother showed up on Roman coins (though the selection of David's story for inclusion in the Bible was not made until more than thirty years after Nero's coins were struck). By the time of Ben Franklin, titillation was a significant selling point for the press, or so Franklin believed.

Today, with people traveling by train, plane, car, and boat, many feel it is unnecessary to know everything about a specific community. Instead, many people have chosen to limit their awareness to certain aspects of life—their jobs, methods of travel, and family concerns, for example. This often means that people lack the depth of understanding that comes from intimately sharing the full spectrum of life's experiences with those in their community.

The village of the past united rich and poor, men and women, powerful and weak. The more recent concept of the "global village" tries to explain how the development of sophisticated communications equipment, such as broadcast satellites, enabled widely disparate people to again share experiences simultaneously. Through television and radio, everyone in the world could learn of a typhoon striking Japan, starvation in Somalia, the plight of a poor family in the South Bronx and of rice farmers in Vietnam. Techniques were developed that allowed radio receivers to be constructed for as little as seven cents each, and such receivers were distributed among the poorest villagers in emerging nations. Television sets, though still relatively expensive, had been reduced in cost to the point where the poorest communities could afford to have one in the town's meeting area, as a kind of electronic newspaper. As a result, when the 1992 Olympic Games were broadcast, the audience was estimated to be one billion or more people. The most remote citizens of the world and the most sophisticated residents of urban centers could share in the athletic events as they happened. The global village seemed to have been achieved.

Ironically, the nations with the technology to achieve the global village now have citizenries that have been stunted by the proliferation of available media resources. Hundreds of television stations receivable by satellite and/or cable, radio programs, and the lure of Internet personal communication with strangers worldwide have all changed the global village concept. The person given the most choices may turn into the person who makes the least effort to utilize them. Instead of feasting from the smorgasbord of news, features, and a vast array of arts programming, some people are staying with the familiar. This may mean conservative religious programming, celebrity talk shows, old Western films, the Sci-Fi Channel, or extremist political diatribes. For every individual who delights in CNN (the Cable News Network) and A&E (the Arts & Entertainment Network) for a broad base of information, there are many more who may watch nothing but ESPN (all sports), MTV (rock music videos), or Comedy Central.

Curiously, it may be the people in underdeveloped nations who are most likely to utilize the best of the electronic access to the world. They have less technology and fewer choices—a situation much like that of Americans in the 1970s before the explosion of information. Thus they are more likely to understand the global village concept.

It is more than access to media that affects who we are, what we experience, and ultimately what we may come to believe—it is also how we choose from the offerings available to us. In the average city, free television programming is available on at least a half-dozen channels (VHF and UHF), and free radio reception is offered by an even greater number of AM and FM stations. These air the greatest numbers of programs most likely to pander to the extremes in taste in order to attract the most viewers and listeners.

The result is that there are reasons to be more concerned today than in the past. Although the issues of ethics have not changed, and the types of stories being told are basically the same, the way in which they are being made available is dramatically different. One concern is access; another is personal censorship through selective reading, listening, and viewing; and still another is how organizations provide us with the menu of choices we have to pick from.

Today, giant entertainment corporations, such as Time Warner, are blending information services, music, and related items as part of their corporate mix. Thus *Time* magazine's stories can affect the sales of Little, Brown's books, Warner Brothers' "gangsta rap" CDs and cassettes, and Warner's motion pictures, as well as the products of several other wholly or partially owned subsidiaries. Each division claims independence from the others, but the reality is that they all affect the parent corporation's profits. Thus there are ethical issues concerning not only what is published but also what is not published. The lack of independence of a media company can lead to certain stories being censored, even when publishing those stories is in the public interest. For instance, will NBC Television News ever do an in-depth study of safety in America's nuclear power plants as long as the network is owned by General Electric, a firm that makes critical components for nuclear plants?

Changes in society also raise ethical questions. There was a time when phonograph records were considered simply means of entertainment. The proliferation of portable cassette and compact disc players, used almost obsessively by young adults, has resulted in music having an unprecedented impact. Many sociologists, psychologists, religious leaders, and teachers fear that the lyrics young people listen to—and even the lifestyles of the entertainers—are having the same influence on the young as television and other media have. Should there be some regulation of content, some standards to which the performers are held—and if so, whose standards?

Added to all this is the issue of the computer, which can be used for everything from a self-contained entertainment medium to a link to information and entertainment worldwide. The Internet now allows access to a vast array of ideas, images, facts, and opinions. Some of it is as meaningless as cocktail party chatter, some as vital as good research, and some blatantly pornographic. Yet who is to decide what should be available?

Finally, if the global village is there for the taking, how do we make choices that will enable us to achieve the best of the concept? How do we select from the proliferation of media opportunities those that will help us both experience and pass on to our children such positive values as empathy, compassion, integrity, and morality?

1

How Journalists Practice to Perceive (and Deceive)

I used to always cover J.F.K. [John F. Kennedy] when he came west to Palm Springs. We knew all about his girlfriends, but the press in those days was a little different than they are now. Everything changed after Watergate. We always looked upon Kennedy's affairs with girls as a hobby, just like Eisenhower's golf. And then when Nixon came and did to the country what Kennedy was doing to the girls, it made it different.

—Jim Bacon, Hollywood columnist and author

It was the police beat reporters who uncovered the story. The mayor was regularly beating his wife, and the cops were always being called out to handle things. Reports were filed and there was no question that he was a wife beater. So when he separated from his wife, we felt the reason should be told. We didn't know if he was a woman hater or cracking from the stress of the job, but if he couldn't handle the stress, that was important news. The publisher told us to forget it. That was about his personal life. The mayor was to be considered untouchable when it came to his personal life.

—a city reporter for one of the largest daily newspapers in the United States (The mayor in question is considered a rising star on course for high political office.)

The year was 1964, and the major cities of the United States were frequently in turmoil. Racial tension was intense as President Lyndon Johnson, claiming to be carrying on the legacy of the recently assassinated President John Kennedy, helped Congress pass a series of civil rights acts that affected everything from education to commerce to education and jobs. During a long, hot summer, riots erupted in several Eastern and Midwestern communities. Although just out of high school, I made extra money by freelancing as a writer and photographer, covering racial unrest in Cleveland and New York. It was my first experience with violent, breaking news stories. It was also my introduction to how the media truly work.

One of the riots took place in a white working-class neighborhood in Cleveland. The city itself was typical of many parts of the Midwest where various immigrant groups settled. The Mayfield–Murray Hill area was known as Little Italy, although many of the people who lived there were from Sicily, a distinction the residents felt was important. The location was notorious for being the center of much organized-crime activity, a history that began during Prohibition, when bootleg whiskey was a major moneymaker. In earlier years, the Mayfield Road Gang had been connected with the Jewish Combination—Sicilian, Greek, and Jewish mobsters, some of whom eventually would also be connected with the Cleveland Gang and involved in the development of Las Vegas.

There was also a Chinatown, as well as neighborhoods where virtually everyone was Polish, or German, or Hungarian, or Irish. There were intense ethnic feelings, and woe to any man who walked into a bar in a neighborhood where he didn't belong.

One of the issues that divided the already fractured city was the school system. There had long been an unofficial policy of staffing the "best" schools (in white middle- and upper-income neighborhoods) with teachers of proven skills, and leaving the other schools (in African American, Appalachian white, and other low-income neighborhoods) with new, unproven teachers and those whose skills were pedestrian at best. Eventually, some of the schools found themselves overcrowded and forced to take measures such as holding half-day kindergarten classes, while other schools continued to provide full-day classes for all. It was decided to experiment with busing some of the children from the overcrowded schools, most of which were predominantly African American, to schools with extra space. The idea was not to integrate the classrooms; the classes would remain as they were, and the bused children would utilize previously unused rooms.

Reactions were swift and often violent. Parents were outraged. Although I spent months covering the stories and talking with older, more experienced journalists on the same assignments, it was never clear exactly what parents were angry about. There was talk of interracial dating and marriage, although most of the schools involved were elementary schools, where the children were still prepubescent. There was vague talk about "those people" affecting property values, the quality of education, and other issues that did not seem to relate to the facts. Yet ultimately it did not matter. Parents began picketing, roving white thugs began going to some of the locations to see who they could hassle, and violence occasionally occurred.

The first time I truly understood what the media faced was when I covered a demonstration. A veteran reporter had taught me that I would get the best story if I arrived early, stayed until after the demonstration was long over, and traveled with a minimum of equipment in evidence. A notebook and pen went into my shirt pocket, I carried two cameras, and I stuffed my pants pockets with film and a couple of extra lenses. I left my gadget bag in the car, and parked a quarter of a mile from the demonstration, walking to where the action was expected.

As the time for the demonstration approached, I watched the people gather. A few residents were out on their front porches, sitting on chairs, sometimes watching raptly, at other times doing knitting, needlepoint, or some other handiwork while periodically glancing toward the school. There were people with picket signs, although they either kept them on the ground or leaned against them rather than holding them up in the air.

I walked about, not picking up my camera, watching what was taking place, talking with people standing about or sitting on porches. A couple invited me to join them on their porch if events became too noisy.

A camera crew arrived. There were at least three people assigned to each television news car at the time—a man with a movie camera, a man handling the tape-recording, and the reporter. A news car would park near the men and women with signs, and nothing would happen. The camera crew would set up, the reporter would check his hair (female reporters were rarely used to cover such demonstrations in those days), the sound technician would check the levels, and the demonstrators would continue talking among themselves. Then the reporter would snap to attention while a test shot and sound level were taken. Immediately the demonstrators grabbed their signs and began parading about just behind the reporter. They would chant various slogans, brandish their signs, shake their fists, and look very angry.

Next, the reporter would interview people, usually trying to get the type of person who was almost irrationally angry yet looked rather benign. If it was a woman, she might seem like your mother or the mother of your best friend. If it was a man, he often looked like the strict but loving father you either had or wanted to have. Only the venom spoiled the image, a contrast that added a touch of drama.

The spokesperson would rant, the demonstrators would march, and the majority of the people at the site would be off-camera, often amused, watching the spectacle.

Then came the radio reporters. A microphone would be aimed toward the demonstrators, who obligingly chanted. Sometimes they would march. At other times, if the television cameras were no longer rolling, the demonstrators would just stand and shout. This would be used as background sound. Quieter, more serious interviews were held one-on-one with the leaders of the various factions involved. The newspaper reporters met with the least reaction. Still photographers, such as myself, would either shoot what was taking place or go to the demonstrators and orchestrate a reaction. "How angry are you?" the photographer might ask. "Wave your sign." "Make a fist." "A few of you get together, take your signs, and walk toward me like I'm the superintendent of schools."

The writers went quietly about, interviewing the people sitting on the porches and standing about. If the demonstrators were truly organized under a leader, that person would be quoted, as would any African Americans who showed up. African Americans were not confrontational at what I came to call "white riots," and almost none came by unless they felt that there was a strong reason for their presence.

The news coverage over the next twenty-four hours was interesting. The television spots, usually thirty seconds in length, would show images of anger and barely contained violence. It was obvious from watching television that this was a community on the verge of exploding. Emotions were high, tempers were flaring, and violence was imminent—or so the images implied.

The radio coverage was reasonably objective. The background sounds of the demonstrators implied more tension than I witnessed, but if the length of the broadcast allowed at least a minute for the story, the quotes seemed to be accurate reflections of what had taken place.

The print coverage was mixed. The story might be headlined "Violence Erupts at School Site," and the photograph chosen for illustration might show someone seemingly threatening violence. But the article was usually objective, explaining all sides of the issue through the words of the people involved. The reporters usually indicated that most of the people were curious, chance passersby, or area residents with no feelings one way or another, despite the actions of a handful of demonstrators.

Some of the stories seemed slanted by their lead-ins. "Tempers flared early this morning . . ." would imply a more hostile crowd than a lead such as "A handful of protesters demonstrated their frustrations . . ." Likewise, the more space given to the story, the more likely it would be that a complete reading would provide an objective picture of what had occurred.

During the time in the mid-1960s when I seemed to be going from one violent demonstration to another, I also noticed what happened when true anger existed. At one protest site, on an overcast morning when the skies threatened rain, a radio reporter was the first of the electronic media on the scene. He stepped from his car carrying the standard recording equipment of the day—a boxlike device, using three-inch reels of tape, the size of a large portable radio (transistors were still fairly new). And because there was no such thing as a built-in microphone, the radio reporter had to carry a large, hand-held mike covered with a windscreen so he could record the voices.

One woman, her eyes ablaze with fury, screamed, "This is none of your business. You don't live here. You've got no right to be here." And with that she picked up her umbrella and jammed it through the side of the tape recorder. The reporter got back into his car and left the scene.

Arriving camera crews were not allowed to unload their equipment, and when one enterprising cinematographer tried to shoot through an open car window while the reporter drove slowly by, several women rushed the car. They used their clothing to block the camera, shouting at the reporter to leave.

I slipped across the street, where a sympathetic neighbor let me stay on her porch provided I didn't try to use my still cameras or ask any questions. She also made a comment that spoke effectively to what was taking place. She said, "You people [the press] have no right to be here. This is something that matters greatly to us [local residents]."

Five years later I was working full-time for a newspaper when there was a race riot in the community. I was the newest reporter on the staff, as yet unproven, and so I was given less interesting assignments. During the week of violence I reported first to City Hall at 4:30 A.M., walking past a National Guard security area where four young men in uniform, each carrying a loaded rifle, kept their weapons trained on me until I showed them my press pass. Most of my time was spent answering telephones and calling various officials for comments about breaking events covered in the street by others.

For the first three days of coverage, a primary source within the predominantly African American area where the rioting was taking place was a well-spoken minister. He had contacted the reporters on the first night of the riot, and had remained a primary source of information. He was articulate and well dressed, and he explained that he was the spokesperson for the African American community. At the time, we believed him.

On the fourth day of the riot, a woman called the paper to complain about the coverage. "Don't you realize that we have block clubs in this neighborhood?" she asked. "Each street has people who meet together regularly to discuss common problems and work out solutions since we're too poor for the city to care. We don't have any spokesman. We're too diverse in our thinking for something like that. No two of us agree about anything other than we want to live decently, just like you people. I've checked around and none of us have ever heard of this so-called minister you're quoting all the time. You want to know what's happening, you send a reporter down here. All of us will talk with him. All the block clubs will cooperate. But we've never heard of this man you keep writing about."

Ten years later I was in Los Angeles covering the story of the Hillside Strangler. Ken Bianchi was a serial killer who, teamed with his cousin Angelo Buono, killed approximately a dozen young women in Los Angeles during several months. Bianchi himself would eventually be connected with seventeen deaths in three states.

The story held an international fascination. Because of intense media interest, the entire county of Los Angeles was held in fear. The killings actually took place within a fifteen-mile radius of the suburb of Glendale, but the terror was everywhere. Visitors frequently came armed, risking being charged with carrying an unlicensed handgun because they felt the need to protect themselves from the serial killer, who had yet to be identified.

The police work was intense and effective. Even in hindsight, few have faulted the thoroughness of the investigation, even though Bianchi was not caught until after he had committed two murders in Bellingham, Washington, several months after relocating from Los Angeles. The basic approach was to investigate all the people in any way connected with each victim, and then try to link the names and addresses to see who had contacts with more than one victim. Some men were found who had ten contacts, others with seven or eight. Ken Bianchi's name came up, but at the time he was known to be connected with only four of the victims. He was on the police list for investigation, although he would not be investigated until after the police checked out men who were known to have had contacts with more of the victims.

After Bianchi was caught, a reporter for the local CBS television affiliate in Washington went on the air, showing the computer printout that linked the killer with four of the victims. His voice angry, his face taut with righteous indignation, the reporter revealed the "startling" information and condemned the Los Angeles Police Department for not catching Bianchi.

I was in Los Angeles and saw the news report, so I called the reporter after he was off the air. I had been writing a book on the case, knew all the details, and had even interviewed this particular reporter because of what I felt was a sensationalized approach that caused more harm than good. "Didn't you know that there were better suspects than Bianchi?" I asked. "He was on the computer list with four contacts, but there were several with eight or more contacts who were being checked out first. It was only after his arrest and confession that more information was known."

The reporter said he did know about the other suspects and admitted they were better ones. He agreed that the LAPD and Sheriff's Homicide Division had done an excellent job, and given what they knew at the time, they were right to place Bianchi lower on the list.

"So why did you air a story that seemed to indicate the task force did not do their job?" I asked him.

Without hesitation he answered, "Because I have to earn points with my boss." The hint of scandal in the high-profile case was good for ratings; telling the truth apparently was not. The reporter never lied and the documents shown were accurate, but a false impression was given by the reporter's telling only a portion of the story.

More recently, during the Jimmy Carter presidency, the Iran hostage crisis occurred. Night after night the television news showed angry youths demonstrating outside the American embassy in Tehran. The impression given was that Iran was a place of endless violence, although according to journalists covering the story, the streets were calm everywhere else. People were living normal lives, going about their daily business. In fact, only a handful of extremists were involved. Later reports indicated that some, and perhaps most, of the demonstrators had been paid to be there.

A still more recent example was the O. J. Simpson trial. The basic facts were these: Simpson's ex-wife Nicole, and a friend named Ron Goldman, who was returning sunglasses her mother had left at the restaurant where he worked, were murdered in June 1994;

the murder weapon was a knife; the wounds were extensive; and the murders occurred late at night, at a time when Simpson could not account for his whereabouts. There was enough evidence linking the former football great with the murders for him to be arrested. But before he could be taken into custody, he and his friend Al Cowling seemingly tried to elude capture by driving along a Los Angeles freeway in a white Ford Bronco. Dozens of police cruisers pursued Simpson and his friend at speeds that never exceeded the fifty-five-mile-per-hour limit, and television cameras in helicopters covered the "chase." The arrest was broadcast as it happened, and for a couple of hours, television shows were preempted so that the low-speed pursuit could be viewed as it took place.

By August of 1995, when the trial had been going on for months, the major issue for the press was racism in the Los Angeles Police Department. Former homicide detective Mark Fuhrman was found to have worked with a screenwriter as a source of information about how the LAPD operated. She had tape-recorded him extensively, although it was unclear whether the tapes reflected his own personal racial views or simply documented dramatic moments that could have occurred given the nature of the department. But whether the tapes represented a scenario of fiction based on fact or one of accurate memories, the controversy was over hate speech. Fuhrman allegedly used the defamatory word "nigger" forty different times on the tapes, according to statements made to the press by defense lawyer Johnnie Cochran Jr. and as confirmed on the stand by the screenwriter. Neither the tapes nor the transcripts were made public, but the presumption of racism was never challenged after the testimony. This occurred despite Fuhrman's previously having claimed under oath that such hate speech had not been part of his vocabulary for the previous decade.

The focus of the majority of the reporters covering the trial turned to the issue of racism in the LAPD. They also began exploring Fuhrman's personal background, the shooting of an unarmed African American suspect in 1987, his psychiatric reports, and other details of his life and work.

The defense attorneys had long wanted to create the impression in the minds of the jurors that Detective Fuhrman may have planted a bloody glove that seemed to link Simpson with the murders. The idea was called into question much earlier in the trial when the prosecution called numerous uniformed patrol officers who felt that a glove could not have been planted without their seeing it happen. Their testimony seemed genuine, and the defense team's argument seemed to be an effort to try anything to get their client acquitted. They did not seem to have a firm belief in the truth of the scenario they were weaving.

Once the tapes were found, the focus of the media turned to racism. The LAPD homicide unit came under scrutiny. Mark Fuhrman was investigated. Television news anchors discussing what had been heard on the audiotapes often lowered their voices to what seemed a conspiratorial level. Then, after allowing time to hook the viewers, the anchors spoke of the "N word" Fuhrman had used. There were editorials about Fuhrman and his allegedly foul language. There were hints of disdain in the voices of the news anchors when the subject was discussed. And in the midst of this was one man, attending the courtroom sessions, trying to bring sense back to the media coverage. This man was the father of Ron Goldman, one of the two victims, who tried to remind the reporters that the criminal case was not about Fuhrman's life and racial attitudes but about the murders of Nicole Brown Simpson and Ron Goldman, two people who seemed to have been forgotten amid a story that was actually only a small aspect of the case.

Justice Potter Stewart, in the time between his retirement from the U.S. Supreme Court and his death, regularly lectured journalists about the fact that there is no public "right to know" under the

Constitution. There is only a right to publish. Material that is published does not have to be accurate. It can include lies, distortions, and half-truths. There may be civil penalties for irresponsible publishing, such as for libel and defamation, but the right to publish anything, regardless of how biased or outrageous, is what is held sacred under the First Amendment. Thus, reporting the news has always required judgment calls on the part of someone, whether the publisher, editor, radio or television station manager, or other responsible individual.

When most people think of media ethics, they think of the honesty of the reporting. They want to believe there is no bias, that if a story leaves the impression that someone is guilty of a crime, the impression is based on truth, not solely on the reporter's personal beliefs.

In most cases, news stories are indeed reliable, because most reporters covering the majority of stories have no reason to be inaccurate. They are chronicling events many others have witnessed, such as city council meetings, local tragedies, business activities, social events, and fashion shows. Even when a reporter develops a feature story on an unusual event or person, there are others who review his or her efforts, check copy, and confirm sources. However, the rare instance where the internal control system fails can result in great embarrassment, as the *Washington Post* discovered in connection with a story it ran on Sunday, September 28, 1980.

The feature article was written by Janet Cooke, a young African American woman who seemed typical of the future of journalism in America. She was a bright and aggressive, with brilliant writing skills and a sensitivity to the problems of the low-income ghetto areas too long ignored by all major newspapers in the country. Fearless on the streets, Cooke had encountered a "precocious little boy with sandy hair, velvety brown eyes and needle marks freckling the baby-smooth skin of his thin brown arms." He was a heroin addict, perhaps the youngest in the city. The tragedy was compounded by the details of the boy's plight. Jimmy was too young to buy heroin for himself, too young to learn to prepare the solution and to inject himself. He could steal, but such theft was unlikely. Instead it seemed that Jimmy was being victimized by one or more adults who were providing the heroin either to keep him quiet or because they found such a young junkie to be humorous. Jimmy's parents had failed him, neighbors had failed him, churches and other community resources had failed him. Only Janet Cooke seemed to have championed Jimmy's cause by writing her story.

The outrage was immediate. Mayor Marion Barry was forced to announce that Jimmy had been found and was undergoing therapy, a lie either of his creation or of the city agency that had failed to help the boy. Other reporters wanted to help Jimmy, but Janet Cooke was vague about his address and would not show colleagues where he lived.

Still the *Washington Post* was thrilled. Bob Woodward, the man who had been part of the reporting team that had helped to force Richard Nixon to resign from office rather than be impeached, producing the bestseller *All the President's Men* in the process, was Cooke's boss in the Metro section. He had overseen her progress, had approved the story, and was delighted that she had come up with something that would grab readers by their heartstrings. Countless others agreed, and the article won the Pulitzer Prize for feature writing that year.

The only problem was that Jimmy did not exist. Janet Cooke had fed the paper what it wanted, a story so dramatic that everyone in Washington was discussing it the following day. They could point with pride to the work of their star African American woman reporter, just as the paper I worked for years earlier could delight in its access to the minister who served as the "community spokesperson" during the riot.

Ben Bradlee, the executive editor of the *Post* at the time, later noted that, to him, "the story reeked of the sights and sounds and smells that editors love to give their readers."[3] He continued, "The possibility that the story was not true never entered my head. After the fact, some reporters, particularly Courtland Milloy, a streetwise black reporter, told me that they had questioned the story. Milloy had taken Cooke in his car to look for Jimmy's house. When she couldn't find it, he shared his doubts with Milton Coleman. . . . Coleman told others he thought Milloy was jealous."

The difference between the Janet Cooke incident and similar incidents involving other newspapers was the magnitude of the mistake and the way it was handled by the *Post*. The Pulitzer Prize was returned, of course, but the *Post* went further. Bradlee ordered the staff ombudsman, Bill Green, to investigate what had happened. Green was to treat the *Post* staff as he would any outside agency that had lost the public's trust. He was to investigate every aspect of the incident, from Janet Cooke's background (fraudulent credentials, including a claim that she had graduated magna cum laude from Vassar College) to the way in which Bob Woodward ran the Metro section. In the end, Green produced an article so insightful and so devastating that it was the type of piece that any newspaper would love to be able to run about a rival. It was, in the words of billionaire Ross Perot, "gotcha!" journalism at its best— but in this case produced by the newspaper that was the subject of the critique. What led to the *Post*'s gloomiest hour was also the avenue for what was, ethically, its finest hour.

The greatest concern the public should have about the media is the one that few people ever consider—what a newspaper, magazine, radio station, or television station does *not* cover. Yet this is one of the first areas where there are ethical breakdowns in all the media. Someone chooses which stories are assigned. Someone chooses how the stories will be covered, including which people will be interviewed. Someone chooses the amount of time (TV and radio) or space (newspaper and magazine) that will be devoted to each aspect of a story.

It is the issue of the "gatekeeper" that makes many media experts fear the results of conglomerate purchases of information distributors. When one person or one company begins to dominate the ownership of large sections of the media, the stories chosen for coverage may become limited.

Earlier I mentioned my efforts to cover a community briefly torn apart by a race riot. The owner of the paper had other media interests throughout the United States, but his power was strongest in the city where I worked. In addition to the only daily newspaper, he owned the only twenty-four-hour radio station, the only television station, and the only bank large enough to sponsor a rival paper. Every election was dominated by his political choices. He was the gatekeeper of all local information reaching the citizens of our community.

Sometimes the actions of the newspaper owner did not matter. He expected objective coverage of the riot, for example, and the inaccurate reporting caused by the focus on the so-called community spokesperson was the fault of naive reporters.

At other times the owner's bias slanted coverage. I remember one election in which the owner had a favorite person running for congressional office. Besides being backed in writing on the editorial page of the paper, the candidate was also supported in less obvious ways. Each time a strong rival gave a speech, we reporters were sent to cover it. We were to be objective. We were to be accurate. We were to do the best possible job of communicating what was said, even when it went counter to the interests of the owner of the paper. However, once we had done this, inevitably we would find that most of what we wrote showing the rival in a good light was not printed. "We had fewer advertisements than usual," we might be told, "and so we had to cut back on pages and a few stories we expected to run had to be killed. We were going to run them tomorrow, but they had an immediacy to them. They had to be used today or not at all, and we just didn't have the space. Great reporting job, though."

Was this censorship? Was this an improper way to limit the information the public would have when they went to vote, or was it simply a reasonable response to a legitimate business problem? After all, regardless of how large a daily newspaper might be, a given edition can have only so many pages, and cost cannot be allowed to exceed advertising revenue.

The same is true for television and radio. There is only so much air time. Radio news can be as short as five minutes, including at least one commercial break. Local television news is usually no less than thirty minutes—but that thirty minutes must include sports, weather, and enough banter by the anchors for them to be seen as celebrities, in addition to time for commercials. Because the public's perception of news is that it is all the same, the only reason to choose one network over another is the personality of the anchor. Establishing that personality takes precious minutes from every broadcast, limiting even the best gatekeeper on the production staff.

There are five primary sources of news and information in American society today: radio, television, newspapers, magazines, and computer online services such as the Internet. Before exploring many of the issues that we unknowingly face each day, it is important to understand the strengths and limitations of each of these sources as they relate to the news.

Newspapers are the oldest form of news among the five, and potentially the most objective. They can use as much space as necessary to cover a story if they so choose. A story can include photographs, which help bring an additional perspective to the words. And the reader can check on the accuracy of the reporting at a later time because printed words remain available day after day. However, contemporary opinion polls usually find that the public feels television news is more accurate than newspaper coverage, ironically for the very reason that the opposite is usually true. Television news has the illusion of accuracy because watching it seems to place the viewer in the midst of the story. But there is no way, short of making home recordings of news broadcasts, to ensure that stories are reported accurately. The ability to read back issues of newspapers means that any mistake can be checked; thus accuracy takes on a greater sense of importance.

Magazines appear less frequently than newspapers. Most are monthly, although some, including those inserted as supplements in Sunday newspapers, are weekly.

It is rare for a news magazine to try to cover a story before at least some information about it has appeared in a daily newspaper. Spot reporting is not the magazine's strong point. Instead, a news magazine allows the reader to gain a broader perspective on a story. The reporters can take their time to get all the facts, separating what was blurted out in the passion of the moment from the truth that may underlie the event. Whereas a newspaper might cover a riot as it occurs—showing the looting, the people who have been injured, the fires that have been set, and the heroism of those fighting for a return to order—the news magazine is more likely to report on the underlying cause of the disturbance. A daily newspaper's first concern is *what* is happening. A news magazine's first concern is *why* it is happening.

Radio and television share the immediacy of coverage with newspapers, although there is a difference. Most radio news is headline news and must be important to the majority of the listeners. Local stories about major fires, dramatic car crashes that shut down freeways, and city council announcements of tax increases are perceived to be of interest. But stories about what people are doing on the first day of spring or the hottest day of the summer are left to newspapers and television. Likewise, any story that requires extra time, such as an analysis of a proposed school levy, will either be ignored or be relegated to stations that provide lengthy news and news/feature programming.

Television's first concern is the visual. Radio broadcasters worry about "dead air"—periods of silence long enough to cause listeners to switch stations. Television broadcasters worry about the "talking head" phenomenon—stories that require so much verbal explanation that the viewer is not visually stimulated. Any news story that requires a talking head, such as an analysis of a tax reform proposal, is relegated to an obscure time slot or not covered at all.

Television news often leads with a fire, a shooting, or some other story of violence. If women and children are seemingly in jeopardy, so much the better. There are flashing red and blue lights. There are men and women in colorful uniforms dashing about with guns drawn or making dramatic rescues from ladders placed against a burning building. Tape of a SWAT police unit rushing an abandoned building in which a transient has holed up, shooting a blank starter's pistol into the air, will get a lead on television. Discussion about the first workable budget deficit program ever devised by a committee of both major political parties may rate little more than a fifteen-second "sound bite."

This is the reverse of the newspaper, where an entire page might be devoted to the deficit story, including the reproduction of some key provisions, but the SWAT team's operation might get no more than two sentences if a space filler is needed.

Lengthy television news programming is no different. Perhaps the most respected television news program of the last two decades has been *60 Minutes*. It provides in-depth (for television) reports on major stories. Often there is much information that must be spoken, creating a potential "talking head" situation. Yet if you watch *60 Minutes* without sound, you will see how this problem is solved. The program is visually fast paced. A reporter and camera operator will be running after a subject who has avoided being interviewed, perhaps chasing the person as he or she leaves an office, shouting questions as they run. There will be quick cuts during an interview, the camera going from the subject to the reporter to anything of visual interest in the room. A variety of different camera angles will be used in showing a manufacturing plant, a business, a scenic area, or whatever the story requires. In fact, you may find that the visual component is entertaining enough that you do not miss the sound, even though you do not know the story being covered.

This is not to diminish the high quality of *60 Minutes*. The reporting is frequently among the best in the TV news business. But maintaining strong visual interest is a major priority. The same story told with less interesting images would not be as successful.

PBS has long been known for news analysis shows that are well researched, objective, and respected. However, these programs are frequently of the "talking head" variety, without exciting visuals or a fast pace. As a result, they appeal to the type of people who are also likely to read newspapers and news magazines and who do not rely on a single medium for news and entertainment.

The only way to make sure you receive the most complete and objective news coverage on a daily basis is to utilize all the media—newspapers, magazines, television, and radio. Together they offer the best chance for understanding the events of the day—unless, of course, the media in your community are dominated by a single owner.

The Internet is a new phenomenon for communicating information. It is at once the most accurate and the least accurate resource available. The Internet allows a user to bypass the gatekeepers of the traditional media. It is conceivable that everyone involved with a story can take to the computer and tell the details as they experienced them. Experts in related fields can use the Internet to discuss all aspects of what took place, as well as the ramifications. There is no censorship. It is a forum open to all, regardless of race, creed, color, or viewpoint.

Unfortunately, the Internet is a little too much like a town meeting. All parties, including articulate individuals with personal biases, scholarly-sounding misinformation, or limited awareness, have equal weight. An outsider unfamiliar with an event has no idea what to believe. There are too many sources and too few ways to screen them.

The Internet, like the fax machine that preceded it, ensures that all sides of a story can be heard. When the Chinese leadership violently cracked down on student dissent in 1989, reporters were limited in the stories they could file, but the students, using facsimile machines, were able to broadcast information throughout the world. Anywhere a telephone line existed, the students' stories could get out.

The Internet takes the fax a step further in that the recipient can interact with the sender, asking questions and getting more information. But the lack of censorship that makes the Internet a potent news force is also what makes it a questionable one. The parameters of the more traditional media allow for the exploration of ethical issues. The lack of such parameters for the Internet means that ethics is usually not a consideration. Everyone online has his or her own soapbox. The rantings of the articulate psychopath are given the same opportunity for expression as the reasoned analysis of the best-informed scholar.

News is just one area of concern in the arena of ethical issues. However, it is arguably the most controversial, because most of us have a tendency to feel that the current emphasis on sex and violence, on the worst aspects of humanity, is somehow a new phenomenon. Many people long for a return to the past, when newspapers were more numerous, with most communities having at least rival morning and afternoon papers, and the content was more carefully prepared. Yet the truth is that the problems with the print media, from which both television and radio news evolved, go back a long way. The legacy of Benjamin Franklin's *Pennsylvania Gazette* has long been with us. And the pioneer city for recent U.S. newspaper development has been New York, where many of the worst excesses have occurred.

The earliest newspapers in the United States were written and edited for men and women with relatively sophisticated educations and higher-than-average incomes. They were also sponsored by special-interest groups wanting to reach such an audience.

For example, some of the papers were sponsored by one or another political party, and thus all the news was filtered through the bias. For example, the Federalist Party (of which Alexander Hamilton was the most famous leader) sponsored the *Gazette of the United St; Minerva;* and the New York *Evening Post.*

These papers were opposed editorially by pro–Thomas Jefferson papers such as the *National Gazette* and the *Aurora.*

Other papers were compilations of foreign news. The editors would take overseas newspapers shipped to the United States, and either quote or rewrite their stories for the American audience. They might or might not have had a domestic political bias, but their income came from the distillation of stories from the overseas press. The competition was intense, and some New York papers even established a pony-express-type relay to transmit news between New York and Washington.

Accuracy was never assured. September 25, 1690, marked the birth of what was probably the first American newspaper—*Publick Occurrences Both Forreign and Domestick.* The Boston publisher, Benjamin Harris, was a printer who had emigrated from England, fleeing his native land because of a question of honesty. Before coming to the colonies, he had claimed to reveal a plot by the Catholic Church to topple the British government. Not one word of the story was true, but when his predictions failed to occur, he refused to admit that he had he lied. Instead, he stated that his publishing of the story had foiled the plot. He never learned his lesson, and his Boston stories about Indian massacres and other problems of the day were the result of his fertile imagination, not documented events.

Some of the early papers made no pretense about their inaccuracies. The first blend of satire and truth was the *New England*

Courant, a cross between *National Lampoon, Mad* magazine, *The Weekly World News,* and a traditional tabloid. It delighted in deflating the pompous leadership of the day. Some of the stories were true; most were not. The targets ranged from the clergy, who dominated the community, to politicians, who had a sense of humor only when it came to the clergy. James Franklin, who ran the paper with his younger brother Benjamin, was eventually jailed.

In these early days of American journalism, objectivity was not even desirable. There was too much political unrest, with the newspapers fanning the flames of revolution. One of the few publications to attempt to present both sides of the dispute with England was *Rivington's New York Gazetteer,* which brought the wrath of the Sons of Liberty upon owner James Rivington.

By the time George Washington had become the first president, newspapers felt they *had* to be biased. Washington was viciously attacked by the *General Advertiser,* and he used the *Aurora* to defend himself against his enemies. Other politicians, noting how Washington was treated, realized that having control of a newspaper's editorial policy was critical to their success. Some used the press, and a few owned their own papers, but all of them experienced the pressures that newspapers could exert.

Perhaps most interesting is the fact that what today would be considered the new power of the Religious Right goes back two centuries. Thomas Jefferson was hated by the editor of the *New-England Palladium and Commercial Advertiser.* Using a statement that might be made by a religious conservative today, the paper claimed: "Should the Infidel Jefferson be elected to the Presidency, the seal of death is that moment set on our holy religion, our churches will be prostrated, and some infamous prostitute, under the title of the Goddess of Reason, will preside in the Sanctuaries now devoted to the Most High."

By the time of Andrew Jackson, in the early 1830s, literacy had increased dramatically in the United States, and even lower-income Americans were interested in the news. In addition, more Americans had gained the right to vote, and minimal education standards were rising. There seemed to be a growing market among the laboring class, for whom both the mercantile and political papers held only limited interest.

Potential advertisers saw that the laborers were reaching a level of affluence that allowed them to buy more than food, clothing, and shelter. As a result, publishers experimented with what was called the "penny press," low-cost newspapers that featured human-interest news, sex and crime stories, and occasionally even items about government, international affairs, and other topics that dominated the more sophisticated papers. Ironically, the new papers often had excellent writing and in-depth coverage that would rival those of today's dailies. By contemporary standards, they used subject matter that was a cross between contemporary tabloids and *USA Today*, with the depth that might be expected in *The New York Times*. Most were founded between 1833 and 1837, and their success, primarily in the East, led publishers in other cities to experiment with the same approach. Ironically, the success of the penny press caused other publishers to look to the creation of in-depth newspapers reaching audiences broader than those of either the penny press or the politically biased papers. Horace Greeley founded the *New York Tribune* in 1841, and ten years later, Henry J. Raymond established *The New York Times*.

A staple of most of the new papers was crime reporting, some of which was accurate. The *New York Sun*, which editor Benjamin Day began on September 3, 1833, reported on the violence in the city, something more likely to afflict its lower-income readers. Day also presented the latest in scientific "discoveries," such as men living on the moon.

The *New York Herald* was less likely to fantasize in its news stories. However, the editor liked the writers to speculate on the major crimes of the day. Thus, although not claiming outlandish "facts," the writers would discuss the possible ways to interpret the news—in a manner not unlike that in which the Sam Sheppard murder case would be covered more than a century later. In 1954, Sheppard, an osteopathic physician (the case will be discussed later in this book), was accused of killing his wife. His guilt was declared by the *Cleveland Press*, and he was eventually brought to trial, where he faced a jury made hostile by extensive pretrial publicity. He was convicted of the murder in sensational proceedings that seemed to vindicate the biased coverage—until he was given a new trial and found not guilty a few years later.

Horace Greeley's *New York Tribune* had a degree of integrity the others lacked. He tried to separate news from opinion, maintaining a lively editorial page while attempting to keep the rest of the paper objective in its coverage.

The invention of the telegraph and the stringing of wires across the nation provided rapid access to information from around the country. However, the cost was extremely high, so several newspapers shared the cost of telegraph service to critical areas. In 1848, the Associated Press was formed by six New York morning newspapers. They used one telegraph line to receive edited versions of foreign news from overseas papers in Boston. Staff personnel in that city digested what they thought would be of interest to the readers, then telegraphed the details to give them an edge on the competition that had to receive the papers by courier. A second line linked them with Washington, although this line was meant for receiving routine stories.

Truly national efforts for higher-speed news gathering by means of the telegraph were not pursued until the war with Mexico and the increasing tensions preceding the Civil War made such efforts vital. The wars also created a demand for sketch artists who could report the stories in the field, and it was primarily through the efforts of such illustrators that photojournalism emerged.

The growing interest in photographs, the improving ability of photographers to cover news stories, and the awareness of the purchasing power of the average laborer led to experiments with papers that combined blue-collar appeal with pictures. The *Daily Graphic*, introduced in 1872, lasted for seventeen years. Others did not fare as well. The *Daily Continent*, for example, survived only six months. Oddly, the most successful tabloid, the *New York World*, had only a one-day run on January 1, 1901. The *World* was a traditional paper whose publisher decided to experiment with a single issue in tabloid format. To the publisher's amazement, the paper sold 100,000 more copies than usual. However, he was unwilling to risk keeping the format for fear that the additional purchases had been made only out of curiosity and would not continue.

It was the *Illustrated Daily News*, later called simply the *Daily News*, that was the right paper at the right time. It was founded in 1919 by Joseph Medill Patterson, a cousin of Robert McCormack, with whom he was already a partner in the *Chicago Tribune*. Patterson deliberately set out to reach what he considered to be the lowest class of literate Americans. These were people who had little education and extremely low-paying jobs, but could read, could afford a newspaper, could afford some of the items advertised, and had an interest in the news if it was presented in a manner that was easy to follow.

The first issue of the *Illustrated Daily News* set the tone for tabloid picture journalism by running a photograph across half of the front page. Inside, the newspaper was jammed with human-interest stories, entertaining features, and more photographs. Bootleggers, sports figures, the new Hollywood stars, criminal activities, and similar items dominated its coverage. At the same time, the publisher was smart enough to realize that because he was reaching an audience no one had ever before so thoroughly exploited, his success would be determined by the interests of his readers. His staff kept alert to local trends, concerns, interests, comments, and criticisms of and by the readers. As a result, the paper evolved many times over the years, providing consumer information, medical news of importance to its market, and other items that addressed its readers' changing concerns. The target market stayed the same, but the paper changed as the circumstances of its readers were affected by the political and economic ups and downs of society. As a result, by 1924 the *Daily News* was the largest-circulation daily paper in the United States, a distinction it would retain for decades.

The immigrant population was also an important source of readership for tabloids. People attempting to assimilate needed to know what was taking place in their city. As they learned to read English, a heavily illustrated newspaper was far more attractive to them than one, such as the *New York Times*, that was almost solid text. If the reader had difficulty with the words, it was possible to use the photographs to get a sense of the story.

This led to a structuring of the way photojournalists were expected to work. Each time they were sent on an assignment, one of the images they recorded was expected to tell a complete story. Someone who could not read the text was expected to be able to look at the photograph and understand what was happening. By the time the *Daily News* had become a reality, photographic film had been developed that absorbed light quickly enough, and cameras had become lightweight enough, so that photographers could be dispatched to cover any story. ("Lightweight" is a relative term. Few photographers carried less than twenty-five pounds of equipment. But they were no longer in need of a tripod or limited by the need for long exposures. Life was being caught at 1/200th of a second, allowing this new type of coverage.)

In addition, there were special cameras that allowed relatively low-quality photographs to be taken under circumstances in which the larger, better equipment could not be used. Some, such as the Leica, used motion-picture film. Others used a special plate, such as the Ermanox. These experimental devices would allow images to be obtained when no other equipment would work.

Darkroom techniques had also advanced. Composite pictures could be made using two or more separate photographs. An event could be "re-created," just as it had *never* happened. Such composites allowed tabloid rivals of the *Daily News* to appear to have intimate access to the lives of celebrities. The first issue of the newspaper ran the following self-introduction:

> *The Illustrated Daily News* is going to be your newspaper. Its interests will be your interests . . . It is not an experiment, for the appeal of news pictures and brief, well-told stories will be as apparent to you as it has been to millions of readers in European cities.
>
> We shall give you every day the best and newest pictures of the interesting things that are happening in the world . . . The story that is told by a picture can be grasped instantly. Ten thousand words of description cannot convey to you the impression you receive when you look at Millet's painting "The Angelus" . . .
>
> No story will be continued to another page—that is to save you trouble. You can read it without eye strain.
>
> The policy of the *Illustrated Daily News* will be your policy. It will be aggressively for America and for the people of New York . . . It will have no entangling alliance with any class whatever . . .
>
> Because the doings of the very fortunate are always of interest we shall print them as interestingly as possible in our society column. Because fiction will always be appealing we shall print the best and newest that is to be had. We shall print the best features that are to be found.

In truth, the newspaper was focused on the one target audience to whom no one had previously given consideration—the average person on the street. The reader of the *Daily News* was the same type of person who one day would be targeted by the creators of radio soap operas, supermarket tabloids such as the *National Enquirer*, celebrity magazines such as *People*, and similar media concepts. It was the individual whose interests ran to either the very different (glamour, violent crime, scandal among the rich and famous) or the very familiar (problems with employers, children, family, and sex involving either vicarious thrills or personal romance).

For example, among the earliest features were columns in which readers were encouraged to write in about "The Queerest Boss I Ever Worked For" or their "Real Love Stories" or "My Most Embarrassing Moment." Literary ability was not a prerequisite, and many of the entries came hand-scrawled on butcher paper or the torn pages of a child's lined writing practice pad. But if your entry was chosen to be in the newspaper, the editor making it more readable, you were paid from one to five dollars.

There were also "cheesecake" photographs of attractive young women—low camera angle, plenty of leg, usually with the arms behind a slightly arched back, which would cause the subject's breasts to push forward against her blouse or bathing suit. These photographs showed actresses arriving in New York by ocean liner. If they actually had come by car, bus, or train, they were simply taken down to the docks and posed on the rail of a ship, where the wind would blow their skirts, exposing more of their legs. Others showed women on beaches or beauty contest entrants. But whoever the subject might be, there would be a cheesecake shot every day.

The *Daily News*, just as Hugh Hefner's *Playboy* did more than thirty years later, knew how to appeal to its readers. When it held a contest for "The Most Beautiful Girl in New York," the winner of the $10,000 prize—a fortune in those days—was Alice Louise Secker, who worked at a corset factory. Subsequent beauty contests were also invariably won by working girls of the day. The paper knew the value of celebrating the common person, the "girl next door," rather than Broadway actresses.

The entertainment also included the comics, and the *Daily News* introduced the most popular and longest-lived comics in America, including *Dick Tracy*, *Gasoline Alley*—part of whose popularity came from the fact that the characters aged over the years—and *Little Orphan Annie*.

What made the success of the *Daily News*—a daily circulation of 230,000 the first year, one million readers per day at the end of six years—all the more remarkable was its competition. It started in business at a time when New York had seven English-language morning papers and ten English-language afternoon papers competing for customers. In addition, the *Daily News* was often called "pictures and vaudeville for the unintelligent masses" by those in the business who felt it was too low-brow.

When the circulation of the *Daily News* reached approximately half a million, the *New York American* decided to compete for circulation by staging a $1000 lottery. Thousands of people rushed to the locations where they could get numbered coupons, one of which would match a number printed in the paper.

Not to be outdone, the *Daily News* started a $2500 lottery. Then the *American* went to $5000. Eventually the competitors raised the ante to $25,000 each, a sum equal to five to ten years' income for a family of four, depending on their circumstances. Neither paper could afford to pay such prizes, but the *Daily News* was not done with the challenge. The company promised to double any amount named by the *American*.

Desperate for a way out of the contest insanity, the publishers of both papers tried to find a way to end the war and still save face. There was no way they could simply stop the contests without their readers feeling they had been cheated and perhaps abandoning both papers. Instead, the publishers went to the postal authorities. Using their political influence and whatever bribes were necessary, they convinced government officials to order an end to the lotteries. The reasoning used by the government when it declared that both papers had been violating the law made little sense, but when the papers "reluctantly" ended the lotteries, it was the federal government that took the blame.

The writing in these newspapers was usually sensational. The reporters knew what the public wanted—lurid scandal and a reason to feel that the average person, underpaid, overworked, never able to get ahead, was somehow a little better off than the rich and famous. Hollywood and the film industry were all still relatively new in the early 1920s. The movie stars made a lot of money, but they were working in farm areas that had little sophistication and almost no nightlife. They lived in mansions, but the more objective writers traveling west to cover the industry talked about how little out of the ordinary took place. They found the industry boring, the actors going to bed early in order to rise well before dawn to put on costumes and makeup in an effort to catch the first rays of sunlight. The cinematographers were almost totally dependent on the weather, and daylight was never wasted. There simply wasn't enough time and energy available for the types of activities that were routine in Manhattan. And even if actors had the inclination, there was no place to go.

Sex and drugs were popular in Hollywood, but they were popular elsewhere as well. Prohibition had begun on January 16, 1920, and bootleg alcohol had become a highly desired beverage throughout the nation. However, the image of Hollywood was one of endless partying. No one wanted to read that most of the stars spent their money on their homes and cars, or that the community lacked the sophisticated night spots that appealed to easterners.

When bachelor Hollywood director William Desmond Taylor was murdered, the *Daily News* sent a writer to tell the story of the unsolved case in a manner that would most appeal to the fantasies of its readers. A former British army officer in World War I, the handsome Taylor was known to be actively pursued by several beautiful actresses. Mabel Normand, one of the stars of the Mack Sennett comedies, was one of the last people to see him alive, though she was never a suspect in the case.

Taylor lived in a four-room apartment where he had once kept a live-in staff of three—a manservant, a butler, and a chauffeur. The staff, however, was down to two at the time of the murder. Taylor had fired the butler several months before his death, after discovering that the man had been forging Taylor's name in order to steal money. Taylor also had a daughter in a private school on Long Island, and an ex-wife he rarely mentioned to anyone. Those were the facts. The killer was probably waiting in hiding for Taylor, because Taylor was shot in the back while he worked at a writing desk. Witnesses said the killer may have been a man because of the clothing worn, but the walk indicated that the person may have been a woman dressed as a man.

Recognizing that truth was not what the *Daily News* readers wanted, and having no information on the case from the police, the writer created a story in the style popular for the day. On February 3, 1922, the paper's report on the murder, complete with photographs including an artist's re-creation of the murder superimposed on a picture of the room where it had occurred, began:

> All Hollywood is being raked for the killer of William Desmond Taylor, all the queer meeting places of the actors and actresses, directors and assistant directors, cameramen and extras—restaurants, beauty parlors, studios, dens where opium and marihuana [sic] and other strange drugs are common, dens where men and women dress in silk kimonos and sit in circles and drink odd drinks—are being visited.
>
> Everyone who has come into contact with the slain director, no matter how remotely, is being questioned. Things that may shock the world of moving picture fans are destined to come out of the mystery, it is said. Popular stars, male and female, may be scorched and smirched before the police investigation is over. And all the sins of the cinema colony will be made known. Dope fiends will figure in the tale before it is all told, and strange effeminate men and peculiarly masculine women.

The story continued from there, the writer taking only two paragraphs to admit that no one knew anything, or where the investigation might lead. All that was certain was that the killer was probably a scorned woman, a jealous husband, or an enemy Taylor had made while working in Hollywood. Considering the fact that the fifty-year-old director was known to enjoy women and was in a position where would-be movie stars were frequently willing to offer themselves to a studio executive who might put them in a movie, the police could logically look nowhere else. But saying those kinds of things was boring. Readers needed more excitement, and the *Daily News* reporter provided the color that lacked all substance.

The *Daily News* created something else as well—a feature called the "Inquiring Fotographer." The first in a long line of employees to hold the title was Jimmy Jemail, who, on a lark, went to Jersey City with camera and notebook in hand. He would stop people and ask them a question such as, "Do you remember your first kiss and did you enjoy it?" He would note their answers and take their photographs, and the next day the *Daily News* would run the question with the answers and photographs of five or six people whose responses seemed most interesting or amusing.

This concept of the "Inquiring Fotographer" was carried over to other publications in the years that followed. Perhaps the most sophisticated was *Vogue* magazine, which hired a young photographer to handle the work. Her name was Jacqueline Bouvier, and one of the subjects she interviewed was a young bachelor U.S. senator from Massachusetts named John Kennedy.

The success of the *Daily News* attracted two competitors. William Randolph Hearst, and Bernarr (formerly Bernard; he thought the double "r" more distinctive) MacFadden in partnership with Fulton Oursler, decided in 1923 to create their own tabloids. Both appeared the following year, starting with Hearst's *New York Daily Mirror*. The more interesting of the two, MacFadden and Oursler's *New York Evening Graphic* appeared for the first time on September 15, 1924, with this editorial statement:

We intend to interest you mightily. We intend to dramatize and sensationalize the news and some stories that are not new.

But we do not want a single dull line to appear in this newspaper. If you read it from first to last and find anything therein that does not interest you, we want you to write and tell us about it.

We want this newspaper to be human, first, last and all the time. We want to throb with those life forces that fill life with joyous delight.

We want to show our readers how to live 100 percent.

Don't be a dead one! Gird up your loins. Make ready to fight for the thing that you want in life and if you read the Graphic with sufficient regularity you can be assured of worthwhile assistance.

The *Evening Graphic* was to prove true to its promise. It not only dramatized and sensationalized the news, but also created a new type of photograph it called the "composograph." Sometimes pictures of unrelated individuals were placed together so that the final picture would look as though they had posed together. This technique would find commonplace use many years later in tabloids, and it was rather complex. Usually the composograph would start with a photograph of models posed in whatever ways were desired. Then an artist would use photographs of famous people, printed so that the head sizes matched those in the photograph of the models. Finally, the artist would cut out the heads of the models, superimpose the heads of the famous people, and rephotograph the entire picture so that it would look as though the photographer had witnessed history in the making.

One of the most famous composographs was that of Edward and Frances Hennan Browning. He was a fifty-one-year-old New York millionaire who had made his money in real estate. She was a fifteen-year-old schoolgirl who married him after a brief courtship, then sued for divorce six months later. The *Evening*

Graphic ran what was supposedly a first-person account by Frances, who was called "Peaches" by her husband; she called him "Daddy." Among other statements, she claimed that Daddy dressed up like a sheik, took his pet goose on their honeymoon, and liked to "come lumbering into our bedroom and growl 'Woof! Woof!' like a bear in my ear."

The newspaper printed a composograph of the honeymoon, and another of the Brownings at home. The honeymoon picture showed Peaches on a chair, her toy dolls near her feet, while Daddy sat opposite her, dressed as a sheik, his goose on a table near his left shoulder. Their conversation was also re-created by printing the words in the same type of balloons used in cartoons.

A more "serious" composograph showed the couple in their home, Daddy's "Temple of Love." This time Peaches was lying on a chaise longue with Daddy leaning over her, while Peaches' mother, who lived with the couple, stood just outside the door, her ear to the wood, trying to learn what was happening.

Whenever possible, the stories the *Evening Graphic* ran were meant to give the impression that they were told by the persons involved. For example, on its first day, the paper ran a story titled "My Friends Dragged Me into the Gutter," which detailed the hard life of a minor motion-picture actress who strayed from the path of goodness and decency.

The *Evening Graphic* owed many of its eccentricities to Bernarr MacFadden. A sickly orphan from Missouri who became one of the first bodybuilders to gain national fame, MacFadden preached a message that seemingly offered something for everyone. He believed that good health required exercise, a vegetarian diet, and an active sex life—though ideally a monogamous one. He declared himself to be a "kinistherapist," a term that sounded professional even though he was discipline's first and only practitioner.

MacFadden opened a health studio in New York City, where he invented exercise approaches, some of which remain standard, others of which seem silly. For example, he invented a pulley-type exercising machine for safely lifting weights, a device that is still found in gyms today and that was the forerunner of such popular modern exercise equipment as the Soloflex.

In a more eccentric phase of his creativity, MacFadden developed a number of exercises to help obese men get in shape. Perhaps the most unusual was having them run around naked (a condition he favored for himself), trying to keep inflated balloons in the air by blowing at them.

MacFadden's first venture into magazine publishing came with his *Physical Culture*. He had been writing and printing pamphlets on health, fitness, and natural living, and the larger forum increased his name recognition.

MacFadden always stayed ahead of popular trends, however. When he discovered that readers were writing to tell him of the troubles in their personal lives, he realized that there was a market for stories that would relate to the dramatic crises people face. The result was *True Story* magazine, which quickly attracted two million readers.

True Story was meant to read like gossip shared by two relatively uneducated neighbors standing by the back fence. The problems almost always had to do with relationships, and they were tales that would later be at home in either the "cheatin' heart" songs of country-and-western music or the early radio soap operas. The staff personnel were all selected from backgrounds like those of their readers, though most were high-school graduates. It was not unusual to have a barber, a hairdresser, a manicurist, or the lowest-level file clerk find himself or herself declared an editor. The salaries were far better than they had been earning, but success in the new position was determined by whether the "editor" was able to improve on the job. Any editor who seemed to be getting too professional, to be using language that was too sophisticated, was quickly fired.

MacFadden's publications were successful, but he had been in trouble with the law since the turn of the century. He felt that there was nothing wrong with nudity, although he somewhat yielded to the times. His first difficulties occurred back in 1901, when he advertised a physical culture exhibition in Washington with posters of women in bloomers or black tights. Later he dressed his women in union suits, still showing far more flesh than the times allowed.

MacFadden also staged physical fitness stunts for publicity. He delighted in being photographed walking, usually barefoot, from his home in Nyack, New York, to his Manhattan office, a distance of twenty-one miles. He organized marathon walks, such as a 325-mile hike to Danville, New York, with elderly participants joining him to prove that good health lasted a lifetime. He died in 1955 at age eighty-seven, having been born when the average life expectancy was almost forty years less than he achieved. He also had the pleasure of having young women tell of being led astray by him when he was in his late sixties.

In the ultimate MacFadden stunt, at the age of eighty-three, he parachuted 2500 feet into the Hudson River. But the high point—or low point—of his literary career was the *Evening Graphic*, whose headlines would later be more successfully used by *True Story* magazine. (The first week's circulation was 400,000. The second week, circulation dropped to 80,000.) The paper grew so slowly that, had MacFadden not been making millions in profits from his other enterprises, money he could use to keep the paper afloat, the *Evening Graphic* would have gone out of business in the first few months.

Nothing was sacred to the press in the 1920s. A photographer would lie, cheat, and steal if it meant getting a picture to market before the competition. And the reporters would act in a similar manner, a fact that inspired one of the most successful Broadway plays of the era.

In 1928, Ben Hecht and Charles MacArthur wrote a true-to-life comedy of reporters in search of the "big story." Although they based their play, *The Front Page*, on a Chicago newsman whose name was changed to "Hildy Johnson" in the script, the New York press delighted in the story because they felt that it was just like their own experiences. As an example of the activities of the reporter with whom Charles MacArthur had worked in Chicago, he once broke into an empty jury room, checked the ballots to determine the outcome of a trial, then called his paper to scoop the other reporters. Moreover, because he knew the others would probably do just as he had done, he then took fresh ballots, changed them from the originals, and replaced the genuine ballots with the ones he had made up, which showed a different verdict.

In an even more outrageous stunt, the same reporter paid a death-row inmate two hundred dollars for the exclusive rights to his story. As soon as he had the story, he challenged the man to a game of gin rummy, during which he won back every dollar he had paid. The money legitimately belonged to the *Chicago Herald & Examiner*, the reporter's employer, but when he won it back, he pocketed it as a bonus. Ironically, the story did not come out until the inmate met with a Catholic priest and warned him never to play rummy with the reporter because the man cheated.

Reporters seldom bothered with facts if they needed fancy to make a story more interesting. For example, when the *New York Daily News* sent Arthur Pegler to a rooming house to learn about a man's death, Pegler discovered that there was no story. The man had died of natural causes. Rather than disappoint his editor, however, Pegler created the fiction that the dead man was Nicola Coviello, an Italian opera composer who had been traveling to Saskatchewan for a performance of some of his work. He had been in New York only long enough to see a few sights, but had made the mistake of traveling to Coney Island. There he had heard jazz, the new form of American music that was becoming so popular with youth. The sound had been so horrible that Coviello had died instantly.

The power of the new tabloids was made most evident in 1926, when William Randolph Hearst's *Daily Mirror* was falling on hard times compared to its rivals. There were no interesting stories to report, so they decided to create their own—with mixed results.

In 1922, the socialite Eleanore (Mrs. James) Mills and her lover, the Reverend Edward Hall, pastor of the Episcopal Church of St. John the Evangelist in New Brunswick, New Jersey, were murdered. Their bodies were dumped on a pig farm owned by Jane Gibson, an eccentric who was dying of cancer and testified from a hospital bed wheeled into the courtroom.

The case was still unsolved in 1926, when Hearst had his staff interview everyone they could find who had any knowledge of the case. It was during one of these interviews that Jane Gibson, dubbed "The Pig Woman" by the press, said for the first time that she was convinced the murders had been committed by the minister's wife, two brothers, and a cousin. Her belief was not based on any evidence, but it was a dramatic "revelation" to pursue.

The paper began pushing to have the case reopened and charges brought against the four. Such was the *Daily Mirror*'s power that criminal indictments were brought despite the case being doubtful to everyone except Hearst's paper, which frequently used biblical quotes—e.g., "And be sure your sin will find you out. (Numbers 32:23)"—as story leads. On July 17, 1926, the paper foolishly printed the following:

A challenge to Mrs. Hall was issued last night by the editor of the DAILY MIRROR. If the MIRROR's story is untrue the editor can be sued for criminal libel. He invites such action as this telegraph shows: "Mr. Timothy Pfeiffer, New York City. This is a challenge to you as Mrs. Hall's legal representative to bring a criminal libel action against me personally if the statements in the DAILY MIRROR accusing Mrs. Hall are not correct. I stand fully responsible for the charges against Mrs. Hall. Philip Payne, Managing Editor."

The four suspects were acquitted because of nonexistent evidence and serious doubts raised about the integrity of "Pig Woman Gibson," who had waited four years to tell what she had "witnessed." Mrs. Hall then took up Philip Payne's challenge, sued him for libel, and won. The out-of-court settlement was substantial enough that rival papers would not print the dollar amount. They did not want to risk being sued for printing falsehoods and exaggerations.

Unlike the *Daily Mirror* stories on the Mills-Hall murders, the most spectacular photograph of the era was an instance of straight reporting. This photograph was printed in the *New York Daily News* in 1928, after Ruth Snyder was executed in the New York State electric chair. She and her lover had been convicted of the crime of murdering her husband, had exhausted all appeals, and were executed by the state.

In an effort to do what had never been done before, the *Daily News* arranged for photographer Tom Howard to be one of the witnesses to the execution. One of the new smaller cameras was strapped to his leg under his pants. An air release—a long tube attached to a bulb that was squeezed to open the shutter—was then brought up into his pocket. When Ruth Snyder was strapped into the chair, Howard crossed one leg over the other, raising his pant leg enough to expose the lens. Then he squeezed the bulb in his pocket and took the picture. That photograph ran on the front page of the *Daily News*, which sold 250,000 more copies than usual. An additional 750,000 copies were then printed, and all of them sold as well.

Reporter Gene Fowler did the finest writing on the Snyder case. His story was sent throughout the country by teletype and actually had far greater impact than Howard's dramatically shocking photograph. Fowler stated:

They led Ruth Brown Snyder from her steel cage tonight. Then powerful guards thrust her irrevocably into the obscene, sprawling oaken arms of the ugly electric chair. That was about 30 minutes ago. The memory of the crazed woman in her last agony as she struggled against the unholy embrace of the chair is too harrowing to permit a calm portrayal of the law's ghastly ritual. . . .

The formal destruction of the killers of poor, stolid, unemotional Albert Snyder in his rumpled sleep . . . was hardly less revolting than the crime itself. Both victims of the chair met their deaths trembling but bravely. . . .

Brief as was the time for the State to slay Ruth and Judd, it seems in retrospect to have been a long, haunting blur of bulging horror—glazed eyes, saffron faces, [so] fear-blanched that they became twisted masks, purpling underlips and hands as pale as chalk, clenching in the last paroxysms. . . .

And as these woeful wrecks passed from life, the shadows of attendants, greatly magnified, seemed to move in fantastic array along the walls, the silhouettes nodding and prancing in a sepulchral minuet. . . .

The tired form was taut. The body that once throbbed [with] the joy of her sordid bacchanals, turned brick red as the current struck. Slowly, after half a minute of death dealing current, the exposed arms, right leg, throat and jaws bleached out again. . . .

At the first electric torrent, Judd's throat and jaws were swollen. The cords stood out. The skin was gorged with blood and was the color of a turkey gobbler's wattles. Slowly this crimson tide subsided and left his face paler, but still showing splotches of red, which were mosaics of pain. The electricity was put on just as the chaplain got this far with his comforting words: "For God so loved the world . . ."

Despite this interest in sensationalism, reporters who covered the White House were unusually discreet in areas where discretion seemed to be bad reporting. Arteriosclerosis and a thrombosis paralyzing his left arm and leg made Woodrow Wilson unable to perform any of his presidential duties for seventeen months. Yet, while the reporters hinted at something terrible being wrong, no one ever learned what had happened during the time he had been incapacitated. Likewise, the press never reported on Franklin Roosevelt's inability to walk, nor did they mention the severity of his physical and mental deterioration when he ran for reelection in 1944. The nation was being led by a walking corpse, a fact so obvious that no one meeting him questioned his deteriorating health. And Jack Kennedy, although notorious for his affairs, also had severe health problems, including a bad back that had troubled him from childhood. His physician often would follow him, carrying syringes and medication needed to help him keep moving if his back froze up on him.

The introduction of television news created an unusual situation. There is little depth to television news. The entire script of a half-hour news program could be written on the front page of the average daily newspaper. The most successful newspapers have recognized this and have stressed their depth of coverage in order to retain readers. Yet the problem with television as a competitor is that it can offer an immediate look at an event. The moment something takes place anywhere in the world, a mobile camera crew and satellite uplink can ensure simultaneous viewing. This is the strength of CNN, for example.

The power of television news is countered by a number of weaknesses that go beyond the superficiality of coverage. A politician has only to look good in order to come across effectively in the eyes of the public. A strong voice, the right gestures, the appropriate body language, and a few words that sound impressive can help a man or woman project an image of leadership. A full analysis of the person's past and present, his or her beliefs and actions as they relate to the public trust, and anything else of substance are the scope of the print media. Thus, television can easily present the reality someone wants the public to believe, even when it is different from the reality that comes from an objective analysis of the person, place, or event.

However, the shortcomings of television news do not make the print media more accurate. The reality of all daily news gathering is that it is limited to what can be learned at the moment, and this means that one day's "facts" may prove to be meaningless or so incomplete as to have led the public to erroneous conclusions. In this regard, print has no advantage over television.

The classic situation occurred in April 1995, when the Alfred P. Murrah Federal Building in Oklahoma City was bombed. The media presumption was that Arab terrorists were to blame, and an Oklahoma City man of Arab descent was one of those named as a suspect. The innocent businessman was a twenty-four-hour villain (actually, stories about him continued for several days), even though at the time there was no evidence that indicated who might have committed the violence. There was also no ongoing domestic terrorism anywhere in or near the state of Oklahoma that would implicate Arab extremists. But each reporter wanted to be the first to provide the latest information on the event, so it was better to report an unfounded rumor than to be the last to name the bomber.

Because of deadline pressures, the daily media operate on the assumption that it is always better to have to say "I'm sorry" than to limit a story because little information is known.

Although such weak reporting is the nature of the beast, the tragedy is that many newspapers will not take the time to engage in self-criticism after the fact. In 1994, the press reported the case of Susan Smith, the young mother in South Carolina who reported her children missing, then told of being carjacked by an African American male, and finally admitted to deliberately murdering her children by strapping them into the back seat of her car and rolling her car into a river. Between the time she talked of a kidnapper and her admission to having been the killer, police were stopping African American men for hundreds of miles around the area where Smith said the abduction had occurred. There was racial tension and great anger, because a similar description of a white male would have been considered inadequate to warrant law-enforcement officers stopping anyone. Thus, not only was Smith using the bias of the people in her community to try to protect herself, but she was also creating what could have been an angry, potentially violent, and quite justified backlash. Yet it was the rare reporter who, upon learning the truth, discussed the very serious racial hatred that was generated by Smith's actions and the media reports of her statements.

There are exceptions. Long-term criminal cases, such as those of serial killers who are caught only after several months or years of investigation, usually result in lengthy analyses of the story after it is over. This is when the false leads and other mistakes are discussed, when mistaken arrests that have caused serious damage to innocent lives are explained, and when the innocent people involved are vindicated in the full context of the story.

The same is true for international events such as wars and disasters—nuclear accidents, terrorist bombings, and the like. But most of the news is allowed to run its course, with reporters' stories being printed daily and the publications hoping that, over time, the truth will come out. The fallout from each day's events being inadequately covered because of time limitations is generally ignored.

This problem also plagues television and radio news, but with these media there is no way for the average person to review past statements and coverage. It is the rare individual who tapes news programs for later review. The stories are accepted passively, the television images giving the impression of the completeness that the medium actually lacks more so than does print.

The complaint most often heard from extremist groups whose diatribes are not printed, and from religious groups whose ideas are enough outside the mainstream not to receive regular coverage, is that the media are biased. Usually the statement is that the media are too "liberal," although the meaning of this term varies with the speaker. Among the mainstream complainers, most of the charges of bias are made by conservative writers and broadcasters using the same media to get their messages across.

There is some truth to the charges, although rarely in the way the accusers mean. First, the media have never been unbiased. Newspapers and magazines have long been used to reflect the interests of their owners. So too, to a lesser degree, have television and radio stations. When Fox Television first went on the air, all of its programming was aimed at a young, urban, predominantly African American audience. Whatever it seemed would be of interest to this audience was the original entertainment fare. And when Fox stations added news shows, the stories they chose to report fell into the category of their perceived viewers' interests. If nothing else, this generally meant a focus on domestic stories over international ones.

Bias in newspapers is meant to attract specific audiences. Some papers go after blue-collar workers. Others are interested in gaining readers from the business community. Still others focus on particular ethnic groups or even specific neighborhoods. For example, there are weekly newspaper chains in which each paper serves a small section of the community, taking its advertising from stores and businesses within a radius of only a few miles. Only stories about people and events within the same area are reported, ensuring a carefully targeted market. Where these people are rich, the tone of the coverage and columns is likely to be conservative. Where these people are of limited means, the paper reflects more liberal attitudes. Yet all the papers may be owned by the same company.

Charges of media bias toward one extreme or another are usually the result of readers/listeners/viewers being limited in the media to which they are exposed. Most Americans watch local news on a favorite TV channel, listen to one radio station, and read a single newspaper, and many of those who charge bias do so on the basis of such a limited sampling.

Bias shown by reporters is generally found among those who cover social issues. Police reporters who cover the violence within their communities are often quite conservative on issues of criminal rights. They are frequently in favor of longer prison sentences and take similar stands normally perceived as conservative. By contrast, those who have spent extensive time with battered women, homeless children, and other unfortunates of society are more likely to be liberal in their attitudes. Everyone is inclined to adopt the attitude of the group they spend the most time with, and the larger the reporting staff, the more specialized the coverage may become. On the largest papers, there may be a reporter whose "beat" is the community's most successful business leaders, another who covers the elite of society, and yet another who specializes in ferreting out corruption in government, law enforcement, and business. A certain cynicism is developed in each of these circumstances, the bias of the reporter varying according to his or her beat.

Sometimes the press is criticized most for its aggressiveness. When Senator Gary Hart challenged reporters to follow him to prove that his personal life was not above reproach, they took him up on the challenge. The result was a series of photographs that showed him cavorting with a girlfriend on a private yacht.

There have been stories of reporters stealing documents or accepting those that have been illegally taken by others. Yet the Constitution allows reporters freedoms it does not give to law-enforcement officers. There are penalties to be paid, as there are for any citizen who obtains something illegally. But the difference is that once a document has been obtained, regardless of how, a reporter can legally publish it.

One's opinions regarding freedom of the press depend on which side of the fence one happens to be on. During wartime, efforts are made to censor the press. Once a reporter learns of a military action that is about to be taken, the tendency is to want to be the first to break the story. Yet, if this is done too soon, the enemy might be able to mount a defense that might otherwise not be possible. Such military censorship is critical before massive invasions such as the D-Day invasion during World War II. By contrast, military censorship must be overcome by an aggressive press to show excesses that might otherwise be covered up. This was certainly the case during the Vietnam War, when American soldiers massacred an entire village at My Lai for reasons that had nothing to do with ordered military action.

The problem with an aggressive press manifests itself when a story becomes such a challenge that the facts get in the way of the deadline. Reporting that can lead to the uncovering of a scandal may also be scandalous in itself if the reporter decides to run the story before it is checked. For example, when White House lawyer Vincent Foster apparently committed suicide in a Washington park, no one knew exactly what had occurred or why. Foster had been a close friend of Bill and Hillary Clinton, and he had been connected with scandals in which they had allegedly been involved. No one knew if his death had been the result of depression, mental illness, a determination to cover up some scandal, or something else. All that was known was that Foster was dead from what appeared to be a self-inflicted gunshot wound. However, the lack of facts did not stop reporters from using the existing rumors *before* any of them had been checked out by either law-enforcement officers or media investigators. Thus, there were stories that hinted at everything from homosexuality being exposed for the first time to an affair with Hillary Clinton.

There are times when rumors are published because they are titillating. The reporters protect themselves by stressing that the statements are not confirmed, as did reporters as far back as the *New York Daily News* coverage of the William Desmond Taylor murder. Yet such titillation can often cause great trauma for those segments of a community that are targeted, such as Americans of Arab descent and African Americans. The Oklahoma City bombing, the Susan Smith claims concerning the "carjacking" of her children, and numerous other stories, both local and national, can foment racial, ethnic, and religious hostilities. Yet for reporters, the stories bring fresh readers on the days they run, from a public anxious for as much information as possible.

Eventually the truth comes out, yet because of the false accusations that have come before, community tensions remain high. Many people remember the original story, often forgetting the later developments that showed it to be inaccurate. And most newspapers will not come right out and say they were wrong in their earlier reports, just that those reports were "preliminary" and part of a "breaking story."

Television can be even more of a problem because there is no easy way to check what was first reported. A back issue of a newspaper or magazine can be checked to determine whether or not a rumor was reported as a rumor. But television news is as fleeting as the words that come over the airwaves. Rumors become history in the mind of the average viewer.

The ethical concerns of journalism are obviously not new. Just as history has been said to be told from the viewpoint of the victors, so the reporting of news is based on the limitations of each medium and the bias of each broadcast or print journalist.

If there is truly a bias in the press, it is not a liberal or conservative bias but rather a bias against the entire issue of religion. The press in the United States has been uncomfortable with matters of faith in a nation where most people feel that some aspect of religion is a cornerstone of society. There are few experts on religion working for newspapers; few reporters do more than take notes on sermons, quote religious leaders about the major holidays, and write stories on controversial issues; and most of those who cover controversial issues lack the training to analyze the bases for disagreements among the various Christian, Islamic, Jewish and other religious groups. For example, during a period of violence in Lebanon, numerous stories were run concerning the extremely conservative Muslims in the country. What was not said, because the reporters were unaware of it, was that at the time, Lebanon had seventeen different Islamic groups ranging from extremely fundamentalist to extremely liberal. There were mosques where devout female followers wearing shorts and halter tops would be tolerated, and there were others where a woman who was not covered and veiled would be condemned as a sinner.

This lack of religious sophistication on the part of reporters is the reason the issue of the Christian Right in politics has been underexplored over the years. The reporters do not understand the social changes that religion and religious leaders can foment. Growing and ebbing religious movements affecting both society and politics have been missed, reported as new phenomena, or written off as aberrations.

At the same time, there is a growing field of religious media, ranging from newspapers and magazines—both nondenominational and for specific religions—to radio and television programming. Access to religious ideas has never been easier. Access to learned analysis or even a fundamental understanding of what these ideas mean, however, is very difficult to find in the media.

To speak of ethics, to speak of right and wrong, is actually to speak of many different concerns and decisions. Newscasting is the area most in need of ethical reform. The entertainment side of the media—especially as it relates to violence, sex, and potentially offensive language—is the area of greatest concern for most people and yet is the easier of the two (news and entertainment) to control, as we will see later in the book. And the most controversial area, the subject of the next chapter, is where the First Amendment is truly challenged: the overlooked ethical concerns of religious broadcasting. When faith is combined with bigotry, fantasy, and greed, issues arise that few people in any way connected with the media industry want to explore. Yet even with religious broadcasting there are ethical concerns that the viewer or listener must understand. Sadly, neither supporters nor critics of what is today lumped together as televangelism have traditionally been willing to tackle these issues.

2

Praise the Lord and Pass the Contributions

M ost discussions of media ethics begin with the issue of children's television programs. Saturday morning cartoon show violence, early evening programming that exposes children to such "humorous" topics as divorce, same-sex parents, and adultery, and the shameless promotion of products are all valid ethical concerns. There are serious questions about how such entertainment influences the behavior of children, but although parents feel comfortable screening and limiting their children's viewing, most adults do not realize that there are ethical issues involved with less obviously exploitive programming. Unfortunately, these issues are normally not tackled by media critics because they fear being attacked on the issue of faith, even when they know that a fraud is being perpetrated.

Religious broadcasting has existed almost as long as radio. Numerous preachers saw the radio as a way of spreading the Word. Some stayed within their own communities, eventually including the listeners in their congregations. They would make house calls or have the people come to their churches for counseling. They felt that they had stay-at-home radio congregations as well as congregations that filled the pews of their churches. Some of the listeners eventually began attending services in person. Others preferred to listen on radio. Certainly this was a help for the elderly and infirm.

There were also Bible schools of the air—educational programs ranging in length from a few minutes to a half hour or longer. Again, these programs were seen as vehicles for spreading the Word.

Gradually a few preachers began doing local broadcasting of traveling revivals. They would set up in a tent or hall, bring in sound equipment, and broadcast the message, the music, and the testimonials to anyone who wanted to listen.

Later the concept evolved into the types of shows now run by the televangelists. The radio became a substitute for the church. It was possible to bring sermons, testimonials, singing, and religious music into the homes of people who would never meet their "pastor." Serving the people meant entertaining and informing them, perhaps baptizing members of the studio audience, but rarely going beyond that. They did not have to visit the sick. They did not have to minister to the elderly and infirm in a manner that would bring them into close contact. They did not have to deal with death and grieving. They did not have to face challenges to the way they thought, as might occur in a real Sunday school Bible class—challenges not meant to be offensive but forcing a clarity of communication often lacking in broadcasting. It was the ideal place for the man or woman who wanted to reach a large audience without ever truly getting involved. It was also the ideal place for fraud.

Healers often used radio because no one could see what they were doing and there was no accountability for statements about their past. It was much like the tent revivalist who speaks of the blind seeing and the lame walking through the healing touch that God has bestowed upon the itinerant preacher. He or she will lay hands on the ill, call out demons, and otherwise act as expected, declaring that in the days and weeks ahead the person who has been touched will be well again. But days or weeks later, the revival leader will be in another town, hundreds or thousands of miles away, again talking of past miracles without accountability. Only the local pastor of the church that sponsored or encouraged participation in the revival will remain and try to explain why the pronouncements did not come true.

The lack of accountability is a tremendous attraction for televangelists. It allows them to engage in outrageous behavior with little fear that the fraudulent nature of what they say will be discovered.

The corruption of religious broadcasting was most evident during the late 1930s, when it became politicized on a national level unlike anything that would be seen again until Pat Robertson made a run for the presidency. The difference was that while Robertson represented a conservative right wing of the Republican Party, the politicization of the 1930s was strongly against the U.S. system of government.

The man who took religious and political speech to a new level of misleading extremism was a Catholic priest named Charles E. Coughlin. At the time he started broadcasting, radio was frequently using a format akin to that of newspapers. Letters to the editor were duplicated in the form of the man-on-the-street interview. Speeches were carried live so that they could be heard as given, not read in newspapers the next day. And entertainment, such as radio plays, was equivalent to the short stories and continuing serials popular with many of the larger newspapers.

By the 1930s, a few unique voices were coming to radio. The half-hour situation comedy, drama, or action/adventure story had been refined into a medium almost as popular as motion pictures. And religious broadcasting had evolved from a simple re-creation of a Sunday service or Bible study to a medium that, in a few instances, included social commentary. Religious broadcasting was becoming an important force in American politics, and the most famous of these broadcasters was the notorious Father Coughlin.

Father Coughlin established his radio broadcasts from the Shrine of the Little Flower in Royal Oak, Michigan. It was also there that he started a political movement called the National

Union for Social Justice, which registered five million members in the first two months, all of them listeners to his program.

"In politics I am neither Republican, Democrat, nor Socialist. I glory in the fact that I am a simple Catholic priest endeavoring to inject Christianity into the fabric of an economic system woven upon the loom of greed by the cunning fingers of those who manipulate the shuttles of human lives for their own selfish purposes," Coughlin explained, creating an image belied by his other actions.

Early on, Father Coughlin's hate speech took on added importance in the minds of some of his followers because of his religious connection. There was a sense that he might be speaking the will of God, whether he was talking theology or politics. It would be the same attitude held by the followers of the Reverend Pat Robertson after his *700 Club* became a platform for political ideas that helped launch a bid for the presidency. However, the message of Coughlin was far different. Robertson wanted to work within the political system. Coughlin was against it. He was a proviolence Nazi sympathizer who had the sense to word his attacks in such a manner that his true message was not always evident to the public. But when he became riled, he could be blatant in describing the violence he felt could be tolerated if "necessary."

"When any upstart dictator in the U.S. succeeds in making this a one party form of government, when the ballot is useless, I shall have the courage to stand up and advocate the use of bullets," said Coughlin in a September 1936 broadcast during Franklin D. Roosevelt's campaign for his second term in office. "Mr. Roosevelt is a radical. The Bible commands 'increase and multiply,' but Mr. Roosevelt says to destroy and devastate. Therefore I call him anti-God."

Coughlin's hate speech was oddly acceptable at the time, and yet it was quite similar to the rhetoric of Malcolm X twenty-eight years later when, in a speech demanding the right to vote, he announced, "The ballot or the bullet. It's one or the other in 1964."

The speech by Malcolm X, which stated the reality of the frustration of illegally disenfranchised Americans, was actually far less incendiary and heard by far fewer people than Coughlin's. Yet, whereas Malcolm X was denounced and investigated by law-enforcement officers, Coughlin was applauded.

The approaching war in Europe revealed Coughlin's odd way of defining the people he hated. Analysts felt he was using the same approach that the Nazi propagandists were using in Germany—promising everyone something they wanted while masking their own true goals. Because his audience was largely uneducated, and because radio made no allowance for comparing what he said with reality, it was only through the study of his written works that he began to be exposed.

Coughlin's tactics were similar to those used by Hitler during his early years of power when he was taking control of people so disheartened and impoverished that any change made sense to them. Hitler told laborers that he would socialize society in order to improve their lot. The landed peasants were told that the great estates would be divided up, increasing their opportunities to do more than eke out a hardscrabble existence. The middle class was told that the big trusts would be dissolved so that they would have economic security. And the upper classes were told that communism would not be tolerated. The elimination of Jews from society, rearmament, and the stabilization of the currency were other issues that delighted the demoralized, frequently anti-Semitic German public.

Father Coughlin used a similar approach to attack democracy. In August of 1938, when he made the following comments in his magazine *Social Justice*, he ignored the fact that most Americans considered democracy to be a way for Christians and Jews to follow a philosophy based on the brotherhood of man. This was certainly how the supporters of Franklin Roosevelt viewed their president's actions. But Coughlin wrote:

Democracy! More honored in the breach than the observance.

Democracy! A mockery that mouths the word and obstructs every effort on the part of an honest people to establish a government for the welfare of the people.

Democracy! A cloak under which hide the culprits who have built up an inorganic tumor of government which is sapping away the wealth of its citizens through confiscatory taxation.

Father Coughlin's remedies frequently paralleled those of the Nazis, although he claimed to oppose both nazism and communism. He also stressed that when his program of Christian leadership was inaugurated, "Millions of American citizens, now followers either of the Communistic or Nazi cause. . . . will abandon the red flag and the swastika as soon as they can discover an active, sound program, in harmony with the Stars and Stripes and the Cross of Christ, a program which, if reduced to action, will liquidate the social, the industrial, the political, and the financial abuses which are responsible for our national misery."

The problem was that the numbers were exaggerated, a technique later used by radio talk show personalities. There weren't "millions" of Americans involved with extremist groups on the left or the right in 1938. The Justice Department's best estimates, based on a partial mandate to prepare Americans for at least thinking about involvement in the European turmoil, listed the Communist Party membership at a maximum of 90,000 men and women, the German-American Nazi Bund at no more than 8300 members, the Silver Shirt Legion at a maximum of 10,000 members, with most accounts seeing half that number, and all the other left- and right-wing extremist groups combined at no more than a few thousand members. Experts felt that the total number had to be fewer than 150,000. But by claiming that there were millions, and by stressing that what he proposed could end this allegedly serious danger to society, Coughlin was assuring himself of support that he might otherwise have been unable to attract.

Coughlin rallied people around nonissues. For example, he demanded that there be: "First, liberty of conscience and of education. A man and his family must be guaranteed the right to worship his God when and how he pleases. A father must be assured that his children belong to him, and not to the state, and therefore that he has the right to educate his children either in public or private schools."

This appeal was effective with Christians of limited education. They did not realize that the "threats" to their liberty that Father Coughlin railed against were not threats at all. Religious freedom was guaranteed by the First Amendment, and no politicians were trying to change it. As for education, it was the same as it is today in that parents had the right to send their children to public or private schools. There were no restrictions.

Father Coughlin suggested that "certain public resources should be nationalized, in the sense that either Federal or State governments may develop transportation, power, and light, through the agency of politically free corporations, but not in the sense that Federal or State governments should monopolize public utilities to the exclusion of private corporations." Again, what he was talking about were the already existing municipal power plants, privately owned public utilities, and the federally owned Tennessee Valley Authority.

The Coughlin search for power through religion was aimed toward the blue-collar worker who was likely to have dropped out of school several years before graduation. He stressed workers' rights, ignoring the fact that he was demanding what was already in place, such as the right for labor to organize unions, a right guaranteed by the Wagner Act. However, he also seemed to be calling for organizations that would combine both management and workers—"Neither capital nor labor should organize against each other, because social justice must be meted out to all without exception"—and this message ultimately proved to be one of many subtle endorsements of the Nazi system. In fact, what he was advocating in this and other writings and speeches exactly matched the structure of an organization called the Nazi Labor Front.

Father Coughlin's agenda became obvious when his followers were encouraged to work with the German-American Bund, an openly Nazi group. The two groups picketed radio stations throughout the United States that refused to run Coughlin's quirky brand of hate, politics, and Christianity. And at Bund rallies in large cities, his newspaper, *Social Justice*, was sold, his name applauded by the men and women who supported Hitler's Third Reich.

Father Coughlin, however, had the right to do what he did, no matter how destructive the potential. It was the American public's first glimpse of the potential danger of the hybrid of religion and extremist politics.

The Bible has stories that seem to call for what are perceived to be political stands. Certainly Jesus was seen as a threat to the political structure of the Roman occupying force. Jesus made clear that he considered politics to be separate from what today might be called social action. For example, upon being shown a coin of the empire, he said "Render unto Caesar what is Caesar's." And even those clergy involved in social protest over the years tend to start with direct help to the poor, the infirm, and the suffering before seeking government assistance for their efforts. They feel that the deed must precede all else.

There are, however, some clergy who feel that God can best be served by simultaneous social and political action. This is especially true with issues such as abortion. Some clergy who are opposed to abortion feel that they must counsel pregnant women and help them understand the alternatives. Others feel that they must demonstrate publicly. And still others feel that God wants them to do everything necessary to shut down abortion clinics, including supporting politicians willing to make the procedure illegal. Some of these clergy run for office. Others use their congregations—whether traditional or electronic—to spread their political messages, and it is over the latter group that there is controversy.

What are the ethics of trying to narrow the focus of a man or woman using a religious show to express personal beliefs? What if you personally believe that the nature of the television ministry is not what it seems? What if you feel that the elderly, the naive, and others without surplus funds are being manipulated with falsehoods in order to get them to send money to the show? The First Amendment requires tolerance of any view, whether eccentric or vicious, if it is truly the belief of the speaker.

For example, one of the most reprehensible approaches to religion is taken by television faith healers who use a sense of personal guilt to keep their supporters. They usually have healing lines where they invoke the name of Jesus, call out whatever is wrong with the person, and strike him or her on in the head, at which time the person falls back, healed and filled with the Holy Spirit. Ernest Angley explains that everyone who is "slain in the spirit" on his show is healed by God. Angley does not claim to heal. He says he is merely God's vessel for healing, a process that many clergy feel occurs through them or through others whom they view as healers. But the key to continuing good health, according to Angley, is never to lose faith. Tragically, some viewers interpret this to mean that they should never go back to their doctors to check on the heart condition, cancer, or whatever other illness they might have.

Angley explains himself in his book *Faith in God Heals the Sick,* in which he writes:

Accept God's Word through faith. Symptoms of your disease may recur after you are prayed for, but never let those symptoms cause you to doubt what God has done for you. [Note how Angley stresses symptoms, separating the symptoms from the underlying problem. It is as though chest pain is a test of your faith that God has cured you of the heart disease for which your doctor has been treating you.]

Do not look back! Lot's wife looked back and lost her life. You, too, will lose yours if you turn back to your city of bondage, the sickness and despair where the devil has held you in captivity. Don't look back to the horrible condition you were in, but look forward to a new life—a life free from sin and sickness.[4]

Angley warns that God is intolerant of deviation from pure faith. He has written, "A young man born deaf and mute came into the healing line. He had never uttered one word in his life. God healed him that night, and he could hear and speak; but a few nights later he got drunk. Because of it, he not only lost his hearing, but the mute spirit re-entered and took his powers of speech."[5]

The result is a show in which those shown going through the healing line, becoming "slain in the spirit" and falling back into the loving arms of the "catchers" who then lay them on the ground, are all supposed to be made well by the power of God. They also receive the message that if they lose faith, they will potentially be made not just sick but actually sicker than they were before the healing. God seems to condemn the medical profession and all other avenues to health. If you go through the healing line, and then want to check the results with your doctor, even if just to better praise God's actions, there is a good chance you will be punished. Fear and guilt prevent people in need of medical care from obtaining it.[6]

Televangelists such as Angley create a problem for broadcasters and the public because they may truly believe what they say. Certainly we know that there is a psychological aspect to wellness. And for many people, the televangelist may be the only medical help they can afford. They are without health insurance. They live in communities that lack free clinics. Turning to a religious broadcaster promising freedom from illness is better than thinking that there is no alternative to their suffering.

Of greater concern are the frauds and semifrauds, the men and women who will use any means to convince people that God is working through them. There is difficulty in discerning them.

For example, there is what is known as "prosperity theology." This is the idea that God rewards the righteous on earth. The more money one has, and the more one is respected by others, the better person one must be. Such an idea inherently condemns the poor, because it implies that all one has to do to get money is to be right with God.

Ignoring the social implications of such thinking, the issue of misuse of funds by televangelists is another ethical question that is difficult to answer. For example, when Jim and Tammy Faye Bakker were disgraced as televangelists, one of the issues was their use of money for personal pleasure. Even their dog had an air-conditioned home of its own.

Jim Bakker eventually went to jail for a period of time, although many of the issues surrounding his crimes were related to off-the-air ministry actions including alleged adultery. Owning luxurious homes, expensive jewelry, and custom-made clothing purchased with contributions from viewers might fit the viewers' beliefs of how a good man should live. They might be annoyed that money sent to help the ministry was spent on personal purchases, but they also might feel that, although somewhat of a scoundrel, the televangelist should have the money. They might even cite a biblical example such as King David, who, although obviously flawed, was still blessed and considered a favorite of God's.

What about other types of faith healers, men and women who are less blatant than Angley. They may use the simple approach of calling out an illness. The televangelist will look into the camera, announce that a healing is taking place at that very minute, and then describe how somewhere in the viewing audience God is reaching out to a viewer of the show. He or she will say something to the effect of: "God is healing a knee. I can feel it right now. It's . . . you know how when you get up in the morning you feel like you have to take hold of your leg and work it a bit to get it going? It has that kind of an ache? I can feel God reaching out and healing that knee right now. It won't happen instantly. It took you how many years to have the problem? But tomorrow or the next day it will be getting better and better because God is healing it."

Or the focus may be chest pains, difficulty in walking long distances without getting winded, or other common symptoms of older, sedentary men and women. The symptoms and problems mentioned are always planned to match the demographics of the viewing audience. Even slang terms used by a large number of viewers might be employed, such as referring to diabetes as "the sugar." It seems that children are never healed during this part of the program, although there may be a story of miraculous healing involving a child at some other point in the show. Such an event may be dramatized, perhaps with a recent picture of the healed child. But during the time when the televangelist speaks into the camera, there is rarely, if ever, any mention of children or of diseases such as AIDS. Instead, the people who are the prime targets for fund raising—older, blue-collar, often of limited education, and usually having worked at physically demanding jobs prior to their retirement—are the ones who are healed.

In the extreme are two common tricks of television evangelists. The first is also used by some traveling evangelists who set up tent and auditorium engagements in different cities. A section of wheelchairs is provided—ostensibly for disabled individuals coming to the program in the hope of being healed. However, although some people legitimately in wheelchairs are placed in the same area, frail-looking elderly people who are quite capable of walking are asked to sit in the vacant chairs. Then, during the time of healing, the evangelist will call the men and women forward, praising God that they can walk to the stage. The audience will applaud—sometimes spontaneously, sometimes encouraged by floor workers—and the act of walking, which these people have always been capable of doing, will seem to be a miracle. Because the director of the broadcast controls which microphones are on and which are off, any microphones in the vicinity of the healthy people sitting in wheelchairs will be cut off. In this way, if they try to explain to the staff that they are not physically impaired, the viewing audience will not hear them.

Another common trick is to proclaim that someone has been healed, and then have him or her attest immediately to the healing. For example, a woman will have a lump in her breast obvious enough that she knows there is a good chance she has cancer. Sometimes she has been diagnosed with cancer and is trying to avoid a radical mastectomy. At other times she goes on the show in hope of avoiding what she knows may be her diagnosis. The healer replaces the doctor.

The healer lays hands on the woman and pronounces her cured by "Dr. Jesus," or whatever term the televangelist uses. Then she will be sent to a private area to check the breast. When she returns moments later, the evangelist says something such as "It's already getting smaller, isn't it? You can already detect that slight change in size which shows God's healing miracle in your life, can't you?"

What person who has gone that far, been publicly touched, and then placed on camera to attest to God's healing power will admit that she sees no difference? And even if she does see no difference, won't she give God the benefit of the doubt?

There is also the rare charlatan who engages in tricks familiar to magicians and some carnival workers. Sometimes, for example, a wireless radio is used to alert the evangelist to information about someone who is being interviewed by a staff member. The healer "divines" the person's problem from the stage and prays for him or her to be healed. The audience, unaware of the trickery, thinks the evangelist is truly of the spirit because this person can seemingly discern even at a distance the demons that plague people.

Then there is the healer who cures people at home by laying hands on the television screen. "Bring your hand to the television screen as I bring my hand to the camera," the evangelist will order. "Do you feel the tingling sensation? That is God working through me to you. That is the healing power of Jesus coming right through your set as you lay your hand on mine on the screen." What the viewer actually feels, of course, is the sensation of the normal magnetic field given off by all television sets. One can feel the same sensation by touching the screen while watching a beer commercial or the Mighty Morphin Power Rangers. But because few people ever touch their screens, the sensation seems to be directly connected to a spiritual power so great that it can pass over the airwaves.

Such tricks often play on the belief systems of the viewers. Television evangelists have been caught embezzling money donated to further their ministries. They have been caught in sex crimes and adultery. They have occasionally had to confess to their "congregations," gathered before television sets hundreds or thousands of miles away. And always there is the sense that because Jesus forgave the sinner, their confessions exonerate them. God simply picked an "unlikely vessel" to be messenger of the Word. If men and women can preach so effectively as to improve the lives of others, and yet have personal lives that are so messy, obviously they are being used by God. Their weakness is proof that their message must come from a power greater than themselves.

Jim and Tammy Faye Bakker were typical of the fallen television evangelists of a few years ago. They were an unusual couple. Jim Bakker was a firm believer in bringing Christians together for worship and entertainment, extending his ministry to what amounted to a Christian amusement park/hotel/retreat/golf course called Heritage U.S.A. His wife, Tammy Faye, was a supporter of Jim's efforts and also a believer in enhancing what God had created through the seeming overuse of cosmetics. She bragged that her husband had never seen her without makeup, yet to many people her use of makeup was so excessive that her face looked like a painted mask.

The show the couple produced was like a soap opera. Their personal lives were often the topic of conversation. One or the other was likely to become so emotional that there would be a flow of tears (and, in the case of Tammy Faye, mascara).

The approach to religion was never a question. Many people responded to Bakker's messages about Christian faith. Many also traveled to Heritage U.S.A., where they, along with the staff, were impressed with Bakker's dedication to giving the visitors a positive experience. They told of Bakker being seen shortly after sunrise, walking the grounds, picking up paper, gum wrappers, and other waste, making certain that everything was spotless for his guests.

Bakker made several serious mistakes. First, he had an adulterous relationship with an employee. He and Tammy Faye also used extensive funds for an elaborate lifestyle that included air conditioning in their dog's outside house. And Bakker's most serious troubles with the law came from overselling the hotel he maintained at Heritage U.S.A. To raise money for the construction, he had created partnerships whereby, in return for a large contribution, each contributor was guaranteed a set number of nights per year. This was a little like a time-share arrangement and was quite popular—in fact, too popular. The hotel was always overbooked because more partnerships were sold than there were rooms in the hotel and nights in a year. The end result was a jail term and fall from grace, a divorce, and the loss of everything he had created.

All of this led to tremendous controversy. Evangelist Jimmy Swaggart ridiculed Jim Bakker, but then was caught having sex with a prostitute and her daughter. Many of their followers became desperate for an understanding of what had happened. They constantly wrestled with the issue of whether or not God's message was tainted by a failed messenger. Even worse, they had to do this without each other's support—the kind of support that is readily available in a traditional religious congregation when a leader fails the people he or she serves.

Perhaps the greatest problem comes with fund raising by televangelists who have themselves as their own product and use God as an endorser. Sometimes the technique is one familiar to older individuals from certain denominations of which most Americans are unaware. When Oral Roberts warned that if he didn't raise the money for his medical center in Tulsa, "God will call me home," the public was outraged. He seemed to be stating that God was blackmailing the viewing audience. "Pay the money or I'll kill the preacher" was the implication. Yet in this case, Roberts was using a technique that was once common among preachers in small Southern areas. There was a job for each person to do, and if the person failed to do it, he or she was "called home" by God.

Likewise, Roberts referred to the "demon" of each different type of illness. Instead of using medical terms, he would talk of the "demon" of cancer, the "demon" of arthritis, the "demon" of diabetes. Yet when he interviewed medical professionals who had worked for him in Tulsa, it was found that his medical knowledge was sophisticated. Only his language seemed quaint.

Television exposes evangelists to a much broader range of people than they could attract to conventional ministries. Some televangelists rise to the occasion by using phrases and style that are comfortable for the broadest possible range of people. Others, such as Oral Roberts, speak as they have always spoken.

At the same time, Roberts talked about encountering a 600-foot Jesus and of fighting for his life with Satan. Even his most loyal followers began to question what was apparently either extreme exaggeration or outright falsehood. And other fund-raising methods he has used, including events where his son declares that God is calling for a specific contribution of twenty dollars or some other specific amount, are equally questionable.

Again, whether they are appropriate or not, does anyone dare to challenge the ethics of such religious broadcasters? What if they truly believe what they are saying? Dare we, the media critics, deny them a First Amendment freedom?

In the late 1950s, the most popular programs on early evening television were game shows. These were question-and-answer programs in which large sums of money could be won by answering questions on art, literature, sports, opera, or any number of other categories. The people who appeared on them—models, professors, cab drivers, and others—were a cross section of American society. It was as though intelligence could be found in everyone, a subtle reminder that the viewing audience deserved respect.

The audience was varied because this was a period when television sets had gone from being expensive to being affordable. It was also a time when many people still were of limited education. Labor jobs paid wages that were often higher than professionals could earn, and so factory workers could afford luxuries. But there was a sense of inferiority for those without some form of advanced training. And the school systems around the country were in shambles to the degree that a best-selling book of the 1950s was *Why Johnny Can't Read.*

The advertisers for these programs were frequently companies making products for a blue-collar audience. Revlon was one of the biggest sponsors, and its marketing strategy during this period was to constantly introduce new cosmetic products, market them aggressively, then remove them from the market in favor of something else. These items—relatively low in cost but producing large profits for the manufacturer—were frequently sold through drugstores. By contrast, the more expensive cosmetic items were sold in department stores and specialty shops where wealthier women did their shopping.

The quiz shows bestowed a dignity on the average person in many instances, and many of the early-round questions were such that the average person might know the answer. It was a technique that would later be used by performers such as Roseanne, who understood the dignity, hard work, and need for respect of working-class men and women. However, whereas *Roseanne* arrived on television following other successful programs aimed toward working-class families, the quiz shows were introduced when most other programming comprised stories of suburban white families, often employing maids or cleaning women.

What went unsaid until the quiz show scandal broke, resulting in congressional hearings and newspaper editorial outrage, was that the games were often rigged. Some people won legitimately. Others were given the answers in advance.

Religious programs seem to fall into the same demographic appeal area as the old quiz shows. They provide information and entertainment. Theoretically, no one is hurt by their ethical violations. Yet just as the quiz show producers discovered that the viewing public wanted to be able to trust the integrity of the programs, so there is also an issue of public trust concerning the information provided through religious programming.

The difficulty with religious programming is that it falls within First Amendment freedoms. Can anyone determine exactly what another person truly believes? And when a religious broadcaster is caught cheating, if he or she turns the action into a morality lesson, is this not right and proper within the context of the show?

The answer, of course, is that all fraudulent programming should be exposed. It is right for the public to hold someone who claims to speak for God to a higher ethical standard than the host or contestant on a quiz show. Yet there are no hearings in Washington concerning deception in religious broadcasting, nor are there ever likely to be such hearings. It is an area in need of ethical reform and improved standards, and yet it is also the one area where the attitude of regulators will remain one of uneasy tolerance. It is better not to rile the true believers than to hold the televangelists to the standards of the holy books they claim to represent.

I would like to provide a set of standards for improving religious broadcasting, but to do so would be to force a personal bias on others. This is a field filled with different interpretations of the same God. One person's false theology is another person's proof of the goodness of the Creator. If a televangelist makes large sums of money, is this contrary to the teachings of Jesus? Or is the televangelist showing the world what prosperity theology is all about, that the good are always blessed with material wealth? There are true believers on both sides of the issue.

What is the answer? First, television evangelism should not be used as an alternative to participation in a conventional religious organization. Attending a church, synagogue, or mosque fits in with the teachings of the three major religions practiced by Americans. It is within the local facility that there can be true pastoring, sharing, and support. For those who are shut-ins, a few telephone calls to area places of worship will reveal one or more groups that make home visitations to the disabled and infirm a part of their ministries. Such genuine social interaction can be critical for both survival and quality of life for the infirm.

Before sending money to a televangelist, request a financial report. Depending on many factors, they are required to give you information on the money they take in and how they spend it. Those who fail to provide such financial disclosure should not receive your support.

Recognize that the products sold may not have great value. Ultimately the money goes to the organization, not to God. In the case of books, many are available through your local library, either directly or from another library through what is known as an interlibrary loan.

Finally, keep in mind that the heart of religious practice is loving God, nurturing others, and being caretakers of Creation. No matter which religion someone follows, these ideas are generally at the heart of its beliefs. A televangelist can entertain and inform, but simply to watch such shows and then send money avoids the heart of the message found in Judaism, Christianity, and Islam and does not represent full involvement in a religious life.

Fortunately, religious broadcasting is only a small portion of the available television programming at any given time, and in most areas there is none during much of the day. But given the trusting attitude of many viewers, televangelism provides greater potential for betrayal of the faithful than do the programs that are most often attacked—television talk shows.

3

Out of the Mouths of Babes, and Studs, and Stars, and . . .

Talk shows, depending on your point of view, are sheer entertainment and the cheapest therapy in America for any emotional problem that ails you, or the corruption of all that is moral and decent and the reason why today's youth are running amok in the streets.

I have appeared on talk shows approximately 250 times in recent years. My topics have been those of the books I have written—the Hillside Strangler, the Kennedy family, why people choose to worship evil, faith-healing frauds, and women who have been "kept" by the rich, the famous, and the powerful. Even my own life has been an occasional focus, such as when I discussed an autobiography dealing with the adoption of two of our four children. I have sat and chatted with everyone from Geraldo Rivera (or "Geraldo!" as he is advertised, the exclamation point worthy proof that he was once sold as the most outrageous interviewer on the air) and Sally Jessy Raphael, to the small-market wanna-be's. I have even been the talk show segment guest for Christian variety shows such as *The 700 Club* and *Heritage U.S.A.*

I was not a typical guest, of course. I have never slept with my son's fiancée after marrying my former mother-in-law because my ex-wife caught us in bed and I had to make an honest woman out of her. I have never experienced sexual dysfunction requiring me to hire a surrogate sex partner coach to give my wife and me step-by-step instructions whenever we try to "do it" together. And I have never engaged in a "May-December" or "December-May" romance that has resulted in a pregnancy test being administered live, on the air, right there on *Sally Jessy Raphael.*

Although I am being facetious about the extremes to which such shows can go, instances such as the live pregnancy test are not unusual. On Monday, November 20, 1995, I happened to tune in *Sally Jessy Raphael,* a program on which I had last appeared after rape charges had been brought against William Kennedy Smith, a member of the influential Kennedy family. That show had been a pretrial exploitation of a tragedy about which I was knowledgeable because of a book I had written on the family's third generation. The more recent show, on which I did not appear, was a follow-up of previous programs on which couples aired one type of problem or another, and the most dramatic story was that of a seventy-three-year-old man and his thirty-one-year-old wife.

In today's society, seventy-three is not particularly ancient, although the man who was the guest seemed elderly beyond his years. He reminded me of the type of men you see in small farming communities—rail thin, their faces weathered by years of working under the sun, their speech rather shaky and slightly impaired by poor dental care. The politically incorrect would call them "geezers" because they lack the vibrant energy of so many men their age who have had better diets, better health care, and less physically demanding lives. I don't know if Sally's guest had the background that I imagined, but his appearance fit the stereotype.

The thirty-one-year-old woman to whom he was married had the face of someone who could have been a model. She was certainly attractive enough to get a man closer to her own age, which is always the issue with this type of program. Conventional reasoning may claim that a fat, unattractive woman will marry any man who asks her and be grateful for what she gets. By contrast, most people believe that a beautiful woman has her choice of men. However, when this woman opened her mouth to speak, her speech was rather harsh. If he was the stereotypical "geezer," she portrayed the image of the "tough broad," probably with a "heart of gold." After all, she had looked past superficial appearance in order to love the man inside.

And love that man she did, which was why, according to Sally's comments and the tape clips of past shows, she was so outraged when he committed adultery. She found him in bed with another woman, something she discussed privately with only Sally and a few million of their closest friends. He claimed no memory of the "dirty deed." She said she had found them in bed, and he did not dispute the charge, but he stated that he had been unconscious at the time.

The audience loved the couple and seemed to enjoy the image of a "geezer" adulterer, and many assumed that the relationship was over. Instead of being grateful for the love of this young, attractive woman, he had defiled their marital bed, even if he was telling the truth and had slept through the act.

What was to be their third appearance was the result of Sally's audience's inquiring minds wanting to know if "May" had stayed with "December." And Sally was quick to point out that not only was the couple still together, they were happier than ever. "May" thought that "December" had gotten her pregnant, a fact she had so far failed to share with him.

In a voice that sounded full of happy anticipation, Sally told her audience that even as the show was unfolding, a staff member from the program and a registered nurse were on their way to the couple's house to administer a pregnancy test. "December" knew nothing about this. "May" thought he would be angry, that he would not want the patter of little feet interrupting his enjoyment of Social Security and youthful sex. However, Sally assured the audience that "May" was determined to keep the child regardless of what her husband might desire. She thus maintained the titillation, hinted at yet another follow-up look at the volatile couple, and assured any abortion foes in the audience that "May" was a good human being at heart.

I never did find out what happened. The show ended before the registered nurse could arrive to administer the pregnancy test. Sally assured all of us, who were breathlessly awaiting the results, that we would see them the next day. She would not let "May" know if she was pregnant unless we were there to share in the experience. Unfortunately I had an unbreakable appointment so I cannot tell you the outcome of this dramatic story.

In years past, cynical radio talk show hosts, who preceded their television counterparts, would have referred to "December" as a "dirty old man." His "May" would have been called a "gold digger" because she could reasonably have expected him to die while she was still young, attractive, and able to marry again. But this is the 1990s, when many television talk shows present compassionate looks at real problems of real people who might also be your next-door neighbors, as long as your next-door neighbor is an anorexic transvestite stalked by an ex-boyfriend who was a priest prior to his marrying a . . . well, you get the picture.

There is a tendency to become flippant about television talk shows. After all, no one forces the guests to go on the air and discuss their problems. Men and women are not kidnapped from their homes, transported in cages, then chained to the sets until they reveal their infidelities, rape experiences, communication problems, and the like. The guests volunteer to go on, often by calling a toll-free telephone number. The talk show producers select a candidate topic, then advertise for people who have the required experience. Everyone volunteers, and everyone receives a free trip, a chauffeured ride into the city, a hotel room, meals, and sometimes a small fee that at least compensates for their missing a day's pay.

In some instances, the chance to be on television seems to affect the actions people take in their daily lives. Christine Lee[7] is an attractive, articulate woman who considered herself engaged to Richard Ramirez, the convicted rapist/murderer known as the Night Stalker. She is one of many women who have become involved with death-row inmates they have met through correspondence. These men have celebrity images, are no longer a danger to others, and could not cheat even if they chose to do so. As one woman now married to a death-row inmate commented to me, "At least I always know where my man is at night."

The chance to appear on talk shows seems to provide some motivation for women like Lee, who also has maintained what would seem to be normal and healthy relationships with other men. She dates "good guys" while declaring her love for Ramirez, a "love" that has ensured that the talk shows will come calling. As she explained:

> My parents have a lot of money, right? He [her father] gave me black eyes a lot, and I'd go to school . . . like then . . . then it wasn't reported, you know what I mean? My aunt has home videos of when I was six and I had two black eyes, and I told her, and she just goes "Oh, shut up, liar." You know what I mean? I don't even talk to them anymore. I just stopped a few months ago.

Christine's home life, as she described it, included what she believed to be abnormal abuse. She talked of violence against children as being normal and was surprised that I considered hitting my wife or son to be wrong. She alleged that she had been abused by her father, who had hit her. The implication of her comments was that as she viewed "proper" childhood, a father was only supposed to hit his son; he was never to strike his daughter.

> I felt like something was wrong [when her father abused her]. Like when I was thirteen and I told my aunt, and she just like . . . "Yeah, yeah, yeah. You're a liar." And she told my father. And then I got in trouble for telling her. He punched me in the face.

And then right after that I dropped out of high school, and had a baby, and I was like, I've got to get away from these people [her parents]. I was like an "A" student.

And now by being near Richard [Ramirez] it's like, *I feel like I'm embarrassing them, and I love it* [emphasis added]. You know what I mean?

And I love embarrassing them. Like they've got really good jobs and they've got a lot of money, so this is like embarrassing them to death, and I love it.

Like I've been on every talk show except *Oprah*, and some I've been on three times, like two or three times. *A Current Affair* like three times. *Inside Edition . . .*"

In a sense, the talk shows have a symbiotic relationship with women such as Christine. Many stay in business only because viewers use the shows for personal ends. Christine, for example, needed the talk shows as a means of seeking vengeance for the wrongs she felt she had suffered at the hands of her family. Regardless of whether or not her allegations were true, she believed what she was saying. She seemed to be using the notoriety of the relationship she had developed as a partial substitute for counseling.

Christine understood what she was doing, although her actions may have seemed to be inappropriate to an outsider. Others allegedly are unsuspecting victims of the producers. In a never-aired *Jenny Jones Show*, the producers arranged for guests to meet their secret admirers. One guest, Jonathan Schmitz, thought he would be meeting a woman who had long desired him. Schmitz was twenty-four, worked as a waiter in Bloomfield Hills, Michigan, and was so certain that a romantic interlude would follow that he spent three hundred dollars on new clothing before being flown to Chicago to appear on the show. Instead, the secret admirer was Scott Amedure, a homosexual bartender.

Because the program was never aired, exactly what happened is not known. Allegedly, Schmitz handled the shock gracefully, with neither humiliation nor rage evident in his demeanor during the rest of the show. However, the humiliation he felt seemed to fester inside him. He bought a shotgun and, a few days later, went to the bartender's home. He fired two shots into Amedure's chest, killing him instantly.

Oddly, the reaction in the television talk show industry was mostly positive—in favor of Jenny Jones. When *Cosmopolitan* writer Marilyn Stasio interviewed producers and other insiders concerning the incident for rival programs, one man told her: "I think that guy was on a bad path. If he was gonna murder, he was gonna murder. No one particular thing can change a docile person into a murderer, whether it's going on a talk show or going into a bar. That guy was definitely disturbed to begin with."

Oddly, although talk shows often pander to the voyeurs in life (titles of programs include "My Mom Is Way Too Sexy," "Confronting the Woman Coming On to My Man," "You're Too Old to Be Dating a Teen," and "I Won't Wait for The Wedding Day, I Want to Sleep with You First"), they are shocked when someone dares to mock them. The *Jerry Springer Show* thought it had another perfect tabloid episode when the father of a young child decided to admit to sleeping with the babysitter.

In the real world, men have been known to cheat on their wives with secretaries, coworkers, and even the family babysitter. In the real world, either they get caught or they don't. In the real world, they confess, if at all, either in the privacy of their own homes or in very public places where the intense emotional reactions that might follow will at least have a chance of being contained.

But producers of talk shows don't think about the real world. In their drive for ratings, they are too likely to encounter people so anxious for their moment on camera that they will do anything, hurt anyone, including themselves. Thus the Jerry Springer staff was delighted to have a program featuring the cheating father, his unsuspecting wife, the babysitter, and the babysitter's boyfriend.

As the audience sat enraptured and the cameras rolled, the husband confessed all. The babysitter was embarrassed. The boyfriend was upset. But the wife began sobbing uncontrollably. She sobbed during the show. She sobbed during the commercial breaks. She sobbed when the show was over. She was devastated, heartbroken, shattered. For all anyone knew, she was so despondent that she might not want to live.

And then came the confession. The tears ended as abruptly as they had begun. The four were not what they seemed. They were actually professional comedians.

Why the staff of the Springer show should have been upset to be duped in this way is hard to understand because the program was great entertainment; and therein lies the issue that is often ignored. Talk television is an entertainment medium. Some of the hosts have news backgrounds, such as Geraldo Rivera, who is also an attorney by training, but most of them are people who simply have the "gift of gab." They understand how to play to their audiences, sometimes because they are professionals from the stage or screen. Ricki Lake got her own talk show in 1993 when she was twenty-four years old, an age that is barely beyond adolescence. She had been overweight, a condition she had had the courage to both correct and discuss, thereby relating to many of the women in her audience. She also had played the ultimate average suburban teenage girl, filled with angst, eating the wrong foods, and in conflict with her parents in movies such as *Hairspray*, and she had learned to handle unpredictable reactions while controlling an audience during her years as a stand-up comic.

The reality is that almost anyone can become a talk show host, which is part of the reason why the number of such shows keeps growing. In the past there were entertainers who frequently did interviews—Johnny Carson, Merv Griffin, John Davidson, and others. Some had been nightclub entertainers, others were popular singers, and a few were intellectuals with a bent for comedy, such as Steve Allen and Dick Cavett. Many worked the late-night audience. Others had shows in the morning or afternoon. Songs were sung, jokes were told, appearances were plugged, and authors were interviewed.

Increasingly, the producers looked for ways to change. A variety show with interviews requires an elaborate set, perhaps an orchestra, and many guests who have to be paid a fee based on rates established by such unions as the American Federation of Television and Radio Artists. Rehearsal time is required for performers. It is a far less expensive undertaking than other shows, but it still does not return as high a profit as it would if there were no one but a host, a studio audience, and one or more "average people" discussing their lives and problems. Thus the shows went from entertainment to pure interviews in what was still meant to be a non-news medium. Some hosts, such as Oprah Winfrey, view themselves as serious presenters of important topics, at least much of the time, even though a ratings fight tends to bring out at least a hint of the salacious. Most have backgrounds that encourage any sense of seriousness to be looked at with a questioning mind because their talk shows are their only outlets for communication off the stage. This is why people such as Lake, Jones, and even comics such as Joan Rivers have all had their one hour a day of talk television.

There is nothing wrong with talk shows being entertaining. For more than a century, traveling carnivals had their freak shows. People with physical abnormalities—the bearded woman, the giant, the midget, the extremely obese fat lady, the lobster boy, and the like—would entertain the audience. Sometimes they gave performances, such as a powerful, unusually tall man (the giant) lifting weights and performing feats requiring great strength. At other times they would sit and talk with people who came by to see them. There was little difference between going to see the fat lady and looking at a caged elephant except that the fat lady could make jokes and trade insults with the crowd.

Today the fat lady is likely to appear on talk television to discuss her food addiction, how much she eats, the traumatic childhood that led to her "disease," and the pain of ridicule that drives her back to the refrigerator. The audience will cheer her efforts, and the talk show will typically have an "expert" on obesity who will give thirty-second sound bites of advice on how she can overcome her problem. There may be a follow-up program that reveals the progress the woman has been making, the show betting on whether the woman is on her way to a svelte figure (applause, whistles, and other sounds of support) or has returned to overeating (boos, hisses, and expressions of sadness and love for her during her struggle). It doesn't matter either way to the host and the staff. Both make for good programs, the freak show having been given new credibility now that it is coming live or on tape from New York, Chicago, or Los Angeles.

The fat lady is increasingly likely to appear on Christian talk television, which often is programmed a little like the old variety shows. They still have singing, sometimes by the host, and always uplifting Christian music. There may be a bit of praying, some humor (often at the expense of liberals and other heathens), some news focused on the greatest concern of the host (evangelical missions and the fight against abortion are strong topics), and the interview. At times there may even be a re-creation of the story being discussed.

For example, the fat lady's story will be briefly told with a voice-over narration. You will see her eating too much, perhaps surrounded by a breakfast of the type she once enjoyed (a dozen or more eggs, a loaf of bread, two jars of jam, a dozen pieces of bacon, a couple of potatoes made into home fries, a quart of orange juice, and a pot of coffee). You will see her husband's disgust, her children's shame, and the way this good woman was ridiculed by the public.

Then there will be the conversion story. Perhaps she is visited by a door-to-door evangelical of the same faith or belief as that of the show's host. Perhaps she is quietly reading the Bible seeking solace as she withdraws from the people around her. Whatever the case, she suddenly feels the overwhelming presence of God, Jesus, the risen Christ, the Virgin Mary, or the Holy Spirit. She realizes she is not alone. She realizes that she is loved by the Faithful One. She becomes filled with the Holy Spirit and is led to change her life, perhaps with the help of a support group, perhaps on her own, her husband and children recognizing the change and helping her through the intensely difficult time. Whatever the case, by the time she is introduced, she is on her way to full recovery. The audience, instead of ridiculing the woman for her obesity, applauds her for having been touched by God and for having changed her life through positive affirmation.

Yet the truth is that a freak show is a freak show in whatever guise it is presented. The woman is not brought on when she is down to a more normal size. She is shown while her appearance is still grotesque to many of the viewers. And if there is a follow-up, and if the woman has not continued to lose weight, the reaction may be as destructive as that of any secular talk show. Some hosts or audience members may see the woman as being possessed by the devil. Others may view her as backsliding, a fallen woman who lacked the faith in God that she needed to sustain her.

If the program provided news rather than entertainment, there is a chance that the host would at least pay lip service to the fairness issue. This issue has to do with giving equal time, or at least a chance for rebuttal, to those who are challenged. This idea was originally embodied in Federal Communications Commission regulations, which required the media to give equal access to all major candidates with the exception of the president (Title 47 of the Communications Act of 1934). The president, by virtue of the importance of the office, is granted unlimited access to the airwaves and does not have to be countered by rivals.

A presidential political speech and address to the nation is usually followed by a brief response by a member of the opposition party. But if a president gives a "fireside chat" of the type originated by Franklin D. Roosevelt and made into a weekly event by Ronald Reagan, there is no requirement for rebuttal. Likewise, a presidential press conference is seen as a news event even though it is highly orchestrated. The conference is usually held with the White House press corps, whose members know that their access is determined by whether or not they are reasonably gentle with the president. The president chooses the people who are called on, how each question will be answered, and whether or not a follow-up question on the subject will be allowed.

But regular news programs traditionally seek to provide alternative viewpoints in the interest of fairness. This usually means that if someone is accused of a crime, deviant behavior, or other impropriety that will make them hated by at least a portion of society, that person will be given a chance to tell his or her side of the story. Entertainment weeklies such as *People* magazine attempt to maintain fairness by giving people a right to respond when challenged. Television talk shows are under no such constraints because they have nothing to do with news. As a result, people can be hurt and information can be presented that is totally false or at least warrants harsh scrutiny, and it is all perfectly acceptable under the law.

Perhaps most dramatic have been the actions of Roseanne, an actress who began as Roseanne Barr, was briefly Roseanne Pentland, then Roseanne Arnold, and finally, because she allegedly hated family and husbands, caring only for that portion of herself that was uniquely her own, simply "Roseanne."

Roseanne was raised in a Jewish family in the midst of Mormons in Salt Lake City, Utah. She and her younger sister Geraldine were born entertainers, with Roseanne having the more biting wit and Geraldine being the more subtle of the two, the intellectual observer. Geraldine had an interest in business and what went on behind the scenes of television. Roseanne was the performer, caring little about business other than making certain she would not be cheated. As they grew up, they decided to take over Hollywood as sisters in the manner of some of the early Jewish brothers who built some of the studios.

Roseanne eventually became a highly successful nightclub comic, with Geraldine working behind the scenes. Then came the television show that made Roseanne a household name, a fight with Geraldine, and the two sisters going their separate ways.

Roseanne's success was a result of the fact that she reflected the blue-collar Everywoman, the same type of person who is the staple of the typical talk show. Phil Donahue, whose talk show dates back to 1967, was the first person to truly understand the audience that was waiting to be tapped. The original topics he tackled were important to the stay-at-home housewife and the reluctant blue-collar worker who was in the job market only because she could not afford to stay at home. Her focus was on her family, and yet she received little respect. She had to spend much of her time with small children, and her husband, who was also likely to have a blue-collar job, did not respect her. As repetitious as his work might be, he was out with other adults, exposed to events of which his wife had only second-hand knowledge. The fact that she might use her spare time to read, that she was self-educated to an extent that elevated her abilities beyond those of her husband, meant nothing to either of them. He did not feel the need to listen to her. He did not feel the need to take her opinions seriously. And he did not want to spend his evenings listening to her discussion of the children, the most familiar and important topic in her life.

The talk show that Phil Donahue crafted not only addressed issues of interest to blue-collar women, but also empowered them. Here was an attractive, well-educated, articulate, and highly paid man who was willing to listen to the women in his audience. He used such phrases as "Come on, ladies, help me out here" when imploring them to question the guests. They were able to ask any-thing that was on their minds, and they knew that if the guest did not respond, it was the guest, not them, who would look foolish. Nothing was scripted. They were the show, and they were re-spected accordingly. For the first time, ordinary women could get involved in ways that previously had been impossible. Humor writer Erma Bombeck was quoted as saying that Donahue was "every wife's replacement for the husband who doesn't talk to her," and he did indeed fill that void.

More important for writers was the fact that the women in the audience, although undereducated in many instances, were intel-ligent and avid readers. They were the readers once targeted by *Redbook* magazine in the 1950s and 1960s when it won awards for presenting complicated medical and social information and issues in a form that educated women who would otherwise not be ex-posed to such material. And they were the readers of the *National Enquirer*, perhaps the largest-circulation weekly in the United States.[8] Thus, although blue-collar women were ignored and were often derided for being uneducated stay-at-homes, they were seri-ous about information. Authors whose subjects attracted their in-terest on the talk shows were rewarded with increased sales at the bookstores.

Roseanne understood this world. Her first child—a daughter who was the result of a brief affair—was given up for adoption. Roseanne had little interest in formal education, preferring to learn about life by living it, including hitchhiking across large por-tions of the country. She lived in a tiny home with her first hus-band and their children. She witnessed how women of her low income level would do anything to help their families, which was the reason why so many of them got involved with catalog sales and companies such as Tupperware. She saw them buying lottery tickets as cheap potential investments. She saw them putting up with husbands who, although hardworking, were chronically overtired and were frustrated enough with life to retreat into drunkenness. She understood the insensitivity of men who, for any number of reasons, failed to think of their wives' needs and desires during sex, but she also recognized that although these men lusted after the centerfolds in male-oriented magazines, they still made love to the overweight, often physically rather dumpy women they had married.

Such women were intelligent and caring survivors who dominated the American scene, and a woman who could reflect their beliefs, values, goals, and lives in her comedy could become very rich. This Roseanne did, making millions of dollars by portraying herself as the blue-collar "Everywoman" despite the fact that her income afforded her a lifestyle to which almost no one is accustomed.

Family members feel that there has always been another side to Roseanne, a fantasy side.[9] They have expressed the attitude that she will say anything that attracts attention. And Geraldine has called her the "drama queen," a woman who will say outlandish things with a straight face because people will believe her. Geraldine also feels that there are times when, for Roseanne, the act of saying something is the act of making it "real." Truth becomes whatever Roseanne wants it to be.

The Barrs remain a mildly dysfunctional family in conflict, although the consensus among three of the four children is that there were never the types of problems Roseanne decided to reveal on national television. These alleged problems ultimately led Roseanne to the talk show circuit and the talk show topic of the 1990s—sexual abuse leading to multiple personality disorder.[10]

Roseanne's claims have been many, and they have frequently varied from one appearance to another. In her book *My Lives*, she wrote of her first memories coming back to her as her then husband Tom Arnold was wrestling with his past of genuine child abuse and molestation. Arnold was a drug addict who sought help for his problems in counseling, realizing that he was using alcohol and drugs because he could not deal with his memories of early abuse.

As Tom described his life with an alcoholic mother who abandoned the family, and some of the mother's physically abusive boyfriends, Roseanne convinced herself that she had forgotten an equally horrible past. "I remembered my mother's sadism, and how much abuse she put me through—a certain kind of abuse until I was old enough to talk, and then something ritualistic, sickening and sadistic."[11]

Geraldine felt that Roseanne was jealous of the attention that Tom, once a stand-up comic who had been far less successful than Roseanne, was receiving. The stories, revealed in her writing and eventually on talk shows such as *Sally Jessy Raphael*, explored molestation from the age of six months, even though it is believed impossible for one to have memories of experiences that occurred so early in one's life. She also discussed other problems within the family, problems the family members deny existed. For example, she claimed that the youngest of the three sisters was also molested because she was thin as a child whereas both Roseanne and Geraldine were obese. She allegedly was thin because of the emotional trauma of the abuse. What she failed to mention was that the youngest sister had severe food allergies that limited what she could consume. She was thin specifically because of the allergies, not because she suffered molestation or other abuse.

On the *Sally Jessy Raphael* program that aired on January 8, 1992, Roseanne told the following story:

What happened. OK. I have my first memory of being molested by my mother at six months old. I got all my memories about two years ago. They started two years ago. But it wasn't just like that they came two years ago. I've been in therapy and in a group for two years. And sometimes, several a day come, sometimes one a month comes. Sometimes something will trigger it, like just seeing young people in stores with their kids, and I'll remember. I've had a lot of memories in two years. And so, you know, I want to say that.

But I remember my mother molesting me while I was—while she was changing my diaper. It was real weird, because, like, I have these segments of memory. Like, all my life, I always said I remembered being six months old and everybody would go, "God, you've got such a great memory." And I always did remember—I always remembered remembering something from six months old. And I just thought I was just—you know, had a great memory. Well, two years ago, I figured out why I have that memory and it's that memory, of my mother doing that. And I have—

My mother molested me sexually until I was about three, or until I could talk and tell. And then she changed that to psychological and physical abuse.[12]

Even worse for the family, Roseanne began using her youngest sister's name and exposing her "problems." She never sought the youngest sister's permission. The youngest sister was married, had a child, and lived a very private life in a different state. She wanted nothing to do with what was being said, did not grant interviews to the media, and was outraged that Roseanne would exploit her for what she viewed to be personal ends.[13]

The first time Roseanne's parents heard about her allegations against them was when her father was listening to the radio. As her father explained:

One morning I wake up around five o'clock in the morning. I'm laying in bed and I listen and I'm hearing this radio program, and I hear this story, and it just blows me away. And I nudges the wife, and I say, "Dear, you better get up. They're talking about us."

She says, "Oh, what're they talkin' about?"

I says, "Roseanne's talkin' about us on the radio." On CNN Radio. It is simulcast. When you hear it on CNN Radio, it is also being shown on CNN Television.

She says, "Well, what's she sayin'? Is it good?"

I says, "You won't believe it. Wake up." And she was in a half-asleep situation. I kept buckin' her. Finally she woke up and I says, "Roseanne's in Denver with Marilyn Van Derbur Atler saying that we sexually abused her as a child."

And Helen says, "Roseanne who?"

I says, "Our Roseanne. Our daughter."

So I says, "Come on. We'll go watch it on TV." So I pulled her out of the bed half asleep, took her in here in the front room, turned on the television, and every thirty minutes—I don't know if you're familiar with CNN—it comes on every half hour. They do the news over, you know. And every half hour, here we are. They got us on television. Me and my wife, and Roseanne at the Kemp Institute on the stage addressing five hundred therapists—eleven hundred people and five hundred of them were therapists—"I am a victim of sexual abuse." And me and my wife sit here and we couldn't believe it. That's when we first heard the story.[14]

The television revelation did not require any ethical considerations on the part of CNN. They were broadcasting an event that was unfolding, a speech that Roseanne was giving. However, the next story was released in *People* magazine under Roseanne's by-line. The publication not only gave her a forum, but also let her present it in her own way and in her own words. Roseanne's portrait was on the cover, and the headline was "Roseanne's Brave Confession: 'I AM AN INCEST SURVIVOR': For the first time the TV star tells her harrowing story of childhood sexual abuse."

Although the Barrs would be outraged, the staff attempted to obtain a statement from them. A reporter was dispatched to get a quote from them, but they refused to talk. The parents felt the situation was outrageous, dishonest, and overwhelmingly painful.

The reality of libel law is that a pivotal issue is the absence of malice. This can be shown in a number of different ways, the most important of which is being certain that each side has an opportunity to tell its version of the truth. There were no documents relating to Roseanne's allegations against her parents. It was her word against theirs, especially because she was their first-born. Thus the effort to get the parents to speak on the record was the proper approach to take.

There were two ways the reporter and editors could have looked at the Barrs' refusal. One way would have been that their daughter was telling the truth and that there was no way to deny it. The other would have been that they were shocked by having a reporter show up on their doorstep in order to question them about a nightmare allegation that was without merit. To the credit of *People*, the article was published without mentioning the parents' reaction to the magazine's approach to getting them to talk. To its discredit, there was little or no effort to follow up with the family, to try to learn the accuracy of what had been said.

What was most aggravating was the fact that, although many other magazines later ran stories of their own, all of them used interviews with Roseanne, her husband, and Roseanne's family members to whatever degree they would talk. None of them other than *People* ever let Roseanne write her own story.

The fallout from Roseanne's first revelations were many. Her mother had operated a home child-care business, taking care of preschoolers and slightly older children, for many years. Some of the first children for whom she had cared were now adults with children of their own. And never had there been a hint of scandal.

Once the story hit, many of the parents of the children Roseanne's mother's had cared for came forward with stories of their own—all positive, all supportive, and all expressing outrage at the idea that she could even be accused of such impropriety. Yet these people were not approached by the media. There was no interest in a loving woman being a positive influence on children. There was only interest in the negative, and that meant that Roseanne had an uncontested platform from which to speak.

Tragically, Roseanne's mother had to give up her day-care business. None of the parents wanted her to stop caring for their children, and there was no hint of scandal, but she was terrified of being set up. Her daughter was one of the most popular television entertainers in America at the time, and she feared that some crazy fan might bring a child to her and then accuse her of hurting the child. She feared lies that would perpetuate the image of a situation that had never occurred.

Ultimately, the Barrs went to see renowned attorney Melvin Belli in San Francisco, where their middle daughter was living. They wanted to sue Roseanne to clear their name, but Belli refused to encourage such a suit, saying that it would hopelessly divide the family. He thought there was a chance for reconciliation with Roseanne, and if there was, it would not occur if they sued her. Instead, he had them take polygraph tests and ultimately made the results available to the media when requested. To the best of my knowledge, these results had been quoted only once before—in Geraldine's account of the family's ordeal.

CONFIDENTIAL REPORT   Our Case No. P-22554-J
    Melvin Belli, Attorney at Law
    Belli, Belli, Brown, Monzione, Fabbro & Zakaria
    722 Montgomery Street
    San Francisco, California 94111
    On 27 September 1991, Jerome H. Barr and Helen R. Barr came to the San Jose offices to undergo polygraph examinations in regard to allegations of sexually molesting their daughter, Roseanne Barr. Roseanne Barr, a comedienne and actress, has

recently made public statements before audiences and on television to the effect that her parents both sexually molested her and that at age 16 they forced her into a mental institution.[15] Both Helen and Jerome Barr are denying these allegations.

Prior to taking the polygraph examination, both Helen and Jerome Barr signed consent forms, indicating they were undergoing testing voluntarily. These consent forms are retained in the files of this office, along with other polygraph related documents on this case.

During the pretest interview of Jerome H. Barr, he denied that he ever sexually molested Roseanne in any manner and he advised that Roseanne had turned herself in to the mental institution in Utah against his wishes and that it was her decision to go to the institution. It was his opinion that Roseanne's current husband is somehow instrumental in her suddenly making allegations of sexual abuse.

Polygraph testing of Jerome Barr was conducted utilizing the following negatively answered relevant questions:

"Did you ever engage in any intentional sexual activity with your daughter?"

"Did you ever engage in any intentional sexual activity with your daughter in Utah?"

"Were you ever aware of your wife doing anything sexual with your daughter?"

"Did you force your daughter into a mental institution?"

At the conclusion of testing, it was the opinion of the examiner that Jerome Barr was being TRUTHFUL [emphasis in original] in his denials of the relevant questions asked during this examination.

Helen R. Barr was administered a polygraph examination utilizing the following relevant questions, which she answered "no":

"Did you ever engage in any intentional sexual activity with your daughter?"

"Did you ever engage in any intentional sexual activity with your daughter in Utah?"

"Were you aware of your husband engaging in any sexual activity with your daughter?"

"Did you force your daughter into a mental institution?"

At the conclusion of testing, it was the opinion of the examiner that Helen Barr was being TRUTHFUL [emphasis in the original report] in her denials to the relevant questions asked during this examination.

> Yours very truly,
> Albert L. Lary
> Harman & Shaheen Associates, Inc.[16]

There is no theater in a polygraph test result. There is no drama in having the objective presentation of information on an entertainment program. Thus Roseanne found herself with opportunities to speak on talk television that caused deep pain for others without the talk show hosts truly knowing whether or not what they were hearing was true. There was no fairness, but only the drama of unchallenged allegations the veracity of which the staff made no attempt to confirm. Here is an excerpt from her appearance on *Sally Jessy Raphael* on January 8, 1992:

MRS. ARNOLD [ROSEANNE]: Like I said, you know, their lawyer said that they took a lie detector test, which really cracks me up, because, I mean, everyone knows that you have to have a conscience and feel some guilt to fail one. And they have never had either, or they wouldn't have done any of it.

SALLY [JESSY RAPHAEL]: Why do they need a lawyer? Because—I don't understand, the lawyer keeps saying, "We're not here to sue."

MRS. ARNOLD: No, they're not suing me. And I call them and say, "Sue already. I'm ready." But they just—they can't sue, and I don't think they want to sue.[17] But they do want to go on every jive show and just discredit me and say that I'm, you know, making false charges. And everyone in the world puts them on TV, too. Which kind of is disgusting, because I'd like to just take a minute to talk about the media and the coverage. Because both Marilyn Van Derbur Atler and myself have totally committed the rest of our lives, basically, to try to do something about this problem. And we find ourselves in a weird position, because now we have to educate the media, too.[18]

* * *

SALLY: I have been interviewing and talking to people, as a way of life for 33 years. I have never—I, personally, have never met anyone who lied about being an incest victim or being an abuser of substances. No one would choose that way to go. So if you're saying to me, "What do you think? What do you feel? Do you believe her?" The answer is, darn right, I do. Thank you for being with us today.[19]

Roseanne later announced that she was suffering from multiple personality disorder and that she was in a ten-year treatment program. The statement was accepted without question. On the *Leeza Gibbons Show*, after claiming to have twenty-one personalities, Roseanne commented, "It's a gift that allows you to be multiply gifted."

The truth, as the talk show hosts could easily have learned if they had acted as journalists rather than as entertainers, is that multiple personality disorder is rare and well understood. It is caused by a number of factors, including abnormal, inconsistent abuse, usually with a sexual component, endured before the age of seven. MPD afflicts individuals who have extremely healthy minds and who are usually of above-average intelligence.

Some children enduring such abuse in early childhood suffer what is sometimes called a "failure to thrive." The child, usually a preadolescent, has no will to live. Any minor ailment, such as a cold, seems to worsen until the child is hospitalized and eventually cannot be saved. There are often no physical marks on the body, although there have been cases of adults in therapy for MPD who have had elementary-school pictures in which their black eyes and bruised faced were plainly visible. Yet checks of school records and interviews of former teachers indicate that no investigation was ever made even though abuse was suspected. In any case, some such children who fail to thrive, rather than surviving as multiple personalities, have been found during psychological post mortems to have undergone such abuse. Other children literally go insane.

MPD is not a mental illness in the normal sense. It is not possible to use MPD as justification for avoiding punishment for a crime in most states. And it is certainly not a "gift," because the condition narrows the thought process rather than expanding it.

As to the treatment, psychiatrists and psychologists who have worked with such individuals do not have ten-year plans. The therapy takes place at the patient's pace, and many such individuals are able to recover within a couple of years.

The problem with talk shows is that MPD sells. Apparently, for many viewers, the notion of a person leading several lives without knowing it is great theater.

The trouble with all of this is the risk of misinformation at best, and great pain for the families at worst. Child abuse can be trivialized or made to seem a guaranteed route to extremely abnormal behavior requiring many years of therapy.

Ironically, as dramatic as stories such as Roseanne's happen to be, regardless of whether or not they are true, the ratings have shown that talk show viewers are not interested in the problems of celebrity guests. They want to see people such as themselves, their neighbors, or others they can identify in their communities.

Celebrities may be the mainstay of variety-style news and information programs such as *Good Morning, America* and *Today*, but the talk show world is blue collar and the people want a mirror of what their own lives could have been. Thus, although some of the celebrity programs have been among the most controversial and, in some instances, among the most dramatic, they have not been popular with the audiences. Bookers have told me off the record that they have stopped looking for celebrities with dramatic stories because the public simply doesn't care. What matters to the talk show producer is drama, conflict, and raw emotion meant to capture the viewer's interest.

Perhaps even worse than talk shows allowing themselves to be vehicles for unfounded allegations and erroneous information, presented with conviction but no corroboration, is the competition for stories among such shows. This competition has led to many producers reading newspapers from all over the nation in search of stories that could be exploited.

One classic case was that of Laura Thorpe, an unemployed nurse who made newspaper headlines when she used a razor blade to cut into her breasts and remove silicone that she had previously had surgically implanted. The story, taken superficially, had everything a talk show could want.

First there was the issue of the use of silicone implants for breast enlargement. Newspapers and magazines were filled with stories about the possible dangers of such implants. There were suspicions that the implants might adversely affect the immune system. There were suspicions that they might cause severe arthritis and other problems. Some women were experiencing pain, fatigue, and an inability to function normally, all allegedly from a once-popular way to obtain larger, fuller, and supposedly more alluring breasts.

The silicone implant story had many components. There was the issue of low self-esteem among women, which would lead them to believe that their natural bodies were not attractive enough. There was the issue of secondary medical care for women, who have long been underserved by the medical community, and the idea that a cosmetic procedure might be unsafe was in keeping with the anger that many people felt toward doctors who seemed to trivialize women's health concerns. And there was the story of an educated woman, down on her luck (she was temporarily unemployed, as was her husband), who had been driven by overwhelming discomfort to perform on herself a surgical procedure she could not afford to have done by a doctor.

This was talk show heaven, and the producers wanted Laura Thorpe at all costs. The fact that her family had no telephone was only a minor problem, because her address could be obtained by simply contacting the reporter who had written the original story.

Thorpe, her husband, and their three sons lived in a trailer home. Staff members from *The Maury Povich Show* got there first, but while they were setting up an appearance, Sally Jessy Raphael's staff located Ms. Thorpe, confirmed that she still had the jars containing the silicone implants she had removed, and put the family and the jars on a plane to New York.

The problem for Sally Jessy Raphael's staff was that the hotel they used to house their guests was well known. Each show tends to favor a different hotel for reasons that range from convenience to the obtaining of special rates in return for a plug during the show. Producers of each know where the guests are housed for the rival shows.

The staff of Sally Jessy Raphael wanted the Thorpes to be comfortable. It was Easter, and the family was treated to an expensive dinner. At the same time, the staff relieved Laura of her jars so they could decide whether and how to use them in a visual display.

Maury Povich's staff contacted Laura Thorpe after she returned to her hotel. They convinced her to come to their offices to talk with them. She left without telling her family where she was going, and within an hour she was being recorded.

The introduction Povich used was dramatic. "Just two weeks ago, at one A.M. in the morning, in the privacy of her bathroom, she took a razor blade, just like this one, and attempted to perform surgery on herself. I mean, we can't even imagine—I mean, the audience is breathless, and so am I. I mean, we want to clutch ourselves. Why would you want to do such a thing?"[20]

There were many questions that were never explored by those involved with the Laura Thorpe story. Prior to subsequent appearances on other programs, Thorpe had to be hospitalized. Was the woman emotionally disturbed? There were conflicting stories about whether or not she could have had the implants removed without charge, whether the implants posed an immediate danger to her health (she reportedly had a fear of cancer), and whether she was a seriously disturbed woman for reasons unrelated to the physical act that brought her so much attention.

Thousands of women in America have breast implants. Some have reported health problems allegedly related to the implants, and others have expressed fears of future health problems. Requests for implant removal have become frequent, and the costs of such procedures vary around the country based on hospital and surgeon's fees. But the extreme act of self-surgery, so far as anyone could determine, had been performed only once, by Laura Thorpe. The implication was that she was a highly disturbed woman, especially because, as a nurse, she would have had sufficient knowledge of the medical world and access to the resources in her community to obtain professional help. Yet no one cared about this. The story touched a responsive chord with the producers as they tried to determine what the viewers would want to see. And the best part for them was that, because the issue of implant-related illness was one very much in the news, they could pass off the broadcast as a public service for women.

Although extreme, the breast implant story is typical of the way in which talk shows often try to sell themselves as public service programs. Instead of dealing with issues that affect the daily lives of their viewing audiences, they focus on aberrations. Remember that the implant story was not about the health risks of silicon, but about a woman who deliberately disfigured herself because of her fears.

It is more common to see people with problems discussing them in ways that can be destructive to those involved. For example, a show on adultery will ideally include a man, his wife, and the lover with whom one of them is involved. The discussion will be confrontational and potentially highly destructive. Emotions are meant to be intense during the show because harsh confrontation provides a sense of drama that would otherwise be lacking. The fact that this might ultimately be destructive to everyone involved is not an issue.

In order to provide a semblance of balance, many of the shows have a therapist appear for the more dramatic revelations. Men and women involved in adultery will have someone who can pass as a relationship counselor appearing with them, for example. The problems with this are threefold. First, the therapist's training, experience, and skills may be far less than is assumed by the image the person may project. Many professions have certain basic and ongoing educational requirements for specialized certification. Organizations such as the American Psychiatric Association and the American Psychological Association have standards that are considered minimal for effective practice. These organizations have methods of policing their own ranks and of arbitrating disputes between patients and their therapists.

But not every professional has to belong to an association. And not every title implies a specific course of training. For example, in New York, a person with a Ph.D. in psychology or a related field of human relations may call himself or herself a "psychotherapist" without being connected to any organization. The person may never have applied for membership in any association, may be involved in unorthodox and highly questionable therapy, or may be incompetent or have lost his or her license as a psychologist. Whatever the case, as long as no title is used that requires the meeting of state and/or national standards, there is no restriction on the individual's work.

Relationship counselors, marriage counselors, and sex therapists all fall into a vague, gray area in most states. In theory, anyone can open an office and claim to provide such assistance, and in practice this truly does occur, ranging from well-intentioned individuals with college and/or graduate training in psychology, education, or some similar discipline, to the truly dangerous. Ken Bianchi, a man now serving several life sentences for his role in the Los Angeles Hillside Strangler murders, once opened an office to practice psychology. He had no training whatever, and yet, with neither credentials nor professional affiliations, he still received calls from people seeking help.

Another problem with all this is the fact that fad practices can be seemingly outrageous in their own right, making the well-intentioned nonprofessional sound sensible. For example, a few years ago the idea of using a surrogate sex partner was quite popular with some well-credentialed therapists. Generally women, these therapist's assistants would help men having sex problems learn to better please their spouses through the physical touching of their bodies. Although the women rarely saw themselves as prostitutes, the reality was that they were being paid for sex. They just performed in a manner that was meant to teach the man how to improve his sex life with his spouse.

Many of these variations on legitimate therapy find their way onto television talk shows. Sometimes they are seeking legitimacy. Sometimes they are colorful in ways that enhance the shows.

But even the legitimately trained and credentialed professionals have mixed reasons for being on the programs. Some are seriously interested in reaching the largest possible audience with their ideas. These men and women have messages to impart and will use any medium to reach those in trouble. Often they are idealistic to the point of feeling betrayed when they find themselves having to give thirty-second or one-minute "sound bites" of information concerning complex problems. At other times they adopt the attitude that any information that reaches the viewer is worth what they have to go through.

Another problem comes with two other common types of therapists. The first is the person who is trying to promote his or her personal practice. The therapist sees the talk show as free advertising to the largest possible audience. Sometimes there is also a book involved that the therapist wants to sell and that also is a vehicle for further disseminating his or her views on a specific topic, such as adult children of addicts, adultery, or survivors of sexual abuse.

The second type of therapist commonly found seeking to be on talk shows is the glory seeker. This is the therapist who simply wants to have appeared on television. He or she loves being recognized on the street and will be available for any show, even if it means canceling a patient's session. Such a therapist is easily manipulated by a talk show producer into endorsing a specific viewpoint. If the therapist is told the nature and tone of the program, he or she can be counted on to say as much or as little as is necessary to maintain the desired pace. The therapist can also be called upon not to claim that a given problem is complex. He or she will either provide a simplistic answer, such as "I feel family therapy is called for and will enable everyone to resolve these troublesome issues," or will support the view of the show's hosts. The latter can be something as inane as "I see that the healing has already begun."

In theory, all of this should be rather innocuous. The concerns that have been raised about the ethical nature of such actions by everyone involved fall into several categories, most of which are outside the media.

First, there is the issue of the people who choose to appear on these programs. The fact is that they do make a choice. For many years the most respected news magazine show on television was *60 Minutes*, and although it remains highly respected, its credibility was slightly tarnished when the staff admitted to having occasionally paid one or more people to appear (see chapter 5 for more information on checkbook journalism). But long before *60 Minutes* was embarrassed by being caught paying people to appear, it acted without shame in its use of a potentially more reprehensible form of reporting—ambush journalism. Yet a variation of the "respected" technique of ambush journalism used by "legitimate" shows has now become a serious ethical issue for the talk shows.

The idea behind ambush journalism was to show the intrepid reporter—Mike Wallace, Dan Rather, or any of the other men and women who have been part of the show—tracking down a reluctant witness. The reporter, along with someone handling the camera and sound equipment, might wait outside a restaurant, hide in a corporation's parking lot, or even force their way into a closed office where they knew they would find their subject. Then, with the camera rolling, they would ask questions the person allegedly had been avoiding by refusing requests for more traditional interviews.

Rarely did ambush journalism work for *60 Minutes*. Sometimes the subject was irate because of the embarrassment. Sometimes the subject was overtired, overstressed, and unable to collect his or her thoughts. Either nothing was said or the person rambled semicoherently as anyone might do in the same situation. At other times the person was angry. Some people shouted obscenities as a way to force the camera to stop recording, never realizing that the repeated "bleeping" of the obscenities would be used to make them look like fools.

Ambush journalism was visually dramatic. It had the appeal of a Wild West shootout with the good guy and the bad guy going head-to-head. It proved that the interviewer would go to any lengths to be objective, to get to the truth as it was seen by both sides. It also brought little knowledge to anyone.

The concept of ambush journalism is frequently applied to talk show planning, although with the subjects' consent. There will be surprise guests—a long-lost biological parent, an old lover, a secret admirer—and there will be surprise revelations, such as a woman admitting to having slept with her sister's boyfriend. The responses to talk shows are frequently similar to responses to news stories. There is shock, anger, intense emotion, and strong visuals for the camera. Little truth is uncovered.

The therapist who might be present at one of these on-the-air ambushes is usually as clueless as everyone else. It is rare when the therapist has time to preinterview the guests who will be appearing. It is rarer still when the therapist supplies the guests for the program, ensuring that they are handled with sensitivity.

The vast majority of talk shows treat all of their guests the same. Assuming that they are flown to the city, they are met at the airport by a chauffeured luxury car or limousine. (Large Lincoln Continentals are increasingly popular for shows based in highly congested cities such as Manhattan. Limousines are still popular elsewhere.)

From the airport the guests are taken to their hotel, where they are given rooms and some arrangement is made for their meals. Sometimes this is a voucher or a special menu. At other times it is a check for a set dollar amount. The idea is to ensure that they can eat decently with a range of options without being permitted to go to extremes. Meals of steak, lobster, and expensive champagne are not permitted, although the payment is generous enough so that most guests are pleased with the meal.

There may or may not be contact with the staff before the guests are picked up for the show. This depends on the nature of the guest, any special visuals that are to be used, and other factors unique to each person. Whatever the case, a show employee, usually with the title of segment producer, serves as the contact. The more important guests (sometimes celebrities, but more often ordinary people with unusually dramatic stories to tell), may be taken shopping, to dinner, or to a museum. Some of the bookers for shows claim to have gone to bed with some of their guests, but if such claims are true they are exceptions. Few would stoop to such depths, although nearly anything may occur if the guest is considered important enough to the show's ratings.

The guest arrives at the studio and is taken to what is called the greenroom, so called because the holding areas for guests were originally painted green. Some still are, but the term is used by almost all talk shows around the country regardless of the actual color of the room.

The greenroom may be large or small. It usually has a television monitor so that the guests can watch the program in progress. Coffee, tea, and/or soft drinks are frequently available. There may also be fruit or some sort of snack food. The idea is to keep the guests there, out of the staff's way, and as relaxed as possible.

Makeup is applied in a separate area, to which the guests are called one at a time. Some guests may be provided with a hair stylist to give them a finished look, although this is not common. (My balding head regularly has the "shine" that lighting people hate when trying to set camera angles so as not to distract the audience from the host.) Wealthier guests, usually professionals concerned with their appearances, may bring along hair stylists at their own expense. Eventually, all the guests sit around in the greenroom, sometimes talking among themselves, sometimes waiting silently.

The show's host may or may not greet the guests in the greenroom. Some do so to establish the image of friendship that many of the guests anticipate. Others are too busy with last-minute preparations to bother, relying on staff members to set the guests at ease.

It is in the greenroom where concerns are addressed before the guests go on the air. How much talking the guests do among themselves depends on who they are. Some are withdrawn. Some feel intimidated. Some are being "babysat" by a producer or booker. And some are gregarious, treating their fellow guests almost as a talk show host would do, eliciting as much information from them as possible.

The negative publicity concerning talk shows suggests that at no time is the therapist given time alone with the guests to discuss their problems. At no time are there preassessments of the guests' problems, their individual needs, or their mental states. In fact, in many instances the guest "expert" may not be experienced with the problem at hand but simply looks good on television.

These problems are real, although not as universal as it may seem. Bookers for some of the most offensive talk shows on television have told me off the record that the problems with the therapists are the fault of the therapists themselves. The bookers do not feel it is their job to offer counseling. One booker explained:

This is someone who called an 800 number in response to a request during an earlier show. This isn't an innocent who was ambushed into an experience. I didn't contact the person and tell them that they were going to get free therapy. They were fans who had to have seen the show at least once, and most give me the impression that they are regular viewers. They know what's going to happen on the show.

We have legitimate therapists—people with real Ph.D.s—as our experts. They arrive early. They have a chance to talk with the guests, and many of them do. I frequently have someone ask if it's all right to talk with the guest for an hour before the show. And many of them talk with the guests for at least a couple of hours afterward. Sure we book a flight for them as soon after the show as we can get them to the airport, but I regularly reschedule flights. In some cases, I start rescheduling before I'm asked because I see the therapist talking with the guest and it's obvious they're not going to stop in time for either of them to leave.

The criticism shouldn't be with us. What happens between the guest and the therapist is up to them. Just remember how we get out guests. Nobody is surprised.[21]

In recent years I have been called by bookers for television talk shows because the range of my writing brings me into contact with experts in a variety of disciplines. I have been asked to supply someone who has worked with gays and lesbians, someone who studies cult- and occult-related crime, someone who can talk about stress in marriage, and someone who is knowledgeable about multiple personality disorder. Although these people are supposed to be skilled, and the presumption is that I have been called because I will find someone appropriate, the questions I am asked about the subject eventually chosen have nothing to do with their expertise. Instead, the subject's age and physical appearance are questioned. (What color is the hair? How lined is the face? How enjoyable is the voice? How pleasant is the person to listen to? Can the person speak interestingly yet concisely? Can the person handle anything from speaking for just a few seconds prior to sign-off to going a half hour or more if the guest does not work out as anticipated? Is the person flexible if the show takes a different direction than planned? Will the person dress right for the demographics of the audience?) Little else matters, although, as one booker stated, the person must be a legitimate Ph.D. in a seemingly related discipline.

There are some professionals who are troubled by this reality. There are others who accept whatever takes place and delight in the trip to the city where the show originates. But it is doubtful that anyone who has appeared on these shows as an expert can realistically claim to have made a therapeutic difference in the lives of the subjects.

The therapist is meant to add a semblance of meaning to what is said. The person is part referee, part scholar, and part therapist, although the last of these is more of a credential than something that is important for the show.

Back in the 1950s there was a television show, now still in re-runs, called *Leave It to Beaver*. The program depicted the "typical" American family of Ward and June Cleaver and their sons Wally and Theodore "Beaver" Cleaver. Naturally they were white and lived in the suburbs, and the father spent most of his time in the office or commuting, actually appearing for only a small portion of most programs.

Each episode featured some sort of adventure in which the boys got into a predicament that was resolved during the last few minutes of the show. There was no sex and no violence. Wally and his friend Eddie had reached puberty, but you would never have known it from the shows. And although one must assume that Ward and June had their children in the normal manner, there was no serious intimacy between them.

The end of each program featured Ward Cleaver delivering a "message." He would sit with the boys, often by their bedside as they went to sleep, and talk with them about what they had learned from whatever adventure or misadventure they had experienced that day. This would be the moral of the story, and as a kid watching this program, I can remember hating the last minute or two, frequently using the time to go to the bathroom or sneak a cookie.

Some of the talk shows are like *Leave It to Beaver*. No matter how good the therapist, no matter whether he or she talks with the guests before or after the show, or never, the therapist seems to have the job of summing up the moral of what has taken place. The moral may be "It's not right to keep secrets in a family" or "Adultery is wrong and no one committing it would make a good marriage prospect for anyone." You get the feeling that the therapist's message is the "redeeming social value" of the program.

Are there legitimate issues with which talk shows should be concerned? This is a serious question for which there are no obvious answers.

Certainly the ambush program, the one involving unexpected confrontation, has been challenged as unethical. On rare occasions a booker will also lie to a guest, claiming there will be on-the-air therapy or some other benefit. This occurs when a potential guest has not contacted the program but was the subject of a news article in a newspaper or magazine that caught the attention of the booker. However, few shows do this, and no one defends the practice as ethical.

What is not mentioned in condemnations of such shows is that there is a tradition of confrontational journalism raising far more serious questions in "legitimate" news programs. This approach has been popular with *60 Minutes,* for example, which was once the ethical standard by which all other news shows were judged.

The confrontation tactics of *60 Minutes* and similar programs almost always involve an attempt to get someone to speak who has been avoiding the camera. For example, suppose a corporate executive is accused of embezzling. The fallout from the financial loss has been enormous. Pension plans will no longer be operational. Retirees will face financial disaster. Dozens of employees have lost their jobs and hundreds more are in precarious positions. The fault seems to rest on the shoulders of one man. He refuses to talk with reporters, and yet his statement is crucial if a balanced picture of the situation is to be presented. This is when a reporter and camera operator will stalk the person, sometimes "ambushing" him in the parking lot of his office building, sometimes pushing past his secretary and walking into his office. There is strong visual drama. The reporter is viewed as being intrepid, the champion of the "little man," determined to learn the truth for the viewer.

It is rare that the news value of such an incident goes beyond the visual. After all, the person has been caught off-guard. He may be in the midst of important work. Certainly this is all unexpected and, whether he is guilty or innocent, it makes little sense for him to make any comment. Instead, he reacts in one of several ways.

Sometimes he curses, either because he's angry or because he thinks that foul language will prevent the material from being aired. However, most shows will air the incident, placing bleeps over the curses, making the man sound foul-mouthed and crude. Sometimes he says "No comment" and keeps walking away from the advancing camera and questioning reporter. Sometimes he tries to cover the camera lens. And sometimes—so seldom as to make the practice of ambush journalism highly questionable—he makes a substantive statement.

Tabloid shows use a different form of ambush. They like to catch a subject in a lie or otherwise embarrass the person with a fact the subject has tried to keep hidden. Perhaps the most dramatic instance of this type occurred following allegations by Patty Bowman that William Kennedy Smith, a member of the Kennedy family, raped her on the beach by the family's Palm Beach, Florida, home. Smith denied the charge, claiming that they were having consensual "rough sex." He was later acquitted when the jury felt they could not tell which person to believe.

The rape allegation was a reporter's dream because it had something to offer no matter whom the public believed. The incident occurred over Easter weekend in 1991. William Smith had been in bed when his uncle, Senator Edward Kennedy, decided he wanted to enjoy some of the area night life with his nephew, Smith, and his son, Patrick, both of whom were staying in the house. He waked his son and his nephew, and together they went drinking and dancing. In the midst of this, Patty Bowman went back to the house with William Smith. A woman named Michele Cassone, who then worked as a waitress, was also at the house, although she was not in the area where the sex act occurred and thus did not witness the act.

There were many questions on both sides. Patty Bowman had probably been drinking. She willingly returned to the family estate, although whether it was for "rough sex," as Smith claimed during the trial, or to see the home of one of the most famous families in America, as she claimed, is still debated. What matters is that the police did not act in a timely manner when the charges were filed. The grounds of the Kennedy house, where the rape was alleged to have occurred, were not checked for trace evidence by a scientific unit for three weeks. During that time the grass was mowed and rainstorms destroyed any evidence that might have proven or disproven the allegations. There were delays in questioning family, staff, and potential witnesses, and the Kennedy men were treated with a respect that arguably prevented the truth from being determined.

Given the situation, the press began seeking Patty Bowman for comments. However, the woman remained silent. She did not want to become a public figure. She turned down offers of at least $1 million to tell her story to one of the highly competitive tabloid newspapers. She spoke only to the police and in court. If she had some other hidden agenda, it never came out. She acted as a wronged woman, using the law to stand up for her rights. It was a noble stance, the type that producers of tabloid television shows hate.

Enter *A Current Affair*, a tabloid show that uses confrontational journalism in whatever way it will enhance the story. An ex-boyfriend of Michele Cassone had taken what were allegedly nude photos of Cassone, as well as pictures of Cassone having sex. He then sold them to *A Current Affair* field producer Malcolm Balfour for a fee alleged to be $16,000.

The reason why the photos were taken was never an issue. Certainly their existence called into question the integrity of the photographer as much as it did the character of the young woman. For all anyone knew at the time, she was deeply in love with the man, was emotionally committed for what she thought would be the rest of her life, and acted out of love. Certainly she never expected the photographs to be sold to a national television show.

Steve Dunleavy, the reporter for *A Current Affair* who interviewed Cassone on camera, wanted to get an emotional reaction from the woman. She had not witnessed the sex act that led to the accusations. She could say very little about the Kennedy family. But she was available for a price, in this case the price apparently being $1000 along with a lunch "to die for"—two bottles of 1987 Pouilly-Fuisse wine at ninety dollars a bottle, lobster consomme, and shrimp scampi. She had a girlfriend with her, and Dunleavy had Malcolm Balfour with him. The meal was served at New York's 21 Club, and the two reporters were drinking vodka and tonics when Michele and her friend arrived forty-five minutes late.

Up until the last moment, Cassone had not made a final decision about going on camera to talk about her experience. The celebrity lunch and payment apparently convinced her to talk. It was a classic case of checkbook journalism, and had she been a witness to the sex act, it would have tainted her testimony. That was not a concern in this instance, but even when it is a concern of the prosecution or defense, it is rarely a problem for journalists (see chapter 5).

Cassone's defenses were down. She was ready to talk about the Kennedy home and what had happened that Easter weekend night, including the way in which Ted Kennedy had dressed after returning to the family compound. These were all topics she had discussed on other programs, including *Sally Jessy Raphael*, where I was also a guest.[22]

Instead, Dunleavy began asking her about the possibility of her posing nude for *Penthouse*, a men's magazine featuring pictures of naked and scantily clad women. The question seemed inappropriate and was not what she had expected, and she vehemently denied that she would do such a thing.

Suddenly Dunleavy pulled out four photographs of her, two showing her topless in a swimming pool, and two more showing her engaging in a sex act. The images were not shown on camera or to anyone in the studio. They were shown only to Cassone, who was horrified and outraged. As Dunleavy would later explain, "She tried to strangle me with my tie. She kneed me in the groin. She kicked me. She also bit me. Finally she dragged me by the tie out of the room. I couldn't retaliate because I'm a gentleman. I just had to grin and bear it."

It was great confrontational journalism. Stills from the taping were reprinted in several publications, including the *National Enquirer*. The violence was impressive. The ratings soared. But did it have any news value? Was anything learned about the Smith rape allegation? Of course not. It was just an extreme case of a guest being surprised, and unlike the guests on the talk shows, this guest had no clue that the embarrassing questions would be far afield of the reasons she went on the program.

Aside from the tactics used with guests, there is also the issue of what happens to guests after the program is over. Perhaps the leading expert in this field is Ellen McGrath, Ph.D., a well-respected psychologist who works extensively with the American Psychological Association as it tries to make effective use of the media and to establish ethical standards for its members. She has also appeared on several talk shows as well as on special programs that have involved talk show hosts. She came to national attention when it was learned that the traumatic effect of being on a talk show was so great for some of her fellow guests that she was forced to do counseling afterward in the greenroom. Eventually she saw enough of guests in crisis to understand why they had appeared on television talk shows in the first place.

"I think there were four or five themes that I would see again and again," McGrath states, "and that others [other psychologists] would see, and we talked about this collectively. One of them is that it's a way to blast through anonymity that people have. It's the notion of your fifteen minutes of fame, and there's a complete distortion of how much the spotlight can burn. It feels like the spotlight is going to be a warm, enveloping, wonderful place, and then, of course, the experience to many is that they've been burned, singed. It destroyed something rather than enhanced it. But the hope, and the need, and the drivenness to get that is very strong and it may have really increased in American society as people feel more helpless and out of control." She explains that the motivation is "just wanting to be somebody when you feel like you're nobody." Appearing on the show gives the person a sense that his or her life, seemingly devoid of meaning, has meaning after all.

Dr. McGrath feels that for this first type of person, getting on the show is what is important. Many of these people manufacture or enhance events, she says, in order to satisfy their need to have the moment in the spotlight that the show provides. They make certain that what they say fits into whatever the theme of the show may be.

By contrast, genuine guests may feel that the show provides them with an opportunity to take revenge or to accelerate their recoveries by talking about their experiences. "The ones where it's more of a victim psychology—they kind of walk through life like victims—for them, it's a kind of entitlement, of justification. They go on thinking they can now go on and gather evidence to justify their position and that they can gather forces to talk about how terrible the victimizer is," explains Dr. McGrath. "They'll go on a lot for justification purposes, to justify their own position and to get the other person who did bad things to them. There is often for those people a hope that they will get some kind of education, that they will get some kind of help," she says. "They verbalize to us that they went on to try and get some kind of help. But, of course, if you look at the way they [talk shows] are formatted, the way experts are used, that's a very spurious possibility, not typically going to happen very much."

It is important to note that psychological counseling is not widely used in the United States. Although we see psychologists everywhere in the media, from syndicated newspaper columns to TV talk shows, there are several reasons why most Americans do not use their services.

First, there can be a social stigma associated with going to a "shrink." There is a tendency to confuse the need for counseling with being seriously mentally ill. In reality, the person may simply need an accepting and skilled listener who can provide a different perspective on a problem he or she is too close to. (The first therapists in ancient Rome were paid listeners in the marketplace. In a sense, their legacy is both the contemporary psychologist and the contemporary bartender.) However, many people do not realize this, although some religious groups—most notably the Catholic Church—have procedures such as confession that can sometimes serve this purpose in a nonclinical setting.

The nature of one's job can also prevent the use of a therapist. Schoolteachers, police officers, hospital workers, and others may feel that the stigma associated with seeing a psychologist will jeopardize either their jobs or their potentials for promotion. In far too many instances, this fear is based in reality.

In other instances, the person in need of therapy lives in a community that is underserved. Small towns and even some sections of major cities may not have adequate counseling services.

Cost is another factor. Although some clergy are trained counselors and work without pay, and although there are social service agencies that provide professional counseling on an "ability to pay" basis, such resources are often either unknown or difficult to find. Instead, the person is faced with fees that can run as high as $125 per hour.

In addition, there are medical professionals who prefer the use of pharmaceuticals to counseling. The reasons are many, but it is not hard for them to convince a trusting patient that it is better to take a pill than to seek the underlying cause of a problem through psychotherapy.

The popularity of television talk shows, not to mention the mass purchases of books on coping with personal problems, can be traced, in part, to the unsatisfied need for help. This is why the hope of some talk show guests is valid. An objective person might say that the expectation of treatment or meaningful guidance on a talk show is unrealistic, but many guests rightfully feel that their options are too limited to try anything else.

Dr. McGrath describes the expectations of the guests seeking help.

I think that they view it as a collective community [talk show host, therapist, and audience] that has several different roles, several different identities. One is the "therapist," and that can be audience and host. A second one is "savior." A third one is "jury," so that they're going to make a judgment that this person is right and good, and that person who did bad things to them is wrong and bad. Fourth, a way to connect, a way to break through the disconnection, the loneliness, the anonymity that so many people feel. And a way to feel connected, if even briefly, to other people, to a larger issue.

Sometimes it's a mining for meaning, trying to really find some kind of meaning in these difficulties, and they see the host and the expert as somebody who can give them more meaning.

Often it's a desperate attempt for direction, for ideas about where to go and what to do with it, although many people don't really listen to us or care that much anyway because they just want to be on and tell their story. What we see often are people who just want to be on and put out what's wrong. They don't really focus on what they want to do about it.

They're getting attention for having been victimized or having been abused. And endemic in American society, we [have a] culture of complaint. It's really a part of the culture right now to focus on what the problem is and how I feel about it, but not to focus on what I'm going to do about it and to take personal responsibility.[23]

This is where talk shows really fail on the whole, McGrath believes. She points to exceptions such as Oprah Winfrey's changed format in the 1995 season. Winfrey stressed how women could take more responsibility for their own lives, recognizing that they could change them. Yet this change in format, although subtle, was accompanied, perhaps coincidentally, by a lowering in the ratings. This may mean that the people who watch such talk shows want to be comfortable with their own sense of self as victim. Or it may simply mean that if someone is speaking positively, the drama is not as enjoyable to watch as it would be if they were whining and seeing themselves as helpless.

More commonly, shows that stress personal responsibility for change are found on programs that use news magazine formats. These include 20/20 and a variety of specials.

The current programming approach is not an *ethical* issue, according to McGrath. It is a *ratings* issue. Showing individuals steps for positive change and explaining how they can take charge of their own lives would be far more meaningful. However, ratings tend to go down with such programming, and without good ratings, shows cannot survive. As one critic has noted, the public is getting the television programming it desires.

Explaining how she feels the programs focus their stories, Dr. McGrath says:

There's definite molding and shaping of the thinking [of the guests] and of what to say [by the bookers]. There's also a lot of encouragement to use excess emotions. Your producer will come up in between [the on-the-air segments] and say, "Gee, you didn't cry enough," or "You've got to get more angry," or "Let me see more of that passion about so-and-so."

When we're on the show, you'll hear the producers come up. . . . They'll tell you that ahead of time. They'll come up in between, too, and say, "You've been too quiet. We need to see more intensity." Or they'll guide you. They'll say, "Go after . . . You're really mad at someone so go after him more." Or "You can fight

against the audience when they say something like that to you."
Those are pretty common coaching techniques that really encourage more confrontation, more abusive communication,
and more emotional violence.

McGrath explains that she usually sees the people in the greenroom before they go on the show. She notes that the people are
usually nervous. They are anxious and engage in "a lot of titter-
ing." She also has found that the guests with problems are usually
not comfortable with her and frequently don't want to talk. She believes that they feel that someone who represents the mental
health profession "is going to make them feel inadequate, point-
ing out their inadequacies." McGrath's tries to be warm, friendly,
and caring, and to help them with their fears. She has been told
ahead of time why they are there, what their problems are, and
what they will be discussing. This enables her to be encouraging,
and to anticipate and ease them through their anxieties. However,
it is not common for her to be able to do substantive evaluations of
each individual's problems and needs.

A valid criticism of talk show therapists is that they often have
no choice but to provide brief, multipart answers to guests' concerns when on the air. For example, if a guest is grieving the loss of
her husband and feels guilty because she also has anger toward
him for dying, the therapist might only be able to say that anger is
normal and one of the aspects of healing grief. The therapist—
with the theme music usually coming on—will then list the stages
of the grieving process, including denial and anger, giving the audience the impression that everyone handles things the same way
and in the same period of time. With more serious concerns, such
as recovery following incest, this is simply not the case.

Although some psychologists are truly experts in their chosen
fields, they often lack the television skills needed for rapid, simplistic, yet effective communication of even a fraction of their

knowledge. They also don't know how to break into other conversations to inject ideas of importance.

Sometimes after a show, guests fall apart in the greenroom, and
they need a trauma counselor. McGrath feels that some guests do
so because the staff members of such programs are less prepared
for such reactions than they should be. The post-traumatic reaction
will vary with the individual. "Some shut down and shut up, and are
very disappointed in the experience," McGrath says. "Some are very
critical of themselves and think they didn't say it right or do it right.
You see the lowered self-esteem almost instantly."

There was a time when talk show hosts would attack their
guests, themselves creating the problems later manifested in the
greenroom. However, that style has changed. Today talk show
hosts are more likely to nurture their guests, encouraging them to
tell their stories. Then they encourage the audience to attack them
for what they have said. They become, McGrath suggests, facilita-
tors of the attack.

Ultimately, however, it is the impact of talk shows on the public that
must be addressed. Sociologist Vicki Abt, Ph.D., of Penn State University, and her colleague Mel Seesholtz wrote an often reprinted paper titled "The Shameless World of Phil, Sally, and Oprah: Television
Talk Shows and the Deconstructing of Society," which originally appeared in the *Journal of Popular Culture* in 1994. In it they say:

> In their competition for audience share, ratings and profits,
> television talk shows co-opt deviant subcultures, break taboos
> and eventually, through repeated, nonjudgmental exposure,
> make it all seem banal and ordinary. The addictive nature of this
> lies in the fact that increasingly bizarre stories are constructed
> to maintain audience share. Television talk shows offer us an
> anomic world of blurred boundaries and at best normative am-
> biguity. Cultural distinctions between public and private, credi-

ble and incredible witnesses, truth and falseness, good and evil, sickness and irresponsibility, normal and abnormal, therapy and exploitation, intimate and stranger, fragmentation and community are manipulated and erased for our distraction and entertainment. Nothing makes conventional sense in this deconstructed society.[24]

Although this is true, there are also other concerns. The first is that, despite the fact that talk shows are entertainment, not news, there is a presumption of fairness by the audience. This is not encouraged by the hosts, who pay only lip service to equal opportunity for rebuttal, especially when airing extremists such as members of the skinheads, the Ku Klux Klan, and other such groups. The studio audience may lash back, but the hosts rarely broaden the issue in the greater social context. For example, discussing the facts that so many groups distort, whether about the Holocaust or about the various minorities that these groups hate, would limit the impact of what is said. For some people, it is quite likely that the host's failure to challenge the inaccuracies "proves" that the statements are factual. After all, the host is their friend, the person who lets them look into the personal lives and intimate affairs of fascinating, sometimes frightening, sometimes erotically charged strangers. Thus if there were something wrong with a guest's statements, the host would "of course" correct their errors.

There is also the question of how a subject is covered. Phil Donahue was quoted by Drs. Abt and Seesholtz because of a show he did on child abuse. As is typical with such shows, there is a titillation factor in the ostensibly serious presentation. As a result, a teenage guest, who had agreed to go on the air to talk about her own abuse, wept as Donahue asked, "Do I understand, Lisa, that intercourse began with your dad at age twelve, and oral sex between five and twelve? . . . Do I understand that you were beaten before and after the sexual encounters?"

The stories presented are horrible and tragic. For some people it is necessary to hear such first-hand accounts in order to believe that such horrors can be perpetrated on the innocent. For others, it is approved titillation, like going to a sexually arousing lecture on erotica that is presented as part of a continuing education program on human sexuality. Regardless of whether or not the person needs the information for his or her profession, the reality is that one of the appeals is the chance to experience what might otherwise be unavailable or considered taboo.

All of this is similar to the silent films in which biblical stories were frequent themes. Directors such as Cecil B. DeMille, in the early years of their careers, learned that they could increase their audiences by showing all manner of abominations—scantily clad dancing girls, lustful relationships, and the like—provided that the people who had sinned either repented or were destroyed in the end. The movies claimed to be uplifting, but as in the last two minutes of *Leave It to Beaver*, the redeeming moral lesson was gratuitous.

Do talk shows pose a moral danger to the youth of America? Certainly, if a young adult is looking to such shows to provide a better understanding of the greater culture, there is a definite problem. Learning appropriate behavior from a talk show is like learning interpersonal relationships from pornographic videotapes. But there are several other relevant issues.

First, the shows are a form of entertainment. They are a choice, not the dominant force in popular culture. The viewers can switch channels, read a book, go for a walk, or engage in any number of alternative activities.

Second, these shows are not aired solely during times when young people can watch. Many compete with daytime soap operas aired when young people are—or should be—in school. Those strongly opposed to the talk shows have cited statistics indicating that eight million children of high-school age or younger watch these shows on any given day. I personally find such figures to be self-serving nonsense, especially because pollsters check only a few hundred to a thousand people, then extrapolate from there. Such estimates might be reasonably accurate, but as a probability and statistics professor of mine commented on the first day of every course, "The only accurate sampling is one hundred percent. Anything less than that is inaccurate to some degree, and the smaller the sample, the less you can trust it."

More important, the advertisers do not believe such statistics. They are selling products that are of interest to adults, not teenagers and young children. If so many youths were being corrupted each day, the nature of the commercials keeping these programs on the air would support this theory.

Third, the political decrying of the industry began at a time when politicians wanted to prevent the public from seeing real concerns, such as decreased funding for the poor, the infirm, the elderly, and others in need. School budgets were being cut or stabilized without accounting for inflation. Children from families too poor to afford adequate food were seeing school lunch subsidies attacked when those subsidies assured them of at least one good meal a day, the prevention of malnutrition, and a chance to reach their full potentials as adults.

Perhaps when children receive the financial support and social programs they need from political officials who too frequently are uncaring, other ethical dilemmas will arise within the talk show industry. But what made the talk shows a major story, and a major chapter in this book, is far less significant than the simultaneous attack on the support services for the youth of the nation. A study of the documents put out by members of Congress and special-interest groups related to the talk shows reveals a righteous smoke screen meant to avoid debate on more serious issues.

Even if the only alternative to a particular television channel in some homes is a different television channel, the attack against talk show irresponsibility came at the same time that Congress wanted to reduce funding for public broadcasting. This means that a provably wholesome, informative, and often uplifting series of programs was at risk of cancellation for lack of funds at the same time that the attacks on talk shows seemed to indicate, in part, that they would be "politically correct" if they addressed the same issues in the same manner as did PBS.

I am troubled by the talk shows, despite having frequently appeared on them—primarily to sell one or another of my books. They are often slanted. They make no provision for fairness. They deal with people in crisis, the mentally ill while still in therapy, and others who cannot evaluate how they will be treated by family, friends, and neighbors after they appear. Words are spoken in the heat of anger. Words are spoken in the name of catharsis, the story to be told supposedly therapeutic in nature, a claim that none of the shows can support. And when guests realize that, for them, appearing on the show was a mistake, the postshow support is generally limited. Professionals such as Ellen McGrath are the exception, not the rule, when they attempt to provide legitimate crisis intervention and referral. There isn't time or budget for elaborate follow-up, although this is done on an individual basis by some bookers for some guests.

Still it might be argued that the emotionally disturbed are knowingly exploiting the exploiters. There is a synergistic relationship between host and guests, and between guests and the studio audience, that almost everyone involved thinks they understand and can handle. Sometimes they can. Sometimes they fall apart. And at least once, in the 1995 case of the talk show guest who murdered his secret (male) admirer, the person takes a life—his or her own or that of someone else.

Radio talk shows are not immune from criticism, even though they are more freewheeling and rarely choreographed. However, it is the seemingly open nature of the medium that actually allows for subtle manipulation, not by the hosts and stations but by the listeners—or so some experts believe.

The classic case, still under investigation at this writing, occurred in New York City. Harlem's major shopping area is 125th Street. This predominantly African American and Hispanic area has shops owned locally, shops owned by whites, many of whom are Jewish, and shops owned by African Americans who do not live in the area.

Freddy's clothing store became the focus of protesters during the Christmas buying season. The store was owned by a Jewish man who sublet space to The Record Shack, an African American–owned record store. However, after more than twenty years, Freddy's was to expand, forcing The Record Shack to move.

The issue seemed to be a minor problem for the local residents. Interviews in the newspapers, on radio, and on television revealed that there was little animosity about the event. Freddy's was fair to customers, employed local residents, and offered competitive prices. However, a number of events had occurred in the area that led to picketing of the store by a group of protesters that included the Reverend Al Sharpton, who had long been known for his championing of controversial subjects. The main concern was the fact that street vendors were being banned on 125th Street, and the majority of merchants were street vendors.

New York City is one of the few places in the nation where street peddlers are an important part of the business community. Entrepreneurs, often immigrants trying to better themselves, are licensed to sell from the sidewalks. On any given day, there are carts and tables loaded with perfumes, toys, books, second-hand magazines, scarves, gloves, hats, shirts, neckties, watches, and numerous other items. Sometimes success is measured by the number of businesses someone has. The vendors are heavily patronized, and there are many stores whose customers are primarily street vendors. Signs on their doors say "Wholesale to the trade only. You must have tax I.D. to buy here." Rather than being a nuisance, street vendors represent a business layer of the city on which many people depend for their livelihood.

There were many reasons for banning street vendors on 125th Street, not the least of which was the commercial boost that such a ban would give to the traditional stores that often sold many of the same products. The economic health of the neighborhood would be improved by banning the vendors, who were licensed to sell anywhere in the city, including Harlem.

Even more unusual was the economic arrangement of Freddy's. While it was subletting to the record store, it was itself leasing from someone else—the primarily African American congregation of the Pentecostal church called the United House of Prayer for All People. Thus Freddy's not only provided local jobs, but also put money back into the community.

The owner of The Record Shack, upset with having to close the location he had so long enjoyed, sought the help of Reverend Sharpton and his organization, the National Action Network. Instead of exploring other avenues of protest, Reverend Sharpton allegedly took to both the streets and, to the surprise of investigators, the airwaves.

The incident that brought the picketing at Freddy's to a head was the entrance of a gunman, one of the protesters, who acted on his own to stop Freddy's from evicting The Record Shack. He entered the store, shooting at people and setting fire to the business. Eight people died, and what had been a seemingly minor protest suddenly became a major crime that horrified merchants and residents alike.

The radio talk show issue arose because another controversial group, the Jewish Action Alliance, had tape-recorded talk radio programs in the days between the request for help by the owner of The Record Shack and the deadly conflagration. The Jewish Action Alliance claims to be a protector of "Jewish civil and human rights and the struggle against anti-Semitism, hatred and bigotry." However, when the group has occasionally seen individual Jews and Jewish groups acting improperly, it has attacked them as well.

The tape recordings included violent rhetoric that seemed to be exhorting the African American listeners to take action against Freddy's. The problem seemed to be exaggerated by the radio speakers, who included Reverend Sharpton, and there suddenly arose a question about the influence of the shows. Had the killer, who died in the fire he set, decided to kill because he felt he was doing what the group wanted him to do? He was a follower and a fellow picket, and he was known to have listened to the radio programs. Thus a question that had to be addressed was whether or not the consistent use of talk radio prior to the violence was actually a conspiracy to achieve a destructive end.

The idea of talk radio as a tool of conspirators is highly controversial. One of the first times it was raised was after the bombing of the Oklahoma City federal building. White separatist and militia groups were found to be using the radio as a means of spreading their political and social beliefs. However, because most of them were either expressing their opinions on regularly scheduled shows or responding to the host's questions, the issue of conspiracy on the air was not raised. The difference in the case of Freddy's was that the callers seemed to be deliberately trying to change listeners' opinions in an organized manner.

Most likely the end result will be that the radio programs will not be considered vehicles for conspiracy, even if a conspiracy is found to have existed prior to the Oklahoma City attack. Certainly the perpetrator was a troubled individual whose actions did not have the support of most of the people in the community. But the fact that such an issue can arise demonstrates that talk radio, like talk television, is not immune to ethical questions. Freedom of the air also implies a sense of responsibility without which the rhetoric of talk radio can inspire acts of deadly anarchy.

Regarding talk television, it is important to note that confrontation is what the public desires. The early shows were closer to public service shows. They would offer information on health, relationships, and the like. Many of the hosts were quite gentle, such as Jenny Jones in her early format, in which she radiated such pleasantness that only a true misanthrope would have disliked her. Yet when Jones and others switched to more volatile formats, the ratings picked up. The higher the ratings, the more a show can charge for advertising, and most of the talk shows are very successful financially.

Yet there is one other concern that is overlooked. If young adults were to switch from the talk shows to serious news programs, would the scurrilousness of what they had been viewing pale in comparison with the fact that junk-bond trader Michael Milken, who was jailed for his unethical and illegal activities on Wall Street, was hired as a university lecturer after being released? He was not asked to teach the ethics of business or the proper ways to do business without crossing legal and moral boundaries. Instead, he was hired to share his knowledge of how to conduct the very type of trading that had landed him in jail.

And what about news of corporate downsizing—the wholesale elimination of jobs held by honest, hard-working individuals to increase corporate profits or the breast beating about cigarette smoking among American youth leading to limitations on domestic advertising and sales, while the exporting of cigarettes and other tobacco products to the rest of the world—causing approximately three million deaths a year internationally—goes on unabated and unchallenged? The news is filled with stories of unethical business executives, of schools closing, of teenagers graduating from high school without being able to read or write, of cities fighting to save their sports teams when almost half the students drop out of school before being trained for the work world, of child abuse ignored by neighbors in "good" family areas, and of wholesale rape, murder, theft, and deceit. We read about the mistresses and sex partners of our presidents. We learn that one Speaker of the House of Representatives served his wife with divorce papers when she was in the hospital recovering from cancer surgery.

How can we decry the immorality of the talk shows while ignoring the greater immorality of the society at large? At least most teens understand that the talk shows are carnival freak shows, but what are they to think when they see the legitimate news programs revealing all manner of ugly truths about the people they are supposed to be able to trust and admire?

Yes, the titles of talk shows are frequently offensive. Yes, there is certainly an ethical question about surprising a guest with a deeply hidden family secret. Yes, the people who call in to appear may be ignorant in some way such that they do not know the problems they will face afterward. But anyone who watches these shows, then calls in to go on the air, knows what may happen. There are no valid illusions in this world of admitted perversity.

Early in 1996, Geraldo Rivera took a look at the split personality of his own programs. *Geraldo!* was often excessive in its presentation of guests who believed in everything from devil worship to adultery. He was also a highly respected, award-winning journalist with a highly praised legal program on cable network CNBC. He decided to write a ten-point "Bill of Rights and Responsibilities" for broadcasters. These are:

1. *Integrity and Honesty:* Guests will be fully informed well in advance that this is a forum where misrepresentation and exploitation will have no place.
2. *Solutions over Shock:* We will engage viewers without pandering to them. Shows should help our guests and our audience gain insight and resolve problems they face.
3. *Respect for Our Guests:* Guests should not be used for sport or spectacle. Civility must prevail.

4. *No Studio Violence:* Physical violence will not be tolerated. Any acts of violence will be edited out of the final product.

5. *Professional Responsibility:* Counselors, therapists, trained professionals, and experts will be a prominent show component.

6. *After-Care:* Professional help will continue to be made available in appropriate cases to guests in need.

7. *Light over Heat:* We will continue to tackle tough social issues in a responsible, nonsensational, informational manner.

8. *Children May Be Watching:* While producing for an adult audience, we will bear in mind that some children may be watching. Mature subject matter always will be placed in an acceptable context for daytime viewing.

9. *Community Outreach:* We will link the home audience with resources in their communities, acting as a powerful clearinghouse that is not readily available elsewhere.

10. *Accentuating the Positive:* While taking hard looks at hard topics, we will emphasize the positive aspects of our life and times, rather than dwell on the negative or the bizarre. We will emphasize solutions, values, and community spirit.

Perhaps we should consider that the talk shows are not corrupting American society as we know it. Perhaps it is the character of the people who watch the talk shows that is corrupting the shows and their hosts. After all, these shows respond to ratings, airing whatever will attract the largest audience among the people with televisions turned on.

The problem with this possibility is that talk shows as they are too frequently presented are not a healthy form of entertainment. They are as wrong in their approach as *60 Minutes* and similarly respected programs are when they use "ambush journalism" and let the reaction of the person serve as the response. The fact that there is an audience for them does not change this reality. There is an audience for executions, and Phil Donahue tried for several years to win this audience by having a condemned prisoner die on camera. There is an audience for just about every perversity known to humanity, as history tragically rediscovers every generation. But this does not mean that torture chambers should be used on game shows because there is an audience for graphic displays of pain and suffering.

Talk shows are inexpensive to produce, but they air during the day, when the audience is limited. Many viewers are not actually watching the shows but using the television for background sound to ease their loneliness. It is radio with pictures, something to have on while cooking, cleaning, taking care of preschool children, or working at a home business. Unfortunately for advertisers, this means that few people are watching their commercials. This is why shock is so appealing, because it ensures that at least some people will be jolted into paying more attention than they otherwise would.

Ironically, one of the potential low-cost substitutes for the talk shows that has been considered is to bring back game shows. These programs would be variations of the quiz shows so popular in the 1950s. Some of those shows, such as *Twenty-One*, were ultimately proven to be rigged. The scandals led to congressional hearings and the type of cynicism that has only recently been heard again, cynicism now directed toward the talk shows.

Unfortunately, money talks. In the current glut of talk shows, many have failed to gain the anticipated viewing audience—but many others are highly profitable. The producers blame the audience for the quality of the product, and the audience is perceived as remaining with them despite public outcries. Ultimately, the issue of ethical behavior rests with the viewers themselves, who choose what to watch, and not with the producers of the material the viewers seemingly desire.

4

Corrupting the Young
for Fun and Profit

It may be a sacrilegious—and obvious—statement, but Barney, the purple dinosaur, is the result of marketing genius. Although the Barney show is aired by the Corporation for Public Broadcasting (PBS), the subtler business techniques used on the show are as brilliant as any developed by more sophisticated sellers of children's tie-in products.

Barney is seemingly innocuous, beloved by the two- to five-year-old set (too old for diapers and too young for Power Rangers), and enjoyable to watch—the first time or two. There are songs and lessons about friendship, safety, sharing, the importance of school, and other significant messages. Important life lessons are hidden in the form of entertaining song-and-dance routines by Barney, Baby Bop, and the Backyard Gang. The Backyard Gang is ever changing because, unlike Walt Disney's original Mouseketeers, some of whose female members had their chests bound to hide developing breasts, any hint of impending puberty relegates a Backyard Gang member to the netherworld of big brothers and sisters. Other children then take their places. Only Barney, Baby Bop—green to complement Barney's purple—and a few of their friends continue.

Barney is actually a doll, or so he appears at the start of the show. Identical dolls, available in a variety of sizes in toy stores everywhere, can be purchased by parents who make the mistake of letting their children accompany them into such establishments. On the television show and the videotapes, the Backyard Gang members use their imaginations and Barney becomes a real being. He plays with them. He sings with them. He is their friend, and he shares the joys of the world with them.

Why is this a brilliant marketing device? Try to convince a small child that the toy dinosaur on the shelf is not the *real* Barney, just waiting for a child's imagination to turn him into a valued playmate. Parents are never around when the Backyard Gang turns their Barney into the real thing, and thus the child believes that if the dinosaur is taken to some private place the magic will occur if the child just imagines it will.

One of our sons was three-and-a-half when we adopted him. He came from a foster home without pets to a home with a dog and several cats. The dog soon made friends with our son. At first it stayed away from him until the child understood that he would not be hurt, then it nuzzled him and licked his face. One of our cats did not wait at all, though. He kept walking over to our son, trying to rub against him, purring the entire time. And although the cat is small, there was something about the animal that made our son feel he needed protection from it.

Our son would go to his bedroom, pick up the Barney doll we had purchased for him, and bring it out to the living room. Then, when the cat approached, he would take Barney and push him toward the cat for protection from the unknown and the unfamiliar. The cat, uncertain what was happening, would step back, looking quizzically at both the doll and our son. Once the child was comfortable with the cat, Barney stayed permanently in the bedroom.

The licensing of Barney dolls and other related toys has been limited, because the show was created for children's entertainment, not for profit. The marketing of Barney has also been relatively limited, increasing primarily as funds for public broadcasting have decreased. And even with marketing taking on an importance not originally considered, the focus remains on wholesome entertainment for children that can occasionally provide information of value to those struggling with the first few years of life. This is not a program meant to make substantial sums of money, although the money that has come from the program's success has helped ensure its survival.

By contrast, most children's shows other than those on PBS have merchandising profits as their focus. Sometimes the entertainment is wholesome and perhaps even of some value. But regardless of the circumstances, profits are at least as important a concern as values, and in most instances profits come first.

The idea of licensing is not new, of course. There were commercial tie-ins long before there was television. One such product was a poster showing all the different wounds and scars that Tom Mix, the cowboy star, had received from ranching, rodeoing, and fighting bad guys. There were secret decoder rings, two-way wrist radios, cap guns, toy rifles, clothing, coonskin caps, mouse ears, and numerous other "BUY ME!" tie-ins for Little Orphan Annie, Roy Rogers, Dale Evans, Dick Tracy, Hopalong Cassidy, Annie Oakley, Mickey Mouse, Davy Crockett, and numerous other characters. In fact, as American Greetings learned in the 1980s and the early 1990s, licensing ideas are most profitable when they precede the creation of a television show.

Those Characters From Cleveland (TCFC) was created as a division of the American Greeting Card Company. One purpose of TCFC was to earn profits by exploiting the fantasy lives of children. Young people fall in love with cartoon and other fantasy figures they see on television and in movies, and they want to have these figures as part of their lives. The Walt Disney company has long brilliantly exploited this fact, and every parent knows that when a child is taken to the next big Disney movie, stuffed toys, books, games, and other spin-offs will have to be purchased. But television is a different medium. Parents have not realized the cynicism that goes into weekday before- and after-school cartoons and adventure series, as well as Saturday morning programming.

In 1980, TCFC created Strawberry Shortcake, a delightful alternative to the cartoon violence that dominated the early morning airwaves. Strawberry Shortcake was used as a theme for greeting cards, toys, lunch boxes, and many other products. There were six half-hour television specials and a home video based on this character, who was described by the company as follows:

"In a very little part of the world is a tiny little place called Strawberryland." Strawberry Shortcake had her home there, among a profusion of strawberry patches. "Strawberry Shortcake is happy and comfortable outdoors tending her garden. She is just as at home making jams and jellies in her kitchen."

The promotional material for Strawberry Shortcake added that the character "is direct, honest, and somewhat naive. Like all true optimists, she rarely sees beyond the next sunbeam."

As of the 1992 report being quoted, total sales from all products licensed for the Strawberry Shortcake concept were $1.12 billion.[25]

The Care Bears, which were produced from 1983 through 1988, were even more successful. These characters were designed to be conveyers of messages. According to their creator, "Each Care Bear proudly wears a symbol on their tummy presenting their special mission in life. Tenderheart Bear, for example, wears a beautiful heart on his tummy. His heart symbol is symbolic of the love and acceptance of one human being for another." The company explained that "all the Care Bears are dedicated to one common goal—helping people share their feelings with other people they care about. The Care Bears answer an existing need—they are an emotional bridge between people. They are also designed to appeal to people of many different ages and on many varied levels. The Care Bears are for everyone—but especially for someone you care about."

There were four half-hour television specials and seventy-six half-hour television episodes. The Care Bears also spawned three full-length feature films and a home video. Total sales as of 1992 were $1.41 billion.

The money that was earned from these early promotions seems extraordinary. Herself The Elf, which ran from 1982 to 1985, was one of the least successful ventures. This character appeared in only a single half-hour television special and one home video, and yet the financial return was $26.4 million.

These early licensing ventures all featured gentle stories about gentle characters—the types of programming that parents felt comfortable about having their children enjoy even if they had to buy the accompanying toys, cards, and other items. For example, the Get Along Gang (one half-hour television special, a home video, and thirteen half-hour television episodes for a 1992 total of $58.3 million in sales) was touted as having "learned the value of friendship and the rewards of togetherness." The marketing promotion explained that "they know that when they combine efforts and skills, there isn't much they can't overcome."

Lady LovelyLocks (ten half-hour specials from 1986 through 1989 for a total of $97.2 million in sales) "reigned over the Kingdom of LovelyLocks with the help of enchanted Pixietails, friendly forest creatures with long, shiny tails who possessed the secrets of Hair Magic. With the help of the Pixietails and her two loyal friends, Maiden FairHair and Maiden CurlyCrown, Lady Lovely-Locks kept the Kingdom of LovelyLocks running smoothly and happily." The only conflict was with the Evil Duchess of Raven-Waves, but every conflict led to the triumph of good over evil.

Although there was still a tendency to look toward the original concepts, as exemplified by the introduction of the Popples ($441 million), which were advertised as having "just one goal—to make people happy," and the Nosy Bears ($21 million), a subtle change occurred. It was as though, to a degree, TCFC had been corrupted by the same tendency that had afflicted other product creators. With characters such as the Gargoyles, the X-Men, Spiderman, and The Mask, along with the live-action Power Rangers and VR Troopers, all using a certain amount of violence, TCFC followed suit. The Barnyard Commandos, with thirteen half-hour television shows and a home video ($15.3 million), were created in 1990, and the Mighty Fighters of the Future, for which it was claimed that there was "no more fast, furious, or ferocious fighting anywhere in the galaxy," were introduced two years later.

American Greetings had joined many other companies in creating products with violence as an aspect of the programming. The Teenage Mutant Ninja Turtles, Batman, Superman, and others dominated the airwaves. Violence was a part of their story lines. Special mutating abilities allowed for a variety of support items to be sold, such as Batman's different costumes for his varying crime-fighting activities, which were first seen in the feature films about the "Dark Knight."

All of these programs have attracted valid, often severe criticism. The reality of the current market is that most programming for children is exciting, visually fast-paced, and devoid of any value. Worse yet, unlike past efforts in which the story lines were generally innocuous, these programs use fight scenes as a way of maintaining interest.

There are exceptions, of course, and these shows are usually lauded by the same people who want the federal government to stop supporting PBS, the one network where concern for children is a priority. *Mr. Rogers' Neighborhood, Sesame Street, Magic School Bus, Barney,* and numerous other regular programs and specials are safe, enjoyable, and often quite helpful. Fred Rogers handles problems that most new parents either find too minor to worry about or do not recognize as concerns for the dirty-diaper set. For example, one of Mr. Rogers' most popular songs is one that tells small children that they won't go down the drain. Small children with no sense of their own size are often traumatized by toilets and bathtub drains because they think they can be swallowed by them.

Fred Rogers focuses on what, to adults, are minor concerns because he is aware that these are serious issues for his audience. Many children learn to count and spell by watching *Sesame Street*, and although many questions have been raised about the quality of the programming, it does provide racial-, ethnic-, and age-diversity lessons that teach children to accept each other for what they are.

Sesame Street has provided a rich legacy in other ways as well. One of the best songs against racism was the *Sesame Street* creation "It's Not Easy Being Green," which was recorded by notables ranging from Kermit the Frog to Frank Sinatra. Yet none of the efforts to teach compassion and tolerance are blatant. There is no "in-your-face" confrontation. Instead, children experience a diverse community of Muppet creations and actors. The mix is quite similar to a version of an integrated urban neighborhood. *Sesame Street* allows children to enter a world of odd characters (Big Bird, Gonzo, Miss Piggy, The Count, Cookie Monster, and numerous others), where they are taught respect for others, compassion, and a variety of other such lessons.

Sesame Street products are widely marketed. There are many Sesame Street books in our small children's home library. The pictures are familiar. The stories are simple enough for our two-year-olds to follow while still being complex enough for our first-grader and his friends. But what makes Sesame Street different from many other children's programs, the merchandising notwithstanding, is that it is nonviolent and mostly educational.

The justification for violent children's programming often is similar to that for adult sexploitation programming. For example, one of the more violent shows on television, one that has two or more fights per episode, is the American version of the long-time Japanese soap opera we call the *Mighty Morphin Power Rangers*. This program is always aired at times when children are home from school, thus making it popular with little children and teenagers alike. It tells of several high-school students "with an attitude" who have been recruited to receive special training and special powers with which to save the world. They can change shape (morph), call on the skills of ancient dinosaurs and other long-extinct creatures, and generally be either teenagers or superheroes as events require. They are a mix of male and female, and engage in politically correct activities (the girls save both the boys and each other, just as the boys save both the girls and each other) in addition to the martial arts sequences.

Because the show is really about fighting, which is obvious from the mock karate that now permeates every elementary-school playground in the nation, the producers have been severely criticized. The supporters who profit from the show have claimed that the programs are about teenagers working together for a higher purpose, thus helping the viewers to be less self-obsessed and more in tune with their own higher moral purposes.

Several years ago, an adult program called *Charlie's Angels* was created by Aaron Spelling. I have never been able to interview Mr. Spelling, who is the king of rather risque television for the young. However, I have talked with friends of his and staff members from the show, who have repeatedly told me the same story about the original sale of the program to the network.

Several times a year, the networks hold what are known as "pitch meetings." These are events in which seemingly anyone can make an appointment with network executives to try to sell them a new show. You are encouraged to come with several ideas. You ideally have a track record and/or an agent that will cause network executives to take you seriously, and a *TV Guide* factor—a title and no more than two sentences that make your show sound so interesting that people will want to view the show after reading the capsule summary in the television listings.

If the network is interested, you provide a treatment that briefly describes a typical story line. You also need to have several additional program ideas ready to prove that the series can sustain itself.

Normally, the networks claim to want "high concept," although what this term means in any given season is subject to debate. Although I am a member of the screenwriters' organization called the Writers Guild of America, West, I am a Hollywood "outsider" living a couple of thousand miles away. I can get away with asking such "dumb" questions as "What does 'high concept' mean this season?" (Guild members living in Los Angeles—the insiders—have to fake it, although they are usually at as much of a loss for such a definition as everyone else.) Generally, the term means that there will be a damsel in distress, although if there is a feminist influence that season, she might be rescued by another woman. Sex usually can never be used unless it is subtle and appropriate to the story line, although writers may feel encouraged to make it appropriate to the story line. There are also repeating fads such as true stories of triumph over adversity—winter storms, severe illnesses, psychological problems, struggles against seemingly overwhelming odds, and the like. Whatever anyone says, however, the reality is that sex and violence are still important focuses of most entertainment for adults, and nowhere was this demonstrated more blatantly than on *Charlie's Angels*.

Basically, *Charlie's Angels* was about three women who graduated from the police academy, so they were trained in self-defense, the use of handguns, and basic investigation techniques. Then they went to work as investigators for a wealthy businessman (Charlie) who was never seen, but only heard on the telephone. A second man, who was the go-between for the women and Charlie, was seen, often working the speaker telephone when he and the three women gathered together to talk to Charlie.

The women were regularly dressed in skimpy outfits and ran around a lot, waving handguns. Sometimes one of them would be tied up, combining two high concept ideas—the damsel in distress and the woman who is saved by another woman. A certain amount of sexual tension was also in evidence, because the women sometimes had to use their attractiveness in order to gain information to solve a crime.

The show was immensely popular and has done very well in re-runs despite having rather unsophisticated, innocuous plots. The selling point was the women, an approach with a long history in the field of entertainment.

The damsel in distress has always been a movie mainstay. Silent films used this theme endlessly, having stolen it from popular stage melodramas. The serials regularly had cliff-hanger endings where the heroine was facing some mortal danger. Sometimes the hero was also in jeopardy, but when he was, he would recover in order to save the woman, who was usually hanging from a cliff (the origin of the term "cliff-hanger"), tied to a keg of explosives with a long fuse set to go off after the villain escaped, trapped in a building that had been set on fire, or in some other life-threatening situation. *The Perils of Pauline* was a classic serial of this type, and one of the more famous episodes was called "Bound and Gagged."

Each week a different episode would be shown in the theaters, and the stories would run for fifteen to twenty weeks or longer. Some were silent. Later ones used sound. But always the concept was the same.

Returning to the origins of *Charlie's Angels*, I have been repeatedly told that the creator was originally not serious. He had other ideas that he felt were far superior. However, he thought of *Charlie's Angels* as a joke, pitching it to get a laugh. (You can imagine the sales talk: "So we get these girls to warm climates where they can wear bathing suits and T-shirts with short-shorts, then get them wet so their figures show. And we give them guns, and we have them controlled by a man you never see, sort of a harem fantasy any man watching can project himself into. And because they went to the police academy, they know how to fight, so . . .") Instead, the ABC television network bought it, and even more important, so did the public.

Today, when *Charlie's Angels* is criticized, supporters contend that the show was good for America. First, it had women in starring roles as investigators and crime fighters, not bimbos and victims to be saved by men. The fact that the bathing suit and T-shirt were the costumes of choice while men wore suits or tuxedos in similar roles is irrelevant.

More important, the women had to work together to solve problems. They were shown communicating, having interpersonal relationships, and demonstrating other skills so valuable in contemporary society and yet not normally shown in association with women. Thus it was "important" television. (Yes, and the Mighty Morphin Power Rangers teach teenagers the importance of working together while "kicking intergalactic butt.")

The fact is that the production companies and networks justify the unjustifiable. There have been many good programs for children. For many years, the ABC television network ran quality after-school specials for children. These were teleplays dealing with a wide range of issues, the scripts as strong as the best of quality adult fare, the acting excellent, and violence nonexistent. Cartoon series can be humorous, outlandish, and sophisticated enough for a wide range of audiences, as the satirical *Rocky and Bullwinkle* revealed. There have been quality satirical productions of classic fairy tales and folktales, such as the work of actress-turned-producer Shelley Duvall. And there have been excellent variety programs for kids. They simply take a little more thought and effort than shows featuring violence as an integral part of the story line. Unfortunately, such efforts to provide wholesome and/or nonviolent material are on the decline.

Is there hope for the improvement of children's television? After talking with insiders, I have my doubts. There is little incentive to change, and there are far more writers willing to knock off another *Teenage Mutant Ninja Turtles* or *VR Troopers* script than those who want to effectively explore a variety of more interesting stories. Even the periodic boycotts have little lasting value.

Although there is always a backlash against the heavy merchandising of products, including their higher cost because of licensing fees, the fact is that the backlash does not last. Toys fit a limited age range, and parents who have learned to say no to one line suddenly find their children wanting something entirely different the next year. This is why Walt Disney periodically re-releases "classic" films, with subsequent new marketing of dolls, lunchboxes, games, and the like. The company waits until the children whose lives were saturated with merchandise are older and new children have come of age to enjoy the films and demand the appropriate toys.

Quality children's programming has a strong, loyal viewing audience who are also willing to buy videos, audiotapes, CDs, books, and toys relating to the shows. (Not all shows market a full range of items. *Mr. Rogers* is not about marketing but helping children, which is why there are no *Mr. Rogers* sweaters, casual footwear, or video games. The licensing of *Sesame Street* products is also highly controlled.) But the full range of exploitation requires marketing people to think sales before entertainment. Such a mentality tends to narrow the scope of creativity to the easy terrain of violence.

In evening programming, sexual innuendo is preferred over violence for those shows that children watch. Some of the humor is lost on young people, which is why small children may be bored by the same inappropriate material enjoyed by teens. But evening marketing is aimed more toward women and those teens with enough money to interest advertisers. The marketing people want to directly influence the buyers, not the children who demand to have toys, cereals, candy, and other items bought for them.

There is also a growing sameness to much early evening network broadcasting because networks are trying to influence the same viewers. No one is willing to risk losing an established audience by attempting to attract people who might have different tastes. This is one of the reasons why cable systems have proliferated.

Early television sought variety. Each network station and affiliate was trying to draw a different audience through a variety of programming. Today, with the exception of reruns on small, independent stations and PBS offerings, the real variety is found on the programs offered on pay channels. Free television is competing for the same audience, and so no one is likely to be as innovative as when free television was the only game in town. The same arts programs, original plays, original movies, and sporting events that once were the staples of free network television are now almost exclusively available for monthly fees or on a pay-per-view basis. This means that the audience for such programs is also drastically reduced because only those who can afford cable are watching them.

Thus there is little incentive to change. Even the critics are likely to be vocal supporters of government-forced change while fighting to discontinue government funding of the limited programming available on PBS. And this sends the message that while violent programming is undesirable, the little competition that exists on the small public stations may be removed from the airwaves. This means that the networks are better off staying with what they are currently doing, waiting for all competition other than cable to die out.

Perhaps the most dramatic study of the results of television violence was conducted by the Aggression Research Group at the University of Michigan Institute for Social Research. In 1977, 750 first- and third-graders in Oak Park, Illinois, were studied to learn the effects of media violence on children. Boys and girls were asked to view such shows as *Wonder Woman, Charlie's Angels,* and *The Six Million Dollar Man,* among other violent programs popular with children and teens.

Fifteen years later, the researchers interviewed most of the women from the original group, and otherwise looked into their current lives. The researchers recorded instances of aggressive and assertive behavior, considering the former to be acts of domestic violence, shootings, punchings, stabbings, chokings, and other forms of violent behavior. Assertive behavior included such positive actions as seeking a good job, defying sexual harassment, and refusing to be victimized by bias in school, on the job, and in the community. It was found that the women who had watched violent shows as children exhibited abnormal amounts of aggressive behavior as adults. It was no different for the men, who were found to be more prone to violence after being exposed to media violence during childhood. The full study, published for the first time in the *Annals of the New York Academy of Sciences* in the spring of 1996, was the first positive proof that there was a direct connection between the viewing of violent programs in childhood and inappropriate aggression in adults.

There are some options, such as the recently developed electronic device called the V-chip, which allows parents to block the reception of shows they deem too violent or otherwise undesirable. But will the chip be used for morning and afternoon cartoons? Will there be alternatives in programming? Or will everyone continue with business as usual, fully aware that children frequently see these programs with their parents and not by sneaking behind their backs. (And, of course, there is the possibility that children will be more sophisticated than their parents and thus able to determine how to cancel the V-chip blockage themselves.)

Children's programming must be considered as only one source of entertainment, not as an electronic babysitter. Even working parents must supply alternatives for their children, such as library books, audio- and videotapes (also available from most libraries), and games. Eventually we may see a computer-designed delivery system for extensive entertainment options whereby parents can plan activities that are in keeping with their morals, ethics, and values (see chapter 5). For now, however, the issue of children's programming is one of ethical abandonment, mixed messages about which segments of the media Congress should support, and failure of communities to provide alternatives.

Should there be specific guidelines? There was a time when it was possible to choose shows that had no commercial product tie-ins as being better for children than those connected with cereals, toys, and other products. Now that funding for public broadcasting has been reduced, even shows that are safe for children, such as *Barney* or *Bill Nye, the Science Guy* have video tie-ins as well as other product connections.

Obviously stories in which violence is used to solve problems—*Gargoyles, Teenage Mutant Ninja Turtles,* and *Mighty Morphin Power Rangers*—are not good for small children, and yet many parents respond that such an argument can be misguided. They note that the *Power Rangers* are a racially mixed group of teenage boys and girls who never fight if they can avoid it. When they must fight evil, they win only when they work together. Kids watching may want to emulate the karate (at the ends of the shows, there are warnings by the actors that karate must be learned through study with a qualified instructor), but when kids play Power Rangers, they usually seek out several friends, understanding that it is not a game to be played alone.

Some superhero shows have evolved in ways that parents need to understand. For example, the latest incarnation of Batman at this writing is as "the Dark Knight." By the same token, a more adult show popular with children is the ABC series *The Adventures of Lois and Clark,* which is the newest form of Superman on television. He is capable of doing only good. He is deeply in love with Lois Lane, who knows his secret. He has doting parents with whom he has an excellent relationship. And at no time do he and Lois, whom adults know full well is sexually experienced, go to bed together, because they want their marriage to be perfect. It is a well-written action adventure show with high moral standards.

Perhaps the best response for parents is to watch children's television objectively and then contact the networks, production companies, and sponsors of both the good and the bad programs.

Praise the good ones, stressing your willingness to patronize the sponsors, as well as asking for similar programs to be added. Likewise, specify your concerns about the bad programs, explaining what is wrong and why you want the shows (sponsorship) discontinued.

This may not seem like much control. But with the enormous amounts of money to be made or lost on children's programming, it has proven to be the most effective method for change.

5

When Money Talks,
Ethics Walks

The media are businesses, first and foremost. They are all underwritten, whether by subscriptions, voluntary contributions, money earned from selling organization memberships, or advertising. Ben Franklin became postmaster of Philadelphia in part so that he could control the circulations of his rivals in the newspaper business. The postmaster determined which newspapers could be mailed, and for how much money. He denied his rivals the potential circulation he ensured for his own *Pennsylvania Gazette*. With decreased circulation, either the advertising rates would be lower or there would be fewer advertisers. Either way, Franklin's paper would be the one of choice.

In Franklin's day, the newspapers were more powerful than the advertisers, and so the person who ran the printing press often could get away with controversy. When there were few or no alternatives to an existing newspaper, an advertiser had to buy space in that paper to stay in business. Advertisers who disagreed with the politics espoused by the paper had to ignore their distaste. This gave the publishers greater freedom when selecting stories because there was no meaningful way for advertisers to boycott their publications. The censorship came from the publishers themselves, who made the ultimate decisions about which stories to cover and how to cover them.

Today the business world has the greater clout. Take a look at your daily newspaper as the weekend approaches. Department stores often take out ads filling one or more pages. Restaurants, movie theaters, nightclubs, and other businesses offering food and entertainment try to catch the attention of people who want to go out on Friday and Saturday nights, as well as families seeking activities for themselves and their children. There are pages and pages of automobile advertisements, and often enough real estate ads to fill an entire section of a large paper.

Magazines are frequently the vehicles of choice not only for some of the same advertisers—albeit on a regional or national scale (car makers advertise nationally and their dealerships advertise locally)—but also for the more controversial ones. Cigarettes and hard liquor cannot be advertised on television, but many magazines would not be able to show a profit if it weren't for the pages of advertising from manufacturers of these items.

Pharmaceutical companies are also major advertisers in magazines, and a few have even experimented with taking what had once been medical journal advertisements and placing them in popular market publications. These ads, often for prescription medicines for ailments common among the demographic mix of readers, suggest that readers who have a heart condition or other health problems should talk to their doctors about the advertised medications. These companies are attempting to get consumers to guide their doctors' treatment plans toward the companies' products.

Advertisers need exposure, and they are sophisticated enough to know that if one medium is closed to them, there are always other alternatives. After paid cigarette advertisements were banned from television several years ago, the cigarette companies started sponsoring sporting events. For years, the manufacturers of Virginia Slims cigarettes received widespread exposure by sponsoring a Virginia Slims tennis tournament. Golf and tennis tournaments regularly have sponsors whose names are repeated endlessly during broadcast coverage, and these sponsors are frequently cigarette companies whose names, if used in association with advertised products, would be banned from the airwaves. A fifteen-second commercial for cigarettes cannot be aired, but a three-hour program sponsored by a cigarette company can be legally broadcast even though the event literally becomes an advertisement.

Even in music there is influence by tobacco companies. For many years the Kool Jazz Festival subtly advertised Kool cigarettes to an audience perceived as being counterculture enough to see smoking as part of a desired lifestyle. Without these companies, many popular sporting and music events would have to be canceled or would have to work far harder to find corporate sponsors.

The same pressure exists in the other media. News stories have been killed or limited to specific areas so as not to offend advertisers. For example, upscale shopping complexes such as malls are known to be relatively high-crime areas. The crimes include shoplifting, mugging, armed robbery, and rape. Malls filled with big-ticket merchandise items and people who can afford them are where the money is. Purses and wallets are filled with cash and credit cards. Shoppers have their guard down, provided the people around them are appropriately dressed for the area. As a result, many professional criminals look to such locations as sources of ill-gotten cash.

By contrast, there are sections of every community that are considered disreputable or unimportant. Often these are lower-income areas without a strong business base from which to draw advertising dollars. Housing values are relatively low. There are no expensive car dealerships and often only an occasional used-car lot. There are few large-scale employers, and when such employers do exist, they are usually businesses (such as manufacturing companies) that advertise to the trade, not to the mass market.

If a newspaper, radio station, or television station has a choice between reporting a crime at a shopping mall where some of its biggest advertisers have stores, and using the same space to cover a crime in the inner city, it will choose the latter. Certainly a major crime, such as a shooting inside the mall, may be reported for its unavoidable shock value, but even in such a circumstance the coverage will be different. It will be more intense, with follow-up stories about the investigation. The media attention will make the incident seem to be an aberration, subtly assuring the public that it is safe to continue doing business there. Yet the same crime in an area without the advertising base is liable to be covered with more play up front, perhaps including area crime statistics, but little or no follow-up. The implication will be that rape, robbery, and murder are business as usual in the one location, but a rare experience in the other, even if the reverse is true. The horror is expressed, but the implication is that if the poor victim's family had lived in a nicer area, there would have been little chance of being victimized.

Sometimes the pressure to kill a story is overt. The publisher or managing editor will be told that the price for running a certain type of story will be a boycott. At other times the pressure is more subtle, such as a reminder of how much money the company spends each week, month, or year. But whatever the case, the message is clear that the story cannot be aired or printed without a negative consequence.

The O. J. Simpson murder trial created a new business twist, although one that unfortunately will become increasingly familiar. This is the issue of media coverage being determined in part by business concerns unrelated to the medium normally handling the news.

When O. J. Simpson was accused of murder, the story was big news. Simpson was an extremely popular professional football player who had retired from the game as a football Hall of Famer. He had been married twice, the second time to a white woman he met when she was a teenager. He was alleged to be an abuser of alcohol and possibly drugs. He would later be found to be a wife beater. Yet he was so popular with the public that he had a second career as an actor and product spokesperson. He helped sell *Sports Illustrated* subscriptions as the voice of its 800 telephone number commercials. He worked with a rental car company, doing both print and television advertisements. And when the police sought to arrest him, he led them on a low-speed chase on a Los Angeles freeway that news departments deemed so important that many of them covered the event as it happened. Eventually his trial would be broadcast by cable's Court TV, by CNN, and by the networks.

All of this could have been seen as a morality story dealing with, among other things, the issue of celebrity worship in America. What was not discussed was the impact of corporate business concerns on the coverage, and there was no more blatant an example than an incident involving Time Warner.[26]

It has already been shown that concentration of media control in the hands of a few is perhaps the greatest ethical concern being faced in the United States today. No matter what ideals may be held by each individual business owned by a media giant, there are corporate controls, although frequently unspoken, that override the concerns of the individual divisions of the conglomerate.

The problem started when *Time* magazine legitimately reported on the murder of Simpson's ex-wife and the young man who apparently had been in the wrong place at the wrong time. *Time*'s facts were as accurate as those of its rival news magazines, *Newsweek* and *U.S. News & World Report*, but what made its coverage different was its cover photo of Simpson, which was computer enhanced to make his skin look darker and his face appear rather sinister. This was quite different from merely selecting a photograph that would put him in the worst possible light. This was an effort to project an image of O.J. that fit the cultural stereotype of the dangerous African American male. He had not and did not confess to the murders. He was eventually acquitted, and although there was intense lingering doubt about the verdict, only the conviction of Simpson would have altered the news media's responsibility in reporting the case.

During the period when *Time* was putting its negative interpretation on the case by means of the chosen photograph, *Sports Illustrated* chose not to mention the case at all. Many staffers and freelancers working regularly for the magazine were outraged. They felt that there was so much violence in the world of athletics, as well as so much prior use of the Simpson name for promotions, that responsible journalism called for full coverage.

No one in management was willing to be quoted, but a number of top editorial people took a different position, although they were unwilling to have me use their names. They explained that there was another reason *Sports Illustrated* did not mention the Simpson case—that the magazine's first obligation was to meet the known interests of its readers at the time they read the publication. Those interests, aside from the sex-oriented annual swimsuit issue, were the outcomes of sporting events that had recently occurred, inside stories about the players, and information on how upcoming games were shaping up. One editorial staffer explained that Simpson's athletic career was old news. He was of no concern to the readers of *Sports Illustrated* because he was no longer a player employed in any capacity as an athlete. In theory, this made sense. In practice, however, he was still connected with the publication, a fact that may have influenced the magazine several months later when it did an article on the abuse of females by athletes, an article that did *not* mention Simpson's name.

Of greater interest than the noncoverage was the way Simpson was reported by *Time* when he worked with author Larry Schiller on a book of letters he had received in prison. The book combined the letters and his responses to the writers. It was his way of giving his side of the story without being subject to cross-examination or having the statements he made investigated for accuracy.

The publisher of the Simpson book was Little, Brown, a wholly owned subsidiary of Time Warner. The book was released during the Simpson trial at a time when the prosecution was presenting its case.

If all of this does not sound very important, it is because normally even a celebrity trial does not generate the coverage that was received by Simpson. The interest in his case was unique among murder trials in the last half of the twentieth century. The Cable News Network (CNN) and Court TV were providing gavel-to-gavel coverage of the trial on cable. The three free networks—ABC, CBS, and NBC—were afraid that people who did not have cable would be so interested in the case that they would order a cable service. This would reduce their audience, lower the rates they could charge advertisers, and ultimately reduce their profits. They made a decision to risk alienating their traditional audience for the soap operas and talk shows that dominate daytime broadcasting by also covering the Simpson trial. The result was that the trial was the primary topic of conversation throughout the nation.

Despite the strong interest, there were many people who did not watch the trial. They gained their information from newspapers and news magazines such as *Time,* and the readers of such publications were presumed to be a primary market for books.

Simpson was well beloved by many people because they remembered his success on the football field and liked seeing him in the movies and commercials he had made since his retirement from football. Following his arrest, entrepreneurs created Simpson-licensed souvenir coins, arranged to sell Simpson autographs, and created numerous other items to be purchased by fans and the curious. Simpson, however, quite apart from the murder charges, was a spouse abuser. Evidence was being introduced that he had beaten the women who loved him over the years, a preliminary to showing the jury that he was capable of greater violence.

The more the story of Simpson's negative side permeated the news, the greater the chance that Simpson's book would be considered self-serving and inaccurate. Although Time Warner could not control most news during the period when the book was being marketed, they could control their own subsidiary. As a result, while *Newsweek, U.S. News & World Report,* and other magazines unrelated to Time Warner were headlining stories of DNA investigation and other evidence techniques, *Time* limited its coverage to a paragraph or two in a small news section at the front of the magazine. This pro-Simpson approach continued when an audiotape of comments Simpson had made in prison was produced by Warner Audio, another subsidiary of Time Warner.

It was only several months later, when all the sales that could predictably be made had been made, that *Time* returned to its normal coverage. Yet off the record, spokespeople for the various Time Warner companies claimed that they had acted independently of each other. The facts are quite different, as proven by what they did and their refusal to speak publicly about the ethics issues involved. The desire to profit from Warner Audio's product drastically altered the legitimate coverage that should have been expected from *Time.*

As to the infamous *Time* cover photo, in an interview that appeared in *Emerge* magazine, which is aimed at an upscale African American audience, the man responsible for the photo's alteration was quoted as saying that, in hindsight, he considered the change a mistake in judgment but felt that it was not meant to be offensive. And that was the end of public mention of the photograph. My request for an interview was turned down by the public relations spokesperson for the magazine.

This was not the first instance of Time Warner letting one subsidiary seemingly dictate what was covered by another. *Time* magazine ran a cover story on author Scott Turow when his book *Presumed Innocent* became a major publishing success. The question that has to be raised is whether the magazine would have felt another author of equal stature deserved the same treatment (few have). What was never stressed in the article was the fact that *Presumed Innocent* was published by Warner Books and would soon be a movie produced by Warner Brothers. Each company was run independently of the other, yet each was corporately connected through the parent organization.

The same is true for television magazine format shows such as *Today*, and *Good Morning, America*. Many times the only reason why a movie star, an author, or a musician is featured is because the parent company is connected with the production company, publisher, or record producer.[27]

Is this wrong? Probably not. Is it misleading? Only in the sense that a rather innocuous event may get promoted beyond its relevance because the network, publisher, or producer has a strong stake in what is happening.

Perhaps the most blatant problem in advertising is the financial influence over news and editorial content by cigarette manufacturers. It is no secret that smoking is addictive and leads to heart disease, cancer, and other severe health problems. This is common knowledge among most people, including those who choose to smoke cigarettes.

Tobacco contains nicotine, a highly addictive substance that provides—at a much lower cost—a variation of the euphoria that is caused by cocaine. Tobacco for cigarettes is also sugar cured, and the sugar causes the adrenalin rush required to metabolize a meal. The sugar is then depleted (hypoglycemia), and the excess adrenalin creates a craving for sugar (in the form of candy, food, even cigarettes). Again, this is nothing new. Such knowledge has existed since the late 1950s.

The tobacco companies have long tried to maintain a presence in the media. When they were allowed to advertise on radio and television, Camel cigarettes was a sponsor of one network's evening news. This occurred well after the time when the first information concluding that smoking was dangerous to health was released (although not reported on the Camel-sponsored evening news).

Respected television personalities were often shown smoking. Edward R. Murrow, a radio broadcaster who became famous for his coverage of the Battle of Britain in World War II, then later switched to television and such shows as *Person to Person*, smoked constantly on the air. He was a man of great intelligence, sophistication, and courage. And when he died of lung cancer, few obituaries mentioned his smoking as a major factor. No one wanted to upset the sponsors.

Television advertising of tobacco products was banned in 1971, when a total of $50 million a year was being spent on advertising in all media. It was not necessary for the tobacco companies to spend more, because smoking was portrayed as being sophisticated and sexy in numerous television shows and motion pictures. Sex scenes usually included cigarettes as part of the seduction and/or the "afterglow." Cigarettes were smoked by the heroes, including rugged western and action star John Wayne, who also died from lung cancer.

By 1975, with retail cigarette advertising limited to the print media, the total being spent on such ads had more than doubled to $115 million. And within a decade, the figure reached $400 million. Such dollar figures imply power to influence, but even such large amounts are misleading when one considers the entire realm of corporate influence.

Cigarette companies did not just manufacture and sell cigarettes. They recognized that the industry was going to change in ways that might cut into their profits. As a result, they began to diversify, usually into food companies. These wholly owned divisions of the tobacco companies had vast advertising power and could use it in any of the media. They bolstered the clout of the cigarette divisions within the print media, and they influenced programming about smoking in the media from which cigarette advertising was banned.

What does all this mean? RJR Nabisco includes what was the R. J. Reynolds Tobacco Company, Del Monte Foods, and Nabisco Brands, and Philip Morris owns Kraft General Foods, which alone controls well in excess of $1 billion in advertising placement. As a result, most magazines and broadcast companies will yield to pressure from tobacco and food advertisers when it comes to their features. If, for example, heart disease is going to be the subject of a television movie, series episode, documentary, or in-depth magazine article, smoking may not be emphasized as a major cause of the problem, even though medical professionals directly relate the two. The first time this blatantly occurred was in 1985 when the American Heart Association was unable to place an advertising supplement in the *Reader's Digest* because it would have mentioned smoking. The *Reader's Digest* did not and does not allow tobacco product advertisements, but its large circulation and public influence are such that the advertising supplement probably would have had an impact on smokers and those considering smoking. The tobacco companies could exert no pressure on the *Digest* staff, but their food products subsidiaries could and did exert such pressure. A study of the Digest's advertising pages at the time indicates that they were a mainstay of the magazine's financial health.

A close look at the current magazines in which articles on health are popular—*Family Circle, Woman's Day, Redbook, Cosmopolitan,* and others—will show that antismoking information is rarely found. When it does appear, it is mentioned only briefly so as to not be overly offensive.

When *Ms.* magazine went from being an advertising-driven publication to one independent of advertisers, the 1990 premier issue included an article by *Ms.* founder Gloria Steinem that stressed why there were financial concerns affecting editorial content. Although she did not directly address the issue of cigarette companies and their subsidiaries, she succinctly described the pressures under which publishers operate. She wrote:

Food advertisers have always demanded that women's magazines publish recipes and articles on entertaining (preferably ones that name their products) in return for their ads; clothing advertisers expect to be surrounded by fashion spreads (especially ones that credit their designers); and shampoo, fragrance, and beauty products in general usually insist on positive editorial coverage of beauty subjects, plus photo credits besides.[28]

The tobacco industry has simply created the same situation that exists with the combining of media companies. It makes no sense for the companies to run articles that are offensive to advertisers (or owners). General Electric bought NBC and suddenly the network did not run stories that would reveal problems faced by its parent company. Tobacco companies raise the issue that you do not bite the hand that feeds you. Their money, and the money from their food and beverage subsidiaries, supplies the funds that help keep television stations, networks, and publishers solvent. Again, the issue is not censorship in many instances but rather the selection of stories that may not include those hostile to the sponsors.

There are other advertising/editorial connections you will find. Take a look at the cover photos of magazines featuring articles on fashion. There will always be credits for the clothing designer or retailer, the hair stylist, and the makeup used by the model. But notice also how frequently the perfume or cologne the model is wearing is mentioned in the photo credit or caption, and then look inside the magazine to see which fragrances are most prominently advertised.

With a photograph, you are drawn by the model's physical beauty, which affects your decision to buy the magazine, and by the clothes and makeup the model is wearing. The sensual appeal of perfume and cologne can be experienced only in person (except for the "scratch and sniff" and fragrance bead devices used for inside advertising). The only reason to mention such items in conjunction with a cover shot is to provide an editorial boost for the advertiser.

Motion pictures use product placements in the same manner. Sometimes a company pays to have its product used as an integral part of the story. For example, several years ago the movie *E.T. the Extra-Terrestrial* became a blockbuster both at the box office and in home video sales and rentals. It was the story of a creature who came to earth and was discovered by some children who helped him find a way to return to his home, despite the best efforts of adults to keep him on earth and subject him to scientific study. There was a scene in the movie in which one of the boys who befriends E.T. uses candy to create a trail that the creature will follow. The producer wanted to use small candies and offered the manufacturer of M&M's a chance to buy into the picture. The company refused, so the right was sold to rival Reese's Pieces, which manufactured a similar product that was less well known at the time. By virtue of being mentioned and shown in the movie, Reese's Pieces enjoyed a major boost in sales that could not have been achieved in any other way.

Sometimes a product placement requires payment of a fee meant to offset the cost of production and thus increase the potential for profits. At other times the film company is simply allowed to keep the product, which is less expensive.

California-based independent computer manufacturers frequently made this type of arrangement when the personal computer was still a new home/small office product and not very popular. The cost was high—$100 to $200 or more per megabyte of memory—and a twenty-megabyte hard disk ran $2000 before the costs of other products, marketing, manufacturing, shipping, and profit percentage were added. Today a hard disk costs less than a dollar per megabyte when retailed, and it costs the manufacturer only a fraction of that to produce. But in those early days, a small-capacity computer could run $10,000 or more while being no more sophisticated than some of today's electronic toys for children.

Unlike today, computer manufacturers were not giants. Other than Apple and IBM, the field was wide open. Every electronic tinkerer's basement might house a would-be computer giant. The builders thought only of getting their products before the public, of gaining a market share, and then growing as consumers learned the usefulness of the products they were making.

Motion picture producers convinced these start-up companies that the appearance of their computers in films would give them unprecedented free advertising. The manufacturers were guaranteed that their computers—and their corporate logo—would be shown prominently. In addition, there would be a screen credit, usually at the end of the picture and usually for a guaranteed time period such as seven seconds.

There would be no fee from the computer dealers for this opportunity. Instead, the production company would get to keep the computers. The equipment was then switched to one or another of their corporate departments after the film was made, saving the production company an investment of $50,000 or more to gain a high-technology advantage.

Product placement today is most noticeable with foods and cars. Family pictures have cereals, soft drinks, and similar products blatantly visible. Adult films have beer, wine, and more sophisticated foods.

Ford Motor Company supplied cars for highly rated, family-oriented programs such as *The FBI*. The only stipulations were that the cars be used by the "good guys" and that they never be shown crashing.

Does product placement have a significant impact on sales? Manufacturers must think so or they would not continue to use this advertisement technique. Certainly the motion picture and television production companies are self-serving in their requests, but product placement has gone on for so long that there is ample evidence it works. The public identifies with the heroes of the stories and wants to do what they do, even if that means drinking beer on their breakfast cereal.

Perhaps more insidious than the interrelated companies owned by tobacco products manufacturers are the news items prepared by companies. Many people have heard the term "infomercial," although they may not fully understand it. An infomercial is a television program, lasting a full half hour or longer, whose sole purpose is to sell a product. Sometimes it is an obvious commercial, such as one for a celebrity's cosmetics company in which the star/business executive and a few of her closest friends (all well-paid, high-profile actresses) sit around and trade beauty secrets. The format is that of a rather casual talk show, and the women never stop mentioning how valuable the cosmetics have been to them. It is informative if you are a potential buyer, but no one misunderstands the nature of the program.

By contrast, there are some infomercials that seem like news or feature programs unrelated to the sale of a product. The people who do the talking are well established in news or business broadcasting, and their names, faces, and voices are quite familiar to the viewers. They will discuss a genuine topic, such as home-based businesses, multilevel marketing, and the potential from catalog sales. They will conduct in-depth interviews with people who have made money in these fields. They will discuss the economy, the cost of overhead when creating your own business, and other details. Often the information is of value to any entrepreneur, at least in part. But ultimately, either by the end of the program or through in-home sales pitches conducted as a result of your calling an 800 number to request that a representative contact you, you will learn that this is a pitch for a specific company. The infomercial, which only has to make one or two references in the credits to the fact that it is a paid advertisement, seduces the public into thinking that the information has been objectively presented.

Less well known, and quite dangerous in its unethical influence, is the public relations videotape that is sent by some companies to their local news media. These slickly produced stories are planned to run for 30 seconds, 1 minute, 90 seconds, 2 minutes, or whatever length is normal for the broadcast outlets that will be receiving them. They are usually well-written, strongly produced visuals. They tell about an innovative manufacturing process, a new invention, a new plant that will be employing locals, or almost anything else that truly is news. The writing is objective, and the story is one that the station might routinely cover if it had time. Thus by using the tape the news department can utilize its resources for other stories, save on the cost of production for that night, and still give the viewers interesting material.

What is not said is that the use of such prepared news releases can be a serious problem. First, because of the savings to the station, the news director is not likely to discourage use of the material. This means the station is not likely to do something that will upset the supplying corporation, a situation that is reinforced if the supplier is also an advertiser.

A friend of mine is a videographer who, though primarily involved with network news production and stories fed by satellite throughout the world, has also been hired at times to record "news" items created by public relations people. He was shocked to find that one manufacturing company ordered him to limit his shooting so that the defective products being produced would not be shown. He later was ordered to choose angles that would not reveal health and safety violations that permeated the company.

Eventually, my friend stopped doing such work because he felt it was unethical. Had any legitimate news team gone into the same place, they would have recorded everything. An innovative product might have been mentioned, but so would the failings of that product, which would still be considered in the developmental stage. And in some instances, instead of the puff piece that was supplied, the reporter would have created a hard-hitting investigative feature resulting in legal sanctions against the business.

The end result is that whenever such PR material is used, you are watching manipulated "news." In many instances you are being cheated out of an important story that could affect the health and/or safety of you or your loved ones. And when the truth does come to the attention of the news department, the issue is likely to be pursued with reluctance, if at all. After all, the decision to take what was presented in a sense made the news department an accomplice in a fraud. Sometimes the decision is made to save face rather than correct past errors—to the detriment of everyone involved.

In a sense, the public relations material provided to news departments has the potential to create problems that are far worse than the denial of information concerning smoking. The pressure exerted by tobacco company food division advertising departments may never be known by most of the public, and the success of that pressure will limit what stories are covered. But the made-for-television-news media features stop the flow of information for which there may be no other source than the news department of the station choosing to use such video news releases. The tobacco companies stop stories from running. The video press releases can prevent stories from ever being uncovered.

The other concern when it comes to financial influence has to do with the paying of sources for information. This is also known as "checkbook journalism," a situation which, surprisingly, is not an international issue. In fact, some countries, such as Japan, have a history of journalists routinely paying the subjects of their interviews.

Payment for information takes several forms. The simplest is a bribe for documents. Remember that it is legal to publish anything in the United States, though there may be any number of civil penalties to be paid afterward. However, it may not be legal to pass information to a reporter.

Journalists like to rely on greedy, unethical, and/or disgruntled employees when working on complex stories. For example, several years ago I was researching a popular tranquilizer that was seem-

ingly highly addictive and was being misprescribed by the majority of doctors in the United States. There were questions of its
safety and whether the tests used to pass Federal Drug Adminis-
tration standards were, in fact, properly completed.

I was invited to Washington, where a government agency was
holding hearings on the drug and others like it. Instead of attending the sessions, though, I was asked by some of the U.S. senate
committee workers to come back to their offices. There they
showed me the files of materials that were being used for the hearings as well as one drawer that contained documents revealing
massive frauds in the industry. "We're sure the investigators will
be making these secret files public record," a senior staff person
told me. They were the files that proved that not only the drug in
question but many other tranquilizers and sleeping pills introduced in the United States during the previous nine years had not
been properly tested. There were hidden health dangers in them
all. "And that is why we're giving you permission to read them
since they were previously classified as being confidential for the
committee's use only."

I was shown the top drawer of the filing cabinet, and the documents were as explosive as the staff person implied. Yet he and I
knew that the pharmaceutical companies had been making carefully placed political donations for years. There was a good chance
that none of the documents would ever be seen or used in the
hearings. (And as matters turned out, when I received complete
transcriptions of the hearings, including copies of the documents
used, the official record contained nothing of the scandal that was
revealed in the files.)

"Now our staff is going to lunch for one hour," he told me.
"That's *everyone* in this office. There will be *no one here but you*."

He paused, making certain I understood what he meant. Then
he continued, saying, "Now you may read everything, but I don't
want you making photocopies for your book. I don't want you

making photocopies on that Xerox machine over there by the window. I don't want you using the photocopier I just loaded with a fresh paper tray, with additional paper just below if you need it. And I don't want you using the toner over here," he added, showing me where it was kept.

"Remember we will all be gone, but just for an hour. And don't copy the documents in the first few folders because those are the ones you will most want to read. Am I clear?"

He was. I photocopied everything. And when the book was released, the doctor with whom I was working made headlines for the revelations that had *not* come out of the hearings. We were threatened with a lawsuit until it was learned what we had documented. And as to the staff person who gave me access to the material, I never asked him his name, and I deliberately forgot what he looked like.

Ethical? Of course not.

Was the release of the information in the public interest? Most certainly.

And this is a scenario that exists in one form or another for many reporters working many different stories. There are whistleblowers of a sort—people who want to alert the public to a problem but don't want to be fired—who will violate the policies of their corrupt employers and pass material to journalists, television reporters, and the like.

There is a second level of information gathering that involves money used as a bribe. (But it is never referred to in this manner; rather, it is a "retainer," a "fee for services," or some other polite term.) For example, at a number of major hospitals throughout Southern California, there are admissions personnel and other staff members receiving regular bribes from reporters seeking to learn who is being admitted and what is wrong with the person. Some hospital personnel are on a monthly retainer. Others are paid as they deliver. The money is excellent. The stories are innocuous.

And though personal privacy has been violated, the end result is usually celebrity material on illness, pregnancy, or spouse abuse. The publications scoop their rivals with material that the celebrities' publicists would probably have released at a slightly later date.

More offensive is the bribe that leads to a photographer or videographer being allowed in to see the celebrity patient. This is mildly traumatic, though usually anticipated. Occasionally the celebrity may hire a security guard to keep the photographers away. And occasionally the celebrity may alert the guard that photographers from specific publications are to "accidentally" be allowed to pass. In fact, some celebrities are paid by the tabloids to tell about their dates or provide the opportunity for the tabloid photographer to "surprise" them. For example, when the comedienne Roseanne was breaking up with her first husband, her soon-to-be second husband, Tom Arnold, admitted he was making money selling stories about their secret rendezvous. The photographers would just "happen" to catch them going on a date and Arnold would receive a check.

The real concern is what occurred with the O. J. Simpson trial and has occurred with other high-profile stories. This is the effort to gain whatever information is available at whatever price it takes. And when this form of unethical behavior is rampant, the public's valid concerns can suffer indirectly. In the case of a crime, money might be offered to the suspect, members of his or her family, surviving victims, witnesses, and others. The journalists want a unique perspective. They want to show the grief, the anger, the madness. They want to be able to predict the outcome of the case based on the information that would normally not be available until it comes out in the trial.

The problems with this situation are many. First there is the issue of free press versus fair trial. The more coverage a case receives, the harder it is to prosecute fairly. And in the not too distant past, there have been excesses that were outrageous.

For example, in July of 1954, in Bay Village, Ohio, a controversial osteopathic physician named Sam Sheppard was allegedly knocked unconscious by one or more intruders who killed his wife Marilyn as she lay in her bed. She was pregnant at the time, and she was severely beaten. Marilyn was the more sympathetic of the two. Sam Sheppard was believed to be a blatant womanizer and certainly led a flamboyant life when away from the hospital he helped run with the other doctors in his family.

The death occurred in the early morning, and by mid-afternoon, one of the investigating Cleveland police officers was convinced Sheppard was guilty of the murder. The doctor was in shock, under sedation, and was being treated for neck injuries he had allegedly received while struggling with an intruder.

Sheppard willingly agreed to be questioned and was interviewed frequently between the July 4 murder and the July 7 false statement issued by the prosecutor, which claimed Sheppard refused his request to talk. It was the start of a campaign to convict the doctor regardless of where the evidence might otherwise lead.

There were several newspapers serving the Cleveland, Ohio, area in 1954, among them the *Cleveland Press*, headed by Louis B. Seltzer. Seltzer understood the power of a newspaper, and his readers were naive enough to believe that anything printed had to be true. For political and personal reasons unrelated to the murder, Seltzer, along with the Cuyahoga County coroner, Dr. Samuel Gerber, wanted to vilify Sheppard. It has never been satisfactorily determined whether they thought he was guilty or simply hated him so much that they refused to be objective about the evidence. Whatever the case, Seltzer used his newspaper to convict Sheppard.

Among the headlines of stories in Seltzer's newspaper that were blatant attacks against Sheppard were: "Someone Is Getting Away With Murder" (July 20, 1954; an accompanying editorial demanded Sheppard be arrested and convicted); "Police Captain Urges Sheppard's Arrest" (July 26, 1954); "Why Don't Police Quiz

Top Suspect?" (July 28, 1954); and "Why Isn't Sam Sheppard in Jail?" (July 30, 1954). Sheppard was actually arrested on July 30, but he was released on bail on August 16—which is normally not possible in a murder case—when the judge found there was no evidence linking Sheppard to the murder. However, with intense pressure from the media and politicians, the grand jury felt itself pressured to indict Sheppard the next day. He was rearrested and would not be set free for almost ten years.

The issue of Sheppard's guilt or innocence is still hotly debated in Ohio. Ultimately, he was found not guilty on November 16, 1966, in a case that made young lawyer F. Lee Bailey a national celebrity. A television series called *The Fugitive,* which was based on the Sheppard case, ran for 120 episodes and had a long afterlife in reruns. Most important, Sheppard's second trial was the result of the June 6, 1966, ruling by the U.S. Supreme Court that Sheppard was denied a fair trial because the presiding judge failed to control the media circus he allowed in his courtroom. He also failed to prevent the jury from being biased by excessive press coverage.

Following the Sheppard fiasco, there were major changes in the way the press handled sensational cases. Trial by the media no longer occurs in so blatant a manner. One-sided coverage still exists, especially in high-profile cases in small towns, but the blatant partisan action shown by the *Cleveland Press* is extraordinarily rare. However, in its place is something equally insidious: the buying of news to the possible detriment of a free trial.

Coverage of a criminal case can obviously affect potential jurors. In the extreme, a trial can be moved to a different city where the emotions are not so strong. The problem with that approach is that the moving of the trial becomes major news in the city where the trial eventually is held. This means that the local media will give it blanket coverage, including explaining in depth why the trial had to be moved (called a change of venue). Although emotions may not run so high, the facts of the case as known to the press will quite possibly influence the new jury pool.

At the same time, press coverage is necessary to ensure a fair trial. There are times when incompetence, political concerns, and other factors enter into the handling of a case. Sometimes the wrong person is tried for a crime. Sometimes there is too little evidence to warrant a trial. Sometimes the prosecution stops investigating the crime when they feel they have a winnable case instead of seeing if other people were involved.

In one city in New York State, three girls were killed by a serial killer. The man in charge of the investigation was planning to quit the police force and go into politics. He needed a conviction in order to boost his standing in the community, but he had no idea who the killer might be. Fortunately for him, a former firefighter, a man who had recently died of a heart attack, was a convicted child molester whose crimes were recently in the news. The investigator announced to the press that the firefighter was the serial killer and would have been arrested had he lived. He then retired to enter politics.

The case was officially closed, but other detectives knew the firefighter was not the serial killer. They kept evidence when they retired, evidence that later linked the killings to another man who had been involved with the murders of fourteen others in California and Washington State. When a journalist linked the three cities, the current detectives came forward and found enough connections for an indictment. Since the man was already serving several life sentences, they decided to wait to bring charges until he is released, an unlikely event, so they can save their city the cost of a trial. There is no statute of limitations on murder, so this delay does not matter. However, had a member of the media not investigated the West Coast inmate's background, the identity of the real serial killer might have been lost.

In another case, a man was convicted of killing his family on a military base. A book was written about the case and there was extensive media attention. The man claimed he was innocent, and a number of top investigators came forward, without charge, to try to help him. But rather than producing what, for him, would be a happy ending, the media attention did not clear him. Instead it brought forward witnesses to events near the man's home, witnesses who lived in the neighborhood and had not been interviewed by law enforcement officers, yet had made note of unusual activities on the street. Several had taken down license numbers of strange cars, then tossed them into a drawer when no one came by. The result, several years later, was the reopening of the investigation because, whether the husband was guilty or innocent, it became known that men and women with records of drug abuse and assault had been in the house. The convicted murderer might be guilty, but if he is, he quite probably did not act alone.

There are numerous other examples, including a Columbus, Ohio, reporter looking at crime statistics for a series of surrounding counties. Using a computer, he found that a series of seemingly unrelated murders, each in a different law enforcement jurisdiction, appeared to have been committed by the same man. There was no routine sharing of case information by the investigators because each thought the murder in his or her community was a unique event. Only the reporter, looking for something interesting to write about, made the connections, then further showed that the killer seemed to be following truck stops. It took two years, but the work resulted in the arrest of a trucker who was a serial killer.

In Florida, author/journalist/educator Fred Rosen was working on a true-crime book about the murder of a man who had been a carnival sideshow attraction. The murder was committed by members of his family who, according to the defense attorney, were reacting to intense brutality. There was even a home video that allegedly proved the validity of the defense argument, a video that was supplied to the prosecution and shown to the jury without sound. The assumption was that there had never been sound, but the truth was different.

Rosen and at least one other member of the media had accidentally been sent a genuine copy of the original tape, and their copies had sound. The dialogue that could be heard belied the defense argument.

Sitting at the trial and witnessing the silent videotape, Rosen was incensed. He felt that he had to go to the prosecution with the copy in his possession or he would be denying the dead man true justice. Once the full tape with sound was played in the courtroom, a conviction swiftly followed, something that probably would not have occurred if the jury had seen only the sound-removed tape that was originally offered.

To Rosen's surprise, the local press shunned him. He was informed that what he did was not something they would do. He was an outsider, traveling hundreds of miles to witness the trial. They were locals, and they needed the defense attorney as a source for future stories. They were willing to ignore the tape and possibly let a killer go free rather than lose a source for future stories.

Rosen, a member of the media, helped resolve the case despite the other media representatives ignoring critical facts. The media can thus be an important force toward ensuring justice in America. Unfortunately the practice of checkbook journalism can create problems at least as bad as those that can occur when a case receives no public scrutiny.

To understand checkbook journalism, suppose a murder occurs in a neighborhood where some of the houses are situated so that the occupants could be witnesses if they had been looking out their windows. The crime is reported and the police flock to the scene. Within minutes, if the police radio has been monitored, reporters also begin to arrive.

The crime scene is sealed off from the public. Photographs and videotape are shot from outside the designated area. This assures the preservation of small items called "trace" evidence. It also allows the investigators to gain clues from the undisturbed crime scene. These clues can come from the way the body is positioned, where objects have fallen, and other details easily changed by accidental bumping by untrained curiosity seekers such as members of the press.

All the reporters arriving at the crime scene have essentially the same story. They were kept the same distance away. They spoke with the same official spokesperson from the police department. If they return to their papers or television and radio stations without further effort, the news will have a sameness to it when it is published or aired. Yet the business of the broadcaster or publisher is to be certain that his or her medium is offering something unique enough to cause the viewer or reader to tune out the rivals. This puts tremendous pressure on reporters to find something else, something that will "scoop" their rivals.

In recent years, the answer has been for the tabloid press and the tabloid television shows to pay people for their stories. The police will ask questions and the prosecutor may request that witnesses not discuss what they saw other than in ways connected with the trial, but no contract exists with these law enforcement personnel. There is no incentive to remain silent when a member of the press is willing to pay witnesses anywhere from $100 to several thousand dollars to tell the same thing they told the police.

The problem is that the payment of money creates the question of whether or not the person will tell the truth. Suppose you heard footsteps going by your apartment at 10:05 P.M. You noticed the time because you had gone to sleep early, heard a bump, and when you went to see what was happening, you looked at the clock.

That story might be critical for the prosecution. That minor detail might set the stage for proving a pattern that included other witnesses who actually could identify the person accused of a murder. Unlike television mysteries, many of the facts that witnesses provide in real cases are rather innocuous in themselves, but together with other details they can prove the charges against someone or result in an acquittal.

The problem is that the witness has often watched tabloid television or read tabloid newspapers. He knows what he has to say is not very exciting, and it has been implied to him that the amount of money he will be paid will be determined by the importance of the details. There is a tremendous incentive to exaggerate or even lie, to claim to have seen far more than was actually witnessed. Once someone lies to the press, his or her testimony can no longer be used with any certainty in court. Assuming that the witness tells exactly what happened, not embellishing the story as was done for the reporter, there is a good chance that the defense attorney will obtain a copy of the story that was written or aired. The attorney will have the witness repeat the truth, then ask the witness about the earlier story for which he was paid. When the witness admits he lied, all credibility is gone. "How do we know you're telling the truth now? How do we know you're not being paid to lie this time? How can we trust anything you say?"

And if the person perpetuates the lie, the defense will show that the details do not match. "What was the person you saw wearing? What color was the shirt? Was it buttoned or unbuttoned? A pullover?" On and on will go the probing, always with the attorney comparing it to the statements of real eyewitnesses who have given a different story.

Eventually there is either disbelief by the jury, who must dismiss the witness in their minds, weakening the case, or an actual mistrial. If you can't tell what is true and what is fake, there is a reasonable doubt and the case must be dismissed.

Checkbook journalism in the United States taints every story that is covered. Is the person being interviewed telling the truth? Is the person leaving out part of the story to make it more saleable? Is the person adding details to make it more exciting?

There are many ways to disguise the payment. An expert might be paid for his or her time, since giving such information is what the person does on a regular basis. And while this seems fair, one of the issues in a libel case is the absence of malice. If someone is a disgruntled employee telling the truth about a corporation to the media, and if that person invests extensive time in an interview, it does seem fair to pay the employee. But by being disgruntled, no matter how justified, the person has created an issue of malice. And under United States libel law, an absence of malice when reporting a story, especially if it involves a public figure, can be extremely important. The use of checkbook journalism that allows the reporter to scoop the nation may also ensure that justice is not done, wrongs are not righted, and what was presented in the public interest (or at least to an interested public) was not in the public good.

And so money is one of the greatest threats to the ethical handling of stories, both real and fictional, in all the media. Yet the role of sponsors, advertisers, and large-budget special interest groups is so accepted in the United States that few people ever think of how insidious their power can be.

6

Are There Ethics in Cyberspace?

It is the great American media frontier. Online communication services ranging from the Internet to America Online to CompuServe to private bulletin boards are following the newest trends in communication. No one is certain what the future will bring, but people in every medium—radio stations, television broadcasters, magazine publishers, newspaper publishers, and motion picture production companies—are looking to see if they need a presence in the online systems. Many have already created special material available to anyone with a computer and a modem. Others are seeing what the near future will hold, and planning to adapt as necessary. But computer access to information is going to be a part of everyone's future, and it is over such services that some of the sharpest ethical debates are taking place.

Before discussing the Internet, it is important to understand another serious concern with computer information services. The role of computers in society as they relate to entertainment and news is still in transition. The computer is now of limited use, but is has seemingly unlimited potential to become the center for sending and receiving all information. The computer will likely be the center for receiving movies on demand, television programming, stereo broadcasts, books, newspapers, magazines, and the like. This does not mean that it will fully replace existing media. However, just as the radio once dominated a family's entertainment thinking only to be displaced by television, so the computer in some form will displace television. The current forms of delivery may coexist (for example, more radios are in use today than in the so-called golden age of radio programming), but the computer-based system will dominate. As this occurs, the idea of Marshall McLuhan's global village will likely die for the most technologically advanced individuals.

The reason for this is that besides requiring instant access to all parts of the world—something that is already firmly in place, thanks to satellite communication—the global village also requires people to take advantage of the concept, and this is where the problem exists.

When the idea for the global village was first put forward, television reception was limited in most parts of the United States. There were usually three VHF stations and maybe one or two UHF stations. Cable was rare. Satellite reception was nonexistent. Programming was broad because the networks were trying to be like a family magazine offering the arts, children's shows, how-to shows, mainstream religious shows, and the like. A day of television viewing would have its soap operas, Westerns, and detective shows, but it would also likely have music, dance, an exercise class, a cooking class, a news feature along the lines of a National Geographic special, and the like. Sitting in front of the set would transport you anywhere in the world where an event was taking place.

With the systems now in place for the immediate future, you can be more selective. If your first love is watching sexually oriented material, you can limit your viewing to such matters. The same is true for sports, music videos, comedy, Westerns, and the like. The global village is still available, but you have to seek it out, and since television has long been a passive activity, the public is not likely to change its habits. The typical viewer, even with remote control, likes to sit back and stay with a particular channel. All contemporary programming revolves around this idea. The networks know that if they can hook a viewer for one show, the viewer will be the lead-in audience base for the next program on the same channel. Thus the more we are able to narrow our choices for an evening's entertainment, the more limited we are likely to make the information we receive. The global village will still exist, and people who are not so technologically advanced as we are will probably still experience it. But the average person using the most advanced forms of communication will probably do what he or she has always had a tendency to do—limit experience to that which is familiar. The more material from which we can draw, the more likely we are to narrow what we do.

Having said that, let us look at the state of online communication today. The Internet is a cross between the world's largest public library and the most sophisticated telephone party line. It has been called the information superhighway because, like the superhighway system that began to link the cities of the United States in the 1950s, it was originally created for the Defense Department. President Eisenhower, a former Army general, felt that high-speed roads were necessary for the rapid movement of troops, tanks, Jeeps, and other military vehicles from city to city in the event of war. That was why his presidency marked the creation of roads today used almost exclusively for business and pleasure travel at speeds illegal on local roads.

Likewise, the Internet was created by the U.S. Department of Defense in the 1970s so that military commanders, intelligence experts, and similar individuals could have rapid access to vast resources of information and to each other. It was later expanded to include defense contractors and universities, many of which had research grants related to military concerns. Today it is available to anyone with a computer, a telephone hook-up (modem), and whatever access fee might be charged. Every imaginable subject can be researched. Everyone using it can "talk" to everyone else if he or she so chooses. There are no age restrictions. There is no censorship. There are no chaperones for the underage, the emotionally unstable, and the violent looking to encourage and be encouraged by like-minded individuals.

"We broke into our first house at approximately midnight," reads a portion of one entry from an Internet user in a small town in Tennessee. It is part of a sexually explicit story written by a man who, with two female friends, went from personal sexual experimentation to gang raping others. "We found the first bedroom of the house, a nine-year-old child slept soundly. We left her alone. We came to the parents' bedroom. As the couple slept (we had no idea who the f— they were) we bound their hands and feet to the bedposts. We gagged them and then shut and locked the door. As Tracy and I yanked on the bonds to tighten them fully, Suzanne pounced on the man and ripped his clothes off savagely. . . .

"I watch for a moment, and then the wife turned to me. She tried her damnedest to scream but the gag prevented her."

The story continued with explicit descriptions of sexual violence, as well as telling of a second break-in where teenagers were the victims. It also detailed the precautions taken to prevent discovery.

The identity of the writer was not given, and though a telephone number was provided for access to the information, the nature of computer sources is that the telephone number was not necessarily that of the writer. The number was for an electronic bulletin board, the computer equivalent of a small-town bulletin board or posting area where anyone, from elected officials to private citizens, can leave messages for others to read.

Perhaps no similar crimes occurred in recent months in the community where the bulletin board was accessed, but the crimes might have occurred thousands of miles away. The rapist could then have sent the story to the bulletin board in a manner that is currently almost impossible to trace, and anyone calling the bulletin board number would be able to read the message.

Or the story could be false, detailing the violent sexual fantasies of someone who might still be a virgin. Individuals using the Internet and other, smaller services such as CompuServe range from doctors, lawyers, businesspeople, and students to men and women who completely lack social skills. Their work often involves computer use to the exclusion of all other contact. Many do not date. Many have few, if any, close friends. If they take their meals in restaurants, they rarely talk with anyone, including the serving staff. It is only behind the anonymity of the computer screen that they lead lives of excitement, adventure, and even romance. Since there is no chance of accidentally meeting the people with whom they are communicating, they can pretend to be anyone they wish.

Mingled in with the voyeurs and the anonymous fantasizers are a number of truly violent individuals. Some have even raped or killed before. Others have been living fantasy lives they want supported in order to act out their desires. The anonymity of the bulletin boards allows their fantasies to be reinforced by others. Stephen Gilbert, an expert in computer security who has appeared on major news and talk shows, has discovered that some users of bulletin boards become increasingly violent because of them. Some share their actions in writing, as in the material quoted above, which came from a bulletin board called Toxic Shock Presents. Others will photograph their victims, then scan the images electronically so that they can "post" them on the Internet and related services. However they do it, several crimes have first been revealed electronically as a small but growing number of violent users reinforce each other. They are a "gang" who live hundreds or thousands of miles apart, supporting each other's violence without ever being directly involved with one another.

A different type of bulletin board accessible on the Internet deals with anarchists' tools that can be made from readily available materials. Among those downloaded for this book were such items as "fire fudge." The ingredients, which are readily found in most grocery stores, hobby shops, and pharmacies (most are so innocuous that a child can buy them without being questioned in any way), are omitted from the quotes for obvious reasons.

Fire fudge, according to the writer, "can be used to ignite most incendiaries, except thermite. It may be used directly as an incendiary on rags, dry paper, dry hay, or in the combustible vapor above liquid fuels."

After detailing the simple manufacture and use of fire fudge, there is a description of an "incendiary brick" which, "when properly made . . . looks like an ordinary building brick and can be easily transported without detection. The incendiary brick will ignite wooden walls, floors, and many other combustible materials." [Note: More details are not being provided here because the information was checked with experts on chemistry, arson, and sabotage, all of whom agree that the simple descriptions and ingredients are accurate.]

After explaining how to make the brick, the instructions state: "When hard, remove the incendiary from the mold, and paint it red to simulate a normal building brick." It goes on to say, "When painted, the incendiary brick can be carried with normal construction materials and placed in or on combustible materials."

The same source provided other information, including how to make such readily transportable high explosives as PETN (pentaerythritol tetranitrate), RDX ("a white crystalline solid that exhibits very high shattering power. It is commonly used as a booster in explosive trains or as a main bursting charge"), and composition C-4, the most common military plastic explosive.

Given the nature of the people involved with such work, it is logical for them to assume that law enforcement might be after them. As a result, the bulletin board also provides details concerning how to build devices that allow eavesdropping on anyone's telephone, and devices for countering an FBI wiretap. The latter includes information not only on how to evade eavesdropping but also on how to sabotage the FBI computer that is likely being used to handle the surveillance.

Again, these are all devices that can be made with items found in your home kitchen, supplemented by materials from hardware and chain electronic stores located throughout the United States. Individually, these are harmless, common products that are legal to possess and are used at one time or another by most adults.

There are other extremists on the Internet. Among the religious zealots are those who are practicing a violent form of Satanism. "Anyone can help spread blood in the name of Lord Satan. If you don't have a career don't worry, neither do we, don't let that stop you from sacrificing. I personally have been doing this for 9 years and I'm still in college while sacrificing young virgins. There is also a need for full-time positions in demon worship."

These items may seem exaggerated and almost humorous, but the quotes are genuine and the information was obtained with the help of law enforcement sources. They all involve people who were spreading genuine information and were involved with real crimes that were later uncovered. The criminals were prosecuted and convictions were obtained.

Yet if you thoroughly go through any large public library, much of what you read on the Internet can be found on the shelves. This does not mean that the bulletin board material is being downloaded, printed, and bound. Rather, books on chemistry, electronics, and physics, training manuals for law enforcement officers, and various scientific journals will give you all the information needed to create bombs, incendiary devices, and the like. Books on all manner of deviant and counterculture religions, including books that detail rituals used by extremists, are all available. Likewise information on various forms of risqué literature, books on sexual deviations, and popular-market tomes of prurience such as Madonna's *Sex* are all available on the shelves. Sexual deviance, torture, unusual ways to have intercourse, erotic literature, and works on similar themes abound. Anyone with a library card and the inclination to look for such products can find them either on the shelves or through interlibrary loans.

Of greater concern is hate speech being spread on the Internet without counter information. Most groups have focused on the issue of censorship. Should Holocaust revisionists be allowed to spread the message that a horrible, well-documented part of twentieth-century history never occurred? Should those who hate blacks, whites, women, Asians, or anyone else be allowed to spread violent hate, often involving lies and half truths to make their point? Should someone who wants to hurt another person "talk" it out in graphic detail with friends?

People have a First Amendment right to free speech, even when that speech is filled with hate, according to Rabbi Abraham Cooper of the Simon Wiesenthal Center in Los Angeles. He is one of the nation's leading experts on all types of hate speech, including postings on the Internet. He explains that the appeal of online services comes from the fact that they are cheap, instantaneous, and anonymous.

Rabbi Cooper—whose knowledge and counsel are sought by governments, universities, and other organizations throughout the world—feels that the biggest problem is that the online services are so wide-open. People who are living their lives on the fringe of society suddenly have instant access to the mainstream population. They have no background in debate or the cultural niceties of intellectual exchange found in a university setting. The anonymity of the Internet also lowers inhibitions because there is a feeling of unconnectedness to the people who will be reading the hate material.

Personal attacks that appear on the Internet are often so anonymous that the victim has no way of responding. Unchallenged hate speech on computers can do great damage to individuals and institutions. Even worse, the literate form, dressed up with graphics, gives the message a potential for credibility that would not otherwise exist.

Another problem Cooper sees is that the older someone is, the greater their knowledge, wisdom, and perspective should be, yet it is the very young, often preteen children, who are most likely to be heavy users of the online services. They lack the discernment of adults, who presumably have the experience and educational background to better place what they are seeing in the appropriate context. Cooper does not see the elimination of such material as being the answer to the problem. Rather, he faults organizations with online access whose leadership fails to provide the information needed to counter the falsehoods and hatred so readily available. He feels that it is critical to be proactive, to be certain that a full range of information is available to users.

As to the issue of children using the Internet, Gail Featheringham of the National Public Telecomputing Network, an organization in the forefront of handling legal issues relating to online services, goes against conventional thinking. She is a former second grade teacher, a generation older than Peter Harter, the attorney who is executive director of the organization. While he is comfortable with the idea of children on the Internet and other online services, she feels that the issue is not the ethics of the information to which they have access. Rather, she is concerned about the focus on computers for the very young.

Featheringham notes that today's children are growing up without the extended families of the past. There was a time when children had parents and grandparents with whom they interacted. Those days are long gone for most families, and today's children are uncomfortable when communicating with adults. Using computers is an isolating act, often involving just their peers.

She feels that there are essential skills elementary-school children need to develop that are more important than computer skills. The social interaction that comes with traditional classroom teaching is critical for the very young. They need to play with other children and with adults. The use of computers can further their isolation and greatly reduce the social skills they will need as much or more than computer expertise when they enter the adult job market.

Another problem with the Internet as it now exists, according to Harter, is that a researcher must have some preexisting knowledge in order to obtain good data. There is no way to be certain that a computer search for information will result in quality material being found.

Featheringham has strong concerns about the availability of information despite the problems. She explains:

> The library, as a foundation, the library has a bill of rights so there is policy in the library. If the policy is nothing more than to protect free speech and lack of censorship, the library does have something called the Library Bill of Rights which means information for all people, essentially. Now, the librarian who purchases materials can say, "Oh, we ran out of money. We can't purchase that hate material," you know, and blame it on the budget, having nothing to do with censorship. But it is the librarian's right to choose, and usually the librarian is an educated person who is trying to represent the community that the librarian serves, so therefore is hopefully making intelligent decisions along those lines.
>
> The bottom line is that there is something in print, a written policy, that they have to go by which doesn't exist right now on the Internet.
>
> Not only am I a librarian, but I'm an educator and past teacher, so I have very strong feelings about kids on the Internet and free speech type stuff. I am totally against censorship.
>
> You would think I would take a more conservative approach, but I don't. I take a very free speech approach to it. Give a child a dictionary, they're going to look up swear words.
>
> So it's not that the stuff isn't out there, it's everywhere. If a child wants it, he's going to get it. And try and regulate some-

thing as vast as the Internet, which is not an American phenom-enon—it's a global phenomenon—is absurd. It's an American ego problem. And I think you [Peter Harter] were the one who said, "On the Internet, the Bill of Rights is a local document." It's kind of ridiculous of us to think that we can monitor it, let alone to legislate it.[29]

Harter and Featheringham note that many of the criticisms of electronic services result from confusion over what they are offer-ing. There are bulletin boards, chat groups, E-mail, and other forms of communication. Some are meant to supply information on a specific topic. They may have been created by an institution or association using the Internet to disseminate factual information concerning a disease, social problem, or other issue. The material is generally objective, accurate, and presented in-depth. It is no different from the written material normally disseminated by such groups, though using this approach saves paper and mailing costs.

The chat groups are ostensibly devoted to a single topic—the latest popular rock star, baseball players of World War II, sexual de-viations, the Kennedy assassination, and almost anything else imaginable. Sometimes the people stay with the subject. Some-times they change the subject. Sometimes two people will move to a more private area for personal discussions.

The chat groups are not sources of accurate information. The people "online" may be genuine experts, or they may be fixated "crackpots" espousing a cause that sounds impressive but is inac-curate, or they may be curiosity seekers, liars, or those with alterna-tive motives. Pedophiles have been known to work the chat groups for children interested in computer games, ultimately working out ways to meet the boys and girls for sex. The targeted child or chil-dren will be told that the meeting is to exchange games, and though these incidents are rare, they periodically make the headlines around the country.

Chat groups meant to foster interpersonal relationships among couples using them as electronic dating services often find that everyone is lying. Men may pretend to be women and women pretend to be men. The young may pretend to be older, and the elderly may claim to be sixteen. Anything is possible.

E-mail is electronic communication sent to individuals in the same manner as regular mail, though without the expense of postage and paper. Bulletin boards are broader-based forms of communication often utilized by special-interest groups to communicate with members and the like-minded. They can be used to create an electronic newsletter, provide training materials, and the like.

Many of the electronic services are designed so that photographs can be downloaded. This is where concerns are most often voiced about access by children to pornographic pictures.

But what does all this really mean?

Peter Harter comments:

I think one area that is important is the role of parents and whether or not they treat the computer as a surrogate parent. I think for years television was treated as a surrogate parent. Television was declared to be a "vast wasteland" in the early sixties by a former commissioner of the FCC [Newton Minnow], and he announced it again in a *New York Times* magazine essay this past spring. It still is a wasteland, and I would agree.

We have a lot of ratings and oversight by government authorities, a lot of civic groups are well established, and they haven't made any headway on it. In fact, despite Rupert Murdoch being a very conservative person morally personally, the Fox Network is one of the most racy networks out there in terms of its content and so forth. More and more violent movies. They're getting the biggest box office receipts. I don't know what to say. All these self-appointed people controlling, rating, and speaking about how bad TV is and nothing has been done in terms of productivity.

In the Net [Internet], however, people have the ability to regulate by themselves what happens in their own electronic communities. And parents, I think, have an obligation to not treat a computer as a surrogate parent. Computers have CD-ROM players and multimedia devices that enable their kids to play very violent games, to get in chat sessions with people who might be much older and lure them to other locations, and pedophiles and child pornographers can find kids on the line as well as they can find them in public or on the phone or in the mail.

So new problems. Old problems. But the responsibility of the parent is still there for them to fulfill. And I think journalists and people who produce content on the Net, general users, have an obligation . . . I think parents really do, and a moral one. If they choose to spend the kind of money on a computer they do these days, don't treat it as just something to take up your kids' time. You can do whatever you want to in your busy life. It's a tool to build ties with your children, to educate them, to learn more about your child's interest, to let them communicate with their friends, and to learn more.

Currently the electronic services are primarily used as glorified party lines, inexpensive communication devices, and the world's largest library. Back issues of newspapers can be read. There is access to many rare books and libraries, and there are numerous other resources. The more physically isolated someone might be, the more valuable are the resources for research and information. But it is still basically a telephone party line and giant library.

What is coming is uncertain, but based on the current research, the probability is that homes will have a communication center that will replace the telephone. A screen will serve as both television and computer monitor, a keyboard will provide fast data access, and there will be a receiver and/or microphone and speaker for voice transmission. The sound system will be high-quality stereo, or at least there will be jacks to allow for the addition of separate speakers for superior listening. You will be able to receive movies both for entertainment and learning. You will be able to read many books and periodicals. You will watch television with the system, and you may be able to listen to radio broadcasts as well. In addition, you will use the unit for work, including tying in to office systems.

This is not pie in the sky. As I write this, there are notebook computers that contain all that is necessary to send and receive messages by telephone, including faxes. Adapters allow them to play music and games, receive television broadcasts, create an electronic photo album, edit photographs, and even play a keyboard instrument much like a piano. Professional photographers have been known to go on location in distant places, take their pictures with an electronic camera, send them by cellular telephone connection to an art director for selection, then reshoot or modify their work according to the reaction, never leaving a beach or other site.

Currently there is a scramble by a number of major corporations to link telephone communication, computer software, motion picture files, television show production companies, and both television and print news services. Although no one is certain of the technology that will be standard in our lives, the ability to create and deliver integrated products is being established by corporate mergers and acquisitions.

Will all of these be fee-for-service products? Will they be available on the Internet? To understand this aspect of the question, you need to know that the Internet is not an American business. It is a communications system used by millions of people throughout the world. These people are operating under different laws and different social constraints. Some countries require censorship of material, which is possible with smaller services such as CompuServe. But no one can censor the Internet.

The attitude among most Internet users is that the freedom to say anything must be preserved. They feel that it is better to allow pornographic material, the violent rantings of anarchists and murderers, and anything else in order to protect the vast majority of material, which is not dangerous, deadly, or obscene. Many even view the Internet as the only resource available to the downtrodden and the oppressed. It is the electronic soapbox for Everyman and thus should never be restricted in any way.

Publishers are finding that, although materials published electronically are covered by existing copyright laws, the copyrights are being ignored. People feel that if they can access the information with their modems, they should be able to download it to their computers and printers without paying a fee. This same situation will exist for the planned information services unless a way is found to send the material only to those who subscribe.

What all this means is that in the immediate future, publishing anarchy will reign on electronic services. Ethical considerations will matter little to most users. They want to be able to reach like-minded individuals with whatever interests them, whatever they are curious about. There is going to be obscene material on electronic services. There is going to be material on a variety of potentially dangerous issues. There is going to be access to radical ideas related to religion, interpersonal relations, and other issues. There is going to be intellectual freedom without a corresponding sense of responsibility. This is not an issue of what is right. It is a reality of how the Internet and other systems have developed.

The world of electronic media allows for the accommodation of special interests. Right now, with the development of cable and satellite systems—the latter including both fee-paid and free downlinks—it is possible to have as many as 150 television channels from which to select at any given time. This selection will only increase with time, as will the proliferation of special-interest programming, as currently occurs with larger cable systems. We have all-cartoon cable networks, all rock video programming, all sports, all news, and so forth. There is even all sexually oriented programming on some cable channels, though usually this is available only during the adult viewing hours of 11 p.m. until early morning. The latter has included a mother/daughter talk show that "stars" two women who go out and have sexual encounters, then discuss what they have done with the different men. And most famous in the New York City area was "Ugly George," a rather nondescript man with a video camera who would openly record himself asking women if they would undress for him, then show them doing just that in his studio if they agreed, which a surprising number did.

The end result of this variety of entertainment will not be the fall of the Western world. Sensually oriented cable channels such as the Playboy Channel have generally been among the most ordered extra-fee services available in larger communities, as well as being the least often renewed. They are sampled out of curiosity, yet the curiosity factor is easily satisfied. Most people do not consider sex to be a spectator sport and prefer X-rated videos to jumpstart a relationship if they want a voyeuristic experience.[30]

The concern that must be addressed is that the proliferation of alternatives will result in an end to Marshall McLuhan's vision of the global village. Although people can be informed of events occurring throughout the world almost as they happen by watching the all-news channels, it will also be possible to stay unaware in all but a narrowed field. It is easy to just watch Western movies, sports programming, science programming, music programming, martial arts movies and sporting events, cartoons, or programs in any other field. It is possible to limit yourself only to ultraconservative political and/or religious broadcasting. It is possible to engage in conversations with people throughout the world while sitting in front of a computer, oblivious to other living beings, and staying in "chat rooms" where there are only neo-Nazis, conspiracy buffs, people who delight in forcing sex on their partners, or almost any other narrowed focus, no matter how deviant. It has become easy to reinforce unacceptable behavior by turning from the society at large to a society of like-minded computer users.

Even more of a concern is that this isolation is beginning with the most privileged within society. The primarily white, primarily upscale urban and suburban families and school systems are making computers with online service access a normal part of their lifestyles. Instead of their children being encouraged to engage in physically interactive programs—sports, music, clubs, church or synagogue programs, dance lessons, martial arts lessons, gymnastics, and the like—it is acceptable (and often encouraged) for them to spend their time alone at the computer monitor. They develop writing skills. They are involved with people all over the world. And they are playing games that will not get them in trouble. But they lack the ability to talk with others face to face. They do not know how to relate to someone of a different generation. They do not know how to interact with customers in stores, restaurants, and other businesses. A child with a lemonade stand on a busy street corner is going to gain more social skills than that same child spending the same time sitting before a computer equipped with the latest in multimedia and Internet access equipment.

There are proponents of such computer use who say that children become blind to the prejudices of society when they are online. They do not know the age, race, sex, religion, ethnic background, or any other details of the person with whom they are communicating. They only know how to share information and communicate on a topic of mutual interest and concern.

This is true so far as it goes. People who communicate by computer are blind to the reality of the person with whom they are interacting. But what happens when they meet those people in person?

No one overcomes bias in isolation. A white child living in a white suburb, going to a predominantly white school, and attending a white church is going to gain nothing from the computer. A white child interacting with children of different races and economic backgrounds in a fully integrated setting will gain compassion, understanding, and the awareness of similarities, not just differences. The computer may be a good meeting place to begin a friendship, especially for someone such as a disfigured, wheelchair-bound individual whose appearance causes others to turn away. But once the relationship is established, the true value comes when the able-bodied person meets his friend already knowing the similarities between them. The differences will not matter at that point, though they would have mattered greatly if there was physical contact prior to intellectual contact. Yet such cases are the rare exceptions.

A society that becomes dependent on its populace having skills that keep most people physically isolated from one another is a society doomed to divisiveness and failure. You cannot have compassion without real involvement. You cannot have consensus without a full understanding of alternatives.

The major ethical question facing the media of the twenty-first century is whether or not we will allow the computer-based information resources to dominate our society. There is nothing wrong with the computer becoming a tool of a society that continues to encourage physical interaction through interpersonal activities. There is nothing wrong with using the Internet as a means of expressing ideas that might otherwise be overlooked, or for reaching people who might otherwise not be reachable. But to let the computer become a substitute for most interpersonal activities, as is now happening, is a potentially dangerous situation.

Playing pick-up basketball teaches cooperation, allows people to have fun and get to know each other through a shared interest, provides a healthy physical release, and can be done anywhere at any age by both sexes. To play computer basketball is to lose everything except the competition, which involves no more than two people and the use of fingers on a control panel.

Venting one's emotions in a chat group may be cathartic, but it does not have the impact of sharing ideas at a coffee shop or other gathering place with people of differing views who can truly explore the topic. Change does not come from throwing words at people but from the interaction that involves all the senses.

Likewise, dating by computer may be a freeing experience. It may allow you to express your fantasies and narrow your choices to people who think like you or excite you with their ideas. But relationships are built on the physical and emotional give and take that come from dating, from exploring sex, from living together, from finding ways to resolve conflict. You cannot turn off a lover who is happy, sad, troubled, scared, or otherwise in crisis at two in the morning when you would rather sleep. You cannot resolve financial concerns, eating choices, decisions about children, jobs, and other matters on a computer. You cannot know the intensity of love that comes from making sex a reality, from finding ways to truly please each other, from experiencing touch, not just ideas about touch. Love grows from sharing life experiences. It does not come from being in a relationship between 7 and 9 P.M., when both of you are able to go online.

The ideas of having a home office for everyone, of eliminating office buildings or downsizing them so that they hold only a skeleton crew, of eliminating people from businesses, such as the replacement of bank tellers with ATM units, are more destructive than having pornography made available to children. To use the computer as the primary source of information and entertainment is fine. As such, it is a tool for everyone. But the idea that society must be adapted to the computer, which is certainly a concept on which many media businesses are basing their future plans, is wrong. It is a step back from what civilization we have achieved in the past few thousand years. It is as isolating as living in extended family groups in caves and villages several days' walk from the nearest neighbors.

If the media truly can corrupt society, as some critics contend, then a society that wants to adapt itself to an electronic communication device is ultimately doomed. Only by overseeing the tool, by making it servant instead of master, can we hope to maintain the social interaction that breeds understanding, compassion, and empathy for all members of society. Moral and ethical values of honesty, respect for life, respect for the limitations of others, and similar concerns only matter when people must interact directly. Otherwise, human life may take on the diminished importance of a character in a video game. Marriage, family, religious practices, and all that forms the best in any culture and community will all suffer dramatically. The social fabric will be weakened to the point where human life is devalued in ways that will diminish us all.

7

Music, Music, Music

In the minds of many critics, there has frequently been a subversive element to music. During the period when Americans held slaves, Negro spirituals frequently were coded songs meant to provide information for the men and women planning a run to freedom. The songs could be sung in the presence of the slave owners without anyone knowing the true meaning. For example, "Go Down Moses," a spiritual that sounds like a retelling of a Bible story, was actually sung to alert people that Harriet Tubman was coming to help. Likewise, a spiritual such as "Down by the Riverside" alerted the slaves that a planned escape would start with a gathering down by the river.

During the rebellious flapper era, songwriter Cole Porter wrote lyrics that shocked the previous generation. One of his love songs has the singer lament that neither alcohol nor cocaine can provide the pleasure he gets from his beloved. He wrote for a generation engaged in counterculture activities, all the while becoming one of the nation's most popular songwriters.

The "good" popular music of the past included lyrics and themes that were highly offensive to moralists, yet generally went ignored. Frank Sinatra might sing "If I'm not with the girl I love, I love the girl I'm with . . ." Taxi-dance girls, some of whom were prostitutes in their off hours, were glorified in the song "Ten Cents a Dance." And there was always the popular ballad "Love for Sale."

In the 1980s, heavy metal and satanic music became a popular part of American subculture. The lyrics were about violence and death. For example, "Tormentor," by W.A.S.P., includes mention of being an amoral, sadistic killer, and "The Skull Beneath the Skin," by Megadeth, includes a graphic description of horrendous torture. Some of the violent lyrics were presented straight, the way we are used to hearing music. Other lyrics were back-masked, a technique that was first explored in the early 1960s as a way to use subliminal messages to sell records. The pioneer in this field was Dr. John Kappas of Van Nuys, California, who was hired to do research both by a major record company and by a popular entertainer of the day. Each wanted to see whether a hidden message could be used to sell more records.

The earliest back masking was technologically crude compared with approaches used today. Dr. Kappas explained:

> They [the recording engineers] would use a method to slow down a word, make it very, very slow in the process of mixing. They would have a regular song with a slow word, hoping the unconscious would pick it up.
>
> It would be a softer track [than the rest of the words and music] and be in the background, and you had to concentrate very hard just to pick up the sound and you had to really step it up [increase the volume] to pick up the word.
>
> So what I did was that I took a pile of songs that were hits. And I took a bunch of young people, thirteen and fourteen years of age to twenty-one years of age, and I would hook them up to what they called biofeedback—galvanic resistance at that time—to see if there were high excitations or high melancholy feelings in the hit songs. I found out that all of the songs that I picked that were hits, all had either high excitation or melancholy. Usually the words had a tremendous effect on people.
>
> We also found out that when we had words that were not understandable, but the beat was very, very prominent, it would give people kind of a wild "up." It would get them moving, almost like a hypnotic state. So we found out that in one respect,

words had a tremendous effect on people. They would create melancholy excitation, and the other would create, without words but just a beat, very heavy, dominating the words, this hype state the people were in.[31]

Later back-masking techniques were more sophisticated. For example, suppose a song is to be recorded on twenty-four tracks. Track number one, and tracks three through twenty-four will be used in the normal way. Then the tape will be flipped. What had been track two is now track twenty-three, and it is on this track that the message will be recorded. For example, in the case of satanic lyrics, the back-masked message might be "I love Satan." Then the tape would be flipped and the record, CD, or cassette made in the usual way from the master.

Regardless of the method, the research showed that back masking did not work. However, people were affected by lyrics when the instruments were miked so that the music was louder than the voices. This was enhanced when an intense, driving beat was used. And it was further enhanced when sensory deprivation was added, the latter being as simple as wearing headphones.

Unrelated to the back-masking research that was taking place during this period was the creation of party records. Back in the early days of blues there were songs that occasionally talked about sex in rather graphic terms. These were sung in nightclubs and other locations where the very adult clientele would never be offended. This same idea, updated, became the basis for party records.

A party record was a novelty item meant to be used by adults during parties or for personal pleasure with a loved one. Rather than being romantic, they were blatantly sexual. They would discuss oral sex and other variations in graphic terms. The language was often crude, though again the target was consenting adults.

"Gangsta rap" was a form of music that came into popularity more than a quarter century after Dr. Kappas's research. It was rap music with an attitude. Frequently the songs were misogynistic, a throwback to both heavy metal and satanic lyrics, which often talked of raping, torturing, and/or murdering women. They also had an intense beat meant for dancing.

"There is a concept called the message unit concept," Dr. Kappas explained about the impact of different types of music, including rap and hip-hop.

Anxiety and hypnosis are synonymous because they use the message unit concept to create the same effect.

A record does the same thing. A record creates a message, an overabundant message into the brain. And if you get too many messages into the brain, you get a primitive mechanism that prepares us for fight or flight. If we can fight, we fight and we go into anxiety. And from the anxiety, which turns into almost an anger, it takes us into the depression. So just by that we can create the futile feelings that kids receive by overabundance of too many messages into the brain.

That is why dope [marijuana, cocaine, crack cocaine, heroin, etc.] is so conducive during rock concerts . . . that what dope does is increase suggestibility of the people using it so that it makes them even worse.

Gangsta rap is a form of popular urban music that is meant to reflect life on the streets of the toughest portions of the inner city. Many of the performers have lived in the areas they sing about. Many have experienced street violence ranging from friends killed in gang wars to police brutality and corruption. Their group names often reflect the image they want to portray, such as N.W.A. (Niggas With Attitude). Their lyrics are filled with expletives, derogatory terms for women, the liberal use of the word "nigger," and occasional mention of killing police.

It is difficult to look objectively at the issue of gangsta rap. Anyone who listens to urban radio stations in cities with large African

American populations will hear extensive playing of rap and hip-hop (rap with music meant specifically for dancing) without ever hearing anything offensive. It is the same with much of the trash metal rock, punk rock, and satanic rock music of a few years back. By contrast, such music is frequently played at brain-numbing levels on car stereos with oversized speakers, portable tape and CD players, and home systems. The impact of it, other than on politicians who have suddenly discovered immorality in the real world and not just Washington, D.C., is questionable.

For a normal, healthy teenager of any color (music is universal, and a popular form that arises within one culture is quickly brought into the mainstream by all cultures), the music is naughty, not an obsession. In fact, the lyrics are often secondary.

My wife and I have four sons ranging from preschool age to nineteen. The youngest three are adopted. The oldest, nineteen at this writing, was "stolen." He is black and comes from the inner city. His father is both alcoholic and a long-term crack cocaine smoker. His mother works two jobs so that she can avoid her children, and his younger sister had her first two children by the age of sixteen.

My son was experiencing physical and emotional abuse in his apartment, a suite directly above the one in which my wife and I were living at the time. He was extremely bright yet hurting so much that he eventually became a tenth-grade dropout. Before we took him in to raise him into adulthood as our own child, he used to escape from home by coming downstairs to our suite. His friends were becoming gang members and several had been crippled or killed. Others were periodically in jail or awaiting trial. All he wanted to do was become a professional chef, a realistic goal for a bright youth, yet with no support, his future was on the streets.

My wife and I would talk extensively with Clifford. He knew I had a small stereo in my office and that he was welcome to use it. Sometimes he would be there when I was out. Sometimes he would be there when I worked. And sometimes I threw him out when I needed quiet. But whenever he played music, it was always angry, violent gangsta rap, often with lyrics that talked about "f—ing white bitches" or killing police in ways they would die in agony.

I never said anything about the music. There was something rather ironic about this black teenager using our home to escape his own, dancing in my office, while the stereo blared lyrics of filth and hatred. At times I found it quite humorous.

That was more than two years before this writing. We helped him get a restaurant job, where he did everything from washing dishes to working as their chef. He went for his GED, getting it on the first try. He began reading books. And today our "surrogate son" is in college. His music of choice is still rap, but he no longer listens to the violent gangsta lyrics. He is experimenting with ballads and jazz. And so far he has avoided the excesses of the streets that have destroyed the lives of so many of his former friends.

By contrast, there are those who have used gangsta rap obsessively, usually with earphones, which is the sensory deprivation Dr. Kappas discussed. Just as those obsessed with satanic lyrics and other negative concepts did before them, many of these young people have become destructive. Some have acted out violently against others. Some have hurt themselves. And the question must be asked with each whether the problem was the music or the family and social circumstances that led them to withdraw into the music.

In the past, studies have shown that the children who are influenced by obsessive listening to destructive lyrics almost always come from homes where their parents have ignored them. Frequently, the children had been withdrawn for years, neither parent making any attempt to reach out. "Adolescence is a hard time," such parents frequently say when their child is found dead or involved with a crime. "I knew he/she was avoiding us a lot and was involved with a bad lot, but isn't rebellion part of adolescence? Don't all kids avoid their parents during the teen years? We just didn't know things were different." Nor did they try to find out.

This is not to say that gangsta rap and other violent forms of music should be considered innocuous or lacking in influence. Quite the contrary. The lyrics are reprehensible. The emotions they convey are usually meant to capture a counterculture audience alienated from the mainstream of society. It is ironic that the groups that become successful enough to be criticized by politicians and others decrying the immorality of the lyrics are also the ones that are rich enough that they are no longer able to relate to their music. It is like the successful folk singers of the 1960s who identified with laborers while driving from appearance to appearance in a customized bus costing at least $250,000.

What is most troubling about many of the critics of gangsta rap music is that they refuse to look at the conditions from which it sprang. Many are politicians who have spoken against programs meant to help children born into poverty or have failed to support public school education programs. Few have spent substantive time in the inner city, either working or living in areas from which the music first sprang. And many ignore the fact that most rap and hip-hop music is not violent, misogynistic, or racist. It is popular dance and listening music.

A few of the rap stars have come forward to challenge the attitudes of the politicians. They claim to be reflecting the realities of the society in which they live. They point to the scandals in Washington, from Senator Robert Packwood being forced from office because of sexual harassment, to Speaker of the House Newt Gingrich serving his first wife with divorce papers while she was in the hospital undergoing treatment for cancer. They point out the blatant womanizing by politicians and many leaders of major corporations. They note the corruption of some police officers, who take free meals, receive bribes from drug dealers, get a percentage of stolen merchandise, and otherwise commit crimes under the color of blue. They point to defense contractors who have huge cost overruns with no checks on their charges. They talk about school systems on the decline while major cities devote millions of dollars to professional sports teams. They claim that their lyrics represent the reality of a hypocritical world.

The truth is certainly somewhere between the two. The problems within the ghettos from which much of the gangsta rap has emerged are many. Low wages mean that even when there are two parents in a home, both may have to work longer than normal hours. Latchkey children have few after-school options other than the streets in communities where both the public schools and outreach programs are strapped for cash. Racism is still common throughout the United States. A major city is likely to have a minority mayor—black, Hispanic, etc.—and yet employ street patrol officers who harass the area minority. And youths, at best, often feel alienated from parents, the government, or the world at large.

Songs that reflect this sense of loveless alienation are a logical outgrowth of the urban experience, just as Depression era blues songs often spoke of rent parties, difficulties on the job, and stress between lovers. The musicians sing about a shared experience, and since their first clubs are often neighborhood bars, the language, style, and theme of their music usually reflects what members of the community have seen.

The hypocrisy of the critics and/or their supporters is also very real. The more we learn the history of the American presidents, for example, the more we see power-driven men who take advantage of others for personal pleasure and/or gain. We see decisions that can affect the lives of many—trade barriers, overseas police actions, war, and similar concerns—made by people looking toward reelection, not necessarily what is best for the nation.

Yet there is hypocrisy among the rappers as well when they try their hand at gangsta rap. Can stories be told in rap without using foul language? And what about the violence of the lyrics? It is one thing to sing about a specific detective or uniformed officer who is violating the trust of his position deliberately or through incompetence. It is quite another to condemn police in general, or to glorify rape, murder, and similar actions.

Most of the politicians focus on the violence of gangsta rap music. The hostility toward women—"bitch" is the mildest word used in many songs; "whore," or the stylized "ho," is probably second—is often overlooked. The put-down of women is not a reaction to hypocrisy in society. It is not a reflection of ghetto life, of up-scale urban life, or of suburban life. It is pure, mindless hatred of half the population.

The trouble with trying to condemn gangsta rap is that it is almost always available solely through stores. A handful of radio stations play it, frequently during time slots when the listeners are more likely to be adults and older teens rather than young children. However, most do not, or they reserve it for late-night play or very low-powered stations (such as dormitory-linked college radio offering counterculture programming). But for the most part, the highly offensive songs do not get aired. Some groups even go so far as to issue two cuts—one for air play and a version with harsher language for the retailers.

What this means is that parental involvement is possible. A child buying such music will predictably play it on a car or home stereo. It will be heard by the parents. It can be stopped by the parents.

The idea of trying to ban such music violates First Amendment freedoms. There is also the question of why this music should be condemned rather than other musical forms. Although obvious cases can be made against rap lyrics, as noted, there are some religious groups that feel that *all* music is connected with Satan. They condemn the use of music in churches. They rightfully note that some of the popular hymns have lyrics that were applied to music heard in bars.

Most mainstream religious leaders, including fundamentalists, note that the psalms are songs. There are many instances in the Old Testament where music is reported to have been used as part of praise worship of God. And certainly Jesus never condemns music in the New Testament. Yet the people who believe music and worship do not belong together would certainly argue for all manner of censorship in the industry.

The reality is that extreme music would not be created if people did not pay to hear it. When certain types of punk and trash metal music were first developed, some of the groups wrecked the nightclubs in which they were playing. They saw it as part of the act. The club owners saw them as an expense too great to continue. The acts were told to play elsewhere. Their artistic freedom was not challenged. They were just denied a place to play. The groups either had to get by on their own in whatever way they could or modify their act.

The same is true with the major-label record company investment in some of the gangsta rappers. The money is spent promoting the groups and their offensive lyrics because money is earned from the sale of their CDs and cassettes. Products last only so long as people buy them, and since this is music marketed toward the young, parents remain in a position to stop the purchase and use of this music.

The proof of the exploitation can occasionally be found in marketing inserts included with the CDs. Some have cartoon figures acting out sexually explicit scenes. They lack the eroticism of even the illustrations in sex-oriented magazines such as *Hustler*. They are naughty, nasty, and offensive, and thus they appeal to adolescents hoping to get a glimpse of a forbidden world. The inserts allow the buyers to send for other products, again within parental discretion to stop.

The trouble with gangsta rap and other violent and/or sexually explicit types of music is that it is a good target for moralists and politicians to rail against. It costs nothing to say that women should be respected, violence is wrong, and language should not be used to shock offensively. Anyone listening to such music can understand the hue and cry against it. Yet within the context of society's ills, this is far down the list. A child reading a newspaper or watching the nightly news encounters far more offensive actions on the part of the political, business, and societal leaders. The words are nicer. The presentation is made in a manner respectful to the listener or reader. But the information is far more shocking and serious. And these problems are not usually addressed by those who condemn gangsta rap.

Equally important, offensive music lyrics are not a new threat to society. Every generation encounters something of this nature, and most people are not hurt by it, grow out of it, then are horrified by what their children and/or grandchildren are singing.

Should parents be alert to the music? Of course. Should the art forms of rap and hip-hop be stopped? Of course not. This is one area where money is a control, and the fewer sales that are made, the faster such music fades from the scene.

It will be followed by something else aimed toward the same demographic or a different one. And it will become a condemned part of the popular culture. But so long as this is not a staple of free television or of most radio programming, it is an issue that has taken the focus from more important ethical concerns relating to the availability of entertainment and information in our society.

It must be remembered that if something has to be purchased to be experienced, certainly the situation with gangsta rap, the control is within the hands of the buyers. Stopping the music is not a question of ethics or free speech. It is a matter of simple economics—controlled, in almost every instance, by parents.

8

What Does It
All Mean?

The late Marshall McLuhan once referred to the impact of radio, television, and the other communication media as having created what he called the global village. He explained that in a village, everyone is able to rapidly learn what is happening with everyone else who lives in the same community. Through the access to media (inexpensive radio receivers, television reception in many remote areas, and the like), almost everyone in the world had gained the ability to experience the same information simultaneously. Hollywood gossip could instantly be known to families in Sri Lanka and nomadic people traversing some of the most barren portions of the Sahara.

Those who heard McLuhan's message were usually convinced that the future would involve more of the same patterns, though somehow intensified. And theoretically this is true. The Cable News Network (CNN) is the perfect example of television giving the world its global village. During the Gulf War, for example, there were reports of CNN being monitored by all the world's leaders. They were able to receive live coverage that was at least as accurate, and often much faster to receive, than information relayed by their intelligence agents and allies. CNN did not "sponsor" the Gulf War, as William Randolph Hearst "sponsored" the Spanish-American War almost a century earlier. But the face of the war was defined by CNN, and the images of the war that the majority of the world's people remember are the images they witnessed on their television sets.

The result was that the Gulf War was a war without bloodshed. The world got to witness Scud missile launches and in-air missile interceptions that, though noisy, were as colorful as a Fourth of July fireworks display. There were journalists risking their lives on top of buildings to show tracer rounds and rocket launches in the distance. There were images of stalwart soldiers and interviews with patriotic American men and women who wanted to stand up to the Iraqi soldiers who had strayed from their nation, sending them home like howling dogs, their tails between their legs in fright. It came as close to being a war designed by Norman Rockwell's paintings as anything that had been covered in recent years.

What was not shown was the face of the civilian population caught in the cross fire of battling armies. We bragged about the limited number of American casualties. Even the tiny handful of American prisoners of war who endured brief stays in enemy hands did not experience the horrors that such individuals can endure. A female soldier was feared raped. A male soldier was feared abused in some manner. But real torture—dehydration, malnutrition, sleep deprivation, and the other horrors that have broken so many captives during this century—was not experienced this time. Nor did the TV reports show the impact on anyone not connected with the military.

The result was two wars. The first was the war of CNN, the war of military objectives, of missile and antimissile technology, of men and women who might have been on a Desert Experience Summer Camp sponsored by a Middle East version of Outward Bound.

The second war was that endured by the civilian men, women, and children who were maimed or killed. There were thousands of casualties in the Gulf War. Some were people too foolish to move from the path of the conflict. Some were people who had no place to go but inside their homes, and if their homes were near advancing or retreating armies, the less than flawless weapons of war often missed their main objectives and destroyed their shelter. And some were people who thought they were safe, who simply discovered how far and how fast a bullet can fly when it misses its initial objective. A gun fired into the air sends a bullet a distance of a mile or more before its momentum is slowed below a killing pace. Just as rural residents fear for their families' lives every hunting season when inexperienced people with guns head for the nearby woods to shoot deer, duck, and other game, so people a "safe" distance from a battlefield can still be felled by a stray bullet. Yet civilian casualties generate real fear, real concern. There can be compassion for the civilian population of even the most hated of enemies. A viewer might think that he or she has been blessed to be living somewhere else and not want to be reminded of the havoc his or her children in uniform might be creating for others. The viewer might change the channel instead of being glued to accurate, though highly limited coverage of the war.

Thus we had what might be called Global Village Lite, to borrow a marketing concept used with beer, ice cream, and other consumable indulgences. We saw an event as it was taking place, never once thinking about where the cameras were placed, or more appropriately, where they were not positioned. We saw the nice side of the war, at least for the victorious. We saw death as the stopping of bad guys shooting guns at our children, parents, friends, or relatives in uniform. We did not see the randomness of death, the bullets without brains, the lives of hope and promise snuffed out by accident, and often without the awareness of the soldier who originally pulled a rifle's trigger.

Modern technology should ensure that the global village remains a reality, and within the limitations of perspective experienced during the Gulf War, it obviously has. Certainly CNN is stronger than ever, both financially and when it comes to the number of viewers. National Public Radio has become famous in the last quarter century for its thorough radio news coverage. And the development of sophisticated still cameras able to create digital images means that photographs taken in the remotest corners of the world can, within minutes, be sent by telephone everywhere there are people with computers and modems. What *Life* magazine once accomplished on a weekly basis even the smallest of newspapers can reproduce daily.

But rather than embracing the possibility that we will be the best informed people in world history, we are emerging into the twenty-first century with the desire to return to the village isolation of ancient times. The ways in which humans use their media access seem to indicate that Americans, the most "wired" people on the planet, are about to become almost as isolated from one another as horseless villages separated by distances too far to walk. And this is occurring when we have access to all the available knowledge that survives in written, picture, audio, film, or video form anywhere humans keep repositories of such material.

Television was an experimental medium when it first began to be popular following World War II. Plays were filmed or shown live, with popular programs such as Kraft Theater dominating the screen. Orchestral programs were broadcast, and one of the great symphonies in the United States was the NBC Symphony Orchestra.

News coverage was limited because the methods for rapidly shipping motion picture film were not yet developed. But efforts were made to cover stories as effectively as possible, and the news/talk shows such as *Meet the Press* tried to provide a depth of information rather than controversy.

Entertainment programs were frequently carryovers from radio. *Amos 'n Andy*, which ironically had to hire black actors instead of the white men who starred on radio; Lucille Ball's *My Favorite Husband* made the transition to TV's *I Love Lucy*; *The Great Gilder-*

sleeve; and numerous others made the jump with varying success. Vaudeville, burlesque, and Catskill Mountain resort comics, not all of whom had enjoyed radio exposure, tried their hand at TV, some successfully and others not. This was the era of Milton Berle, who often dressed in women's clothing and dominated the ratings, Red Skelton, Red Buttons, Bob Hope, and numerous others. There was even the equivalent of Court TV. In 1951, the Kefauver hearings into organized crime, held by a U.S. Senate committee chaired by Tennessee senator Estes Kefauver, were so popular that motion picture theaters set up television sets and allowed passersby to come inside to view them. Usually there was no admission charge, since the hearings were held at a time when most theaters were dark. And the movies remained the most popular form of entertainment in America, well over half the population of the nation attending every week.

No one knew what the public wanted to watch on television. No one knew which shows would be popular. There was a sense that television would change the way in which Americans sought their entertainment, but since no one had any answers, it was easiest to program something for everyone. Thus, in the course of any given day, it was likely that while watching the three network stations or their affiliates (ABC, CBS, and NBC) the average person was exposed to history, science, the arts, news, and pure escapist entertainment. Local programming often included the showing of old Encyclopaedia Britannica films, which were also being used in school classrooms. And there were shows such as *Romper Room* for preschool kids, in which a format was repeated locally in order to allow the customizing of the show for the community in which it was broadcast.

Some local markets experimented with living room learning. Shown at an early morning hour, there would be classes in everything from cooking to ancient history, usually taught by a rather wooden-looking professor from an area college. Later these would become more sophisticated, allowing viewers to buy a workbook and pay a fee to take the course for credit.

And all of this was on the three national TV networks. It was the equivalent of a fine arts major in a liberal arts college, albeit without the depth of learning possible with books and interaction with professors.

Today everything has changed. The networks still exist, but the issue is how much money can a show make. If you want to watch ballet or a symphony, you can subscribe to cable, buy a premium service, and pay to have broadcast what you once could see for free. The only exception is PBS, but public broadcasting does not have the signal reach of the networks.

I remember the day when one of my local television stations bought the rights to broadcast films from the MGM library. I would periodically become seriously ill with whatever would get me out of school and allow me to lie on the couch in the television room. (Today there may be more televisions than rooms in some homes. Back then the television was usually either in the family room or, as in my home, a room set aside for viewing just as a home library was set aside for reading.) Then I would watch every movie that was shown, right through *The Milkman's Matinee*. The latter was so early in the morning that presumably only someone who delivered milk door-to-door from a refrigerated truck would be awake. Milk had to be in place when most families arose, so milkmen presumably had the most tiring hours, along with factory third-shift workers, hospital personnel, police, firefighters, and insomniacs. In the average year I managed to see one hundred or more old movies in addition to going to the Saturday matinee at the local theater (one serial, any number of cartoons, a newsreel, and the feature, all for a quarter until you reached puberty. It was 50 cents from the time you were twelve until you were seventeen, at which time you turned adult and paid 75 cents).

This is not to say that people were not selective in what they watched. My grandmother worshiped Kate Smith's variety show.

My family enjoyed Ed Sullivan. Only occasionally did the sounds of a concert on television fill our home. And a good Western always took precedence over anything more intellectual. But the options were there, and the choice of stations was so limited that most television watchers were regularly exposed to a broader spectrum of art and information than they would voluntarily have chosen. That is why we became a global village. And with the proliferation of information services, including an average of 150 stations via satellite TV systems, that is also why the global village is now becoming a choice instead of the dominant reality of the past.

The vast proliferation of special-interest magazines is a clear indicator of how we fragment our attention. Previously *Look*, *Collier's*, the *Saturday Evening Post*, and similar general-interest magazines would discuss health issues, family activities, hobbies, finance, and related topics. But today we isolate ourselves. Time Warner has a magazine for celebrity gossip, a magazine for people interested in sports, and another for those who want world news and lifestyle features, to name a few. It produces music that ranges from songs your parents and grandparents once enjoyed to music your mother warned you would turn you into a snarling, self-centered, rude, crude, sex-mad beast. It is active in the motion picture and television production business. It has a division that publishes books. And always the divisions are focused on how much money each can make by catering to its limited audience.

In the early days of television, time spent in front of the picture tube forced me to explore areas of knowledge in which I was not always interested. The long "dead" general-interest magazines had a similar impact on reading, boredom assuring that people would at least skim through articles on topics in which they had little interest. The nature of the limited media was such that those who indulged in the experience were taken beyond the narrowed world of the familiar.

Today, the average person is immersed in ever narrowing topics. If you are involved with the financial world, it is possible to read only business-related magazines, watch business news on twenty-four-hour cable television, and communicate with business experts on computer service chat lines. The closest you will come to gaining information outside this narrowed focus is through *The Wall Street Journal*, which has three feature stories on diverse subjects on the front page of each paper. And while those stories are so well written that many people uninterested in finance will read them, those immersed in business may choose to skip them.

In the extreme is a magazine such as *Physician's Management*, a financial publication for doctors. The medical profession receives little training in the business side of a medical practice, something that is increasingly important. To fill this gap there are both broad-based and narrow-market magazines. In addition to *Physician's Management* there are such journals as *Veterinary Economics, Medical Economics, Dental Management,* and the like. However, because these magazines are outside the world in which the doctor trained, they resort to subtle tricks to keep the doctors reading.

For example, more than fifteen years ago *Physician's Management* had an editor who told the writers to write in a manner that would give the doctor/reader no more than two paragraphs of information at a time. The editor set the material in type in such a way that the busy physician could read the equivalent of sound bites about the topic being discussed. The full article was detailed and helpful. But the way the writers presented the material allowed the doctor to read in snatches, thinking about what was said, then returning later for more information. And the reason? The former editor's studies had shown that the average physician had too short an attention span to absorb the content of an article of the regular length.

"Look at the way they train," the editor explained.

These are kids who focus on the hardest math and science courses in high school so they can get into a good college. Then they have to narrow their learning even more so they can get into medical school. After that, they focus down on their specialty, eventually spending as many as twelve years after high school totally absorbed in science. If they have the time to read more broadly, they lack the inclination.

Even worse, once they have that M.D. degree, they are treated like gods. The financial scams we write about usually involve flattery. The person trying to sell them a risky stock plan, an investment in supposedly rare collectibles, or whatever else it may be, flatters them. "But of course you know all about this. You're a doctor. You've had one of the finest educations you can get. I don't need to tell you how great a value this is." And the doctor's got a big enough ego to fall for it, refusing to admit that he knows less about most things than the office receptionist.[32]

Instead of our job being the focus, as with the doctors, we may stay with a special interest when we explore the media. This can be sex, utilizing everything from the men's magazines to cable's Playboy Channel and its clones, to what is called cyberporn—sexually explicit chat groups on the Internet. It can be a hobby. It can be a sport or other special interest. And unless a media outlet relates to one of their special subjects, most people will not allow themselves to be exposed to it.

The global village is not dead, but we have developed so many choices that we must consciously make an extra effort to experience such a community. Otherwise we will live in a self-imposed isolation that matches the limitations of communication that existed before satellite systems, cellular phones, fax machines, and the like.

The only answer to this problem is to address it in the school systems, something which is not currently happening. In part this is because the issue has not yet been noticed. For example, some teachers are thrilled with the breakdown of barriers among the children because they can communicate online without knowing the age, race, religion, or other attributes of the other person.

"Our children have such diversity," one teacher gushed in an article recently carried by one of the wire services. The story told of wealthy, white suburban children whose previous ideas about other cultures came from television and from the type of person their parents hired as a maid, cook, or gardener. When they went online, they came to understand that they were making friends with people who might be black, Hispanic, Asian, Jewish, Gentile, Muslim, Buddhist, atheist, or anything else.

"We became friends without knowing anything but what was in our hearts," one adolescent stated. Another commented about how it was possible to achieve world peace and understanding through the Internet. "We are all the same in cyberspace."

Yet the fact was that bias still remained. There was no real awareness of the other person during such keyboard interaction. Those same loving children reportedly still shied away from other teens who were different when they had encounters in the area shopping mall. Skin color still mattered. For some, the specific religious denomination they professed remained a barrier to friendship. And physical appearance could still lead to attraction, avoidance, or even ridicule.

Only social interaction breaks down barriers. If one does not see the differences between oneself and another person, then the impact of their commonness is diminished. Only when a white person, a black person, and a brown person realize that their basic goals in life and their desires for themselves and for their children are all the same and when they see that families are families, can there be some form of harmony. Try meeting online, becoming friends, and later saying, "By the way, I know you're a famous fashion model, rich, sophisticated, and aloof except when we talk because we have become close friends. Perhaps you should know that I'm really a black midget woman living in a drug-infested inner-city neighborhood using the computer available to the public in a church coalition's neighborhood center. So, friend, when can we have lunch?" Communication online is better than no communication at all, but it is not the answer to society's problems. Cyberspace living—with mental isolation through the careful selection of what one reads, watches, and hears from the diverse array of media offerings—is increasingly common. Certainly the cost has made this far from an epidemic. But we are racing from the potential of the global village far more rapidly than we entered the world of simultaneous knowledge. And the only answer is to expose the very young to the richness of information available to them while still looking upon school yard play at recess, field trips, and other forms of interaction as being at least as important as the three R's.

For example, the Vatican Library is "online." Several museums have digitalized part of their collections so that the artworks can be studied on the screen. Photos taken from outer space are available for study. And historic events can be better experienced through the accessing of film clips, old photographs, and various documents dating back to the period being covered in class.

Children must get hooked on what was once called a liberal arts education or they will never be more than narrow-minded and naive as adults. The early years of education must focus on social interaction, not on seeing how rapidly they can absorb information through self-teaching computer programs, the use of online services, and similar "state of the art" teaching approaches that are becoming increasingly popular.

Instead of focusing on TV corrupting our children—such as the pervasiveness of violence on early morning, late afternoon, and early evening programming—we should realize that it is the educational system that dehumanizes us. The home office is fine for many businesses, but it is at the water cooler where we learn to have compassion, tolerance, and an appreciation for the rich diversity of people in even the smallest community. The fabric of society is not going to be torn by the unethical conduct of the people who create television and radio programming, computer services, books, magazines, or newspapers. In the twenty-first century, the greatest moral threat to society will likely be ourselves and the way we choose the aspect(s) of the media we use in our daily lives.

The other major threat to society is one stressed by such experts as Anne Russell, the editor of *Folio* magazine, a publication that studies the world of magazines. This threat is the ownership of diverse forms of communication by the same companies, with the subsequent risk that corporate decisions will override editorial ones. This does not mean there will be censorship, but that the stories covered will be chosen based on the bias of top management. Certain events, activities, and even divergent points of view will never be known by the public at large. A speech will be given and no one will report what was said to the people who do not attend. A medical problem will arise and go unchecked because no one is interested in reporting it because those who care do not reach the demographics of the viewing audience. Young people will not be exposed to music and art beyond what some "expert" deems of interest in order to keep them watching and listening. The fact that they might like something that is new and different, having previously not known anything about the subject, is irrelevant. The hope of interest does not ensure ratings.

Today, the problem is still limited. Theater and dance groups still make outreach performances in schools. Children are still bused to "young people's concerts." Library story hours still involve a group of children gathering around a real adult who can pace what he or she reads according to the children's reactions. And there is still enough experimentation with the Internet and the various online services so that people are discovering diversity in their curiosity.

But "surfing the net" is little different from the years when many families bought massive shortwave radios for the excitement of listening to the world. But once such experiences became familiar, most people went back to the popular mass programming of the day—*Stella Dallas, One Man's Family, The Shadow, Johnny Dollar, X-Minus One*, and the like. The same is true with the information explosion. Viewers who buy a satellite dish receiver for a few hundred dollars or hook up to cable for a monthly fee are increasingly focusing on personal interests—the cartoon channel, the weather channel, the financial channel, the lifestyle (translation: dating and sex) channel, and similar programming. Likewise, magazines relate to very special interests. And newspaper editors, increasingly fearing that their papers are going unread, redesigned their format to provide special-interest sections promotable to people who would otherwise not buy a daily paper. However, the newspaper at least remains the last vestige of general-interest publishing, even though some are going online and advertising that you can limit your reading to just the news that interests you most.

In the early days of Adolf Hitler's rule in Germany, he stabilized the economy, won back the right of the citizens defeated in World War I to again bear arms, and brought food prices in line with the economy. Then he asked the public if they had any reason to criticize his rule at the time. They said they did not, that he was doing for their country what they wanted to see. And that was when he ended the free press, an action that allowed him to begin destroying his enemies, to establish concentration camps, and to create the horror of the Third Reich.

The information explosion has the potential to let Americans do to themselves what Hitler did to the German people—mentally isolate them from the events of the day. Unless schoolchildren are encouraged to routinely explore a broad area of learning both for knowledge and for fun, we will have adults with blinders. Instead of unethical exploitation by the media, we will have people damaged by their unwillingness to look beyond narrowed interests developed in childhood.

We have the chance to be the most broadly educated people the world has ever seen. We have the chance to use the media to expand our knowledge of the history of human experience. But until the educational system utilizes this potential, the more computer literate a child may be, the greater the access he or she has to satellite and cable television programming, the greater the potential for destruction. Socialization is at least equal in importance to information gathering. Compassion, empathy, true communication, and growing spirituality does not develop through a keyboard, modem, and CD-ROM. Moral judgments are difficult to make on a medium where truth is relative, and people can act out fantasies because the party with whom they are communicating cannot see them.

Information is not knowledge and wisdom. Information does not allow reflection. Information has no history, no context, no past.

Information is critical for the decision-making process. But information added to human interaction can improve interpersonal relationships at all levels of society. The key is to keep the information a tool, not a god that is an end unto itself.

Perhaps the most serious ethical concern is an issue that involves the First Amendment. We have looked at the question of sex and violence on the Internet and the impact on children. We have looked at the issue of television violence. But the creators of the media, who are most influential in society, must understand that they must balance freedom with responsibility.

There is nothing wrong with using sex and violence as plot devices when telling stories. The Old and New Testaments of the Bible, the Koran, the Talmud, and other works that provide spiritual guidance are closely related to the actual lives of people from our past. The moral laws we learn as children, such as the Ten Commandments, were written in response to the human condition, not in anticipation of it. People were coveting what was not theirs. They were making commitments to each other, then breaking them through adultery. They were taking each other's lives. They were focused on themselves, their pleasure, and their pain instead of having a broader concern about those around them. The issue of First Amendment rights is no different. The ability to communicate often unpleasant ideas was being challenged by church leaders, governments, even neighbors who were hostile to what someone was saying. The media were to be a marketplace of ideas, including unpopular ones. But most people, though liking the concept in theory, had their own thoughts about where to draw the line. Rather than have anyone dominate through the restriction of free speech—as even so seemingly liberal a man as Benjamin Franklin was able to do when he became postmaster of Philadelphia in order to limit the circulation of newspapers rivaling his own—the First Amendment became the most important addition to the Constitution. It was the first item of the Bill of Rights, and it remains the most frequently attacked. The problem comes when freedom is accepted without responsibility. This is typically what is happening with the motion picture industry.

The vast amount of "product" (movie scripts for filming) needed by the motion picture, television, CD-ROM, and original video industries is so great, and the average age of many of the new writers so young, that many films rely on shocking content to hide a lack of substance. It is easier to re-create the darkest corners of the human soul or the most intimate of human physical experiences than to create thought-provoking, absorbing entertainment.

There are writers who are exceptions, of course. Some labor in relative obscurity, since the writer of a movie is seldom given the attention that even a first-time book author receives. Others, such as Rod Serling, whose work was a series of morality tales about average people struggling from day to day (*Requiem for a Heavyweight*, *Patterns*, the almost eighty film scripts he contributed to *The Twilight Zone*, among many others), elevate film to a level where entertainment challenges the mind without forgetting to be enjoyable.

But the vast amount of product needed, the relative youth of many writers, producers, and directors, and the insecurity of businesspeople have led to base entertainment without responsibility. Given the history of human literature, including many of the world's holy books, there is nothing wrong with telling a story that includes sex, violence, and the baser aspects of human existence. Unless someone can vicariously live an experience, it is difficult to develop compassion without being either a perpetrator or a victim. A writer or filmmaker who can re-create a rape in such a way that the pain and horror leap from the screen and into the heart of the viewer may be doing a public service. Too many people confuse rape with sex because there is sexual penetration involved. And much soft-core pornography—whether X-rated films, books sold as erotica, or magazines—includes fantasy rape. The restraint of the woman or the man stems from a willing desire to be submissive. Penetration is eagerly awaited. The participants are involved in a sex game, and no matter how frightened the "victim" might be at first, the fear is of the underlying desire that causes the person to want to be submissive. The sex act itself is avidly sought, a radical contrast to the reality of rape in real life.

Likewise war, domestic violence, the realities of street life for teenage runaways, and similar subjects can be effectively told in gritty, hard-edged movies and books. Crimes become more heinous. The pain of people with whom the viewer or reader might previously not have been able to relate—slaves, blacks, Hispanics, Asians, or whoever has been defined by the person as "different"—suddenly is understandable.

Irresponsibility arises when the vehicle chosen to convey these feelings will predictably reach the wrong individuals. And this is the primary remaining ethical concern few people wish to address.

In December 1995, the film *Money Train* was released by Columbia Pictures. During its filming, the script was reviewed by New York City's Transit Authority, the organization responsible for running the subways and buses that are the heart of the city's transportation system. The review occurred because the producer wanted to film two scenes involving violence against subway to-ken-booth workers. The subway system is a dramatic underworld for people who live outside New York. Here is one of the largest, most expensive, vibrant cities in the world, where people walk down some steps in order to travel rapidly underground. Hundreds of thousands of people descend to this hidden world each day, paying the price for a token, passing through a turnstile, and heading for jobs, shop-ping, entertainment, friends, or home. The wealthy mingle with the poor because the streets are so jammed and parking so expen-sive that it is not practical for most people to own a car.

There are homeless and/or mentally ill people who attempt to live in the subway system. Some try to find a slightly hidden corner of the waiting area, then create a "home" from cardboard, dis-carded rags, and anything else that will give them privacy and warmth. Others panhandle enough money to ride the subway, sleeping from one end of the line to the other.

Occasionally there are fights or deranged men and women hav-ing animated conversations with people only they can see. And everywhere are law enforcement officers, a police force as large as that of most other major cities, yet with almost all of the officers patrolling underground.

It is in this world that the token-booth workers spend their days locked in a glass cage. The booths are equipped with instant fire-extinguishing devices, bullet-resistant glass, and other security measures. Yet at any given instant the token workers may be alone. The police may be patrolling elsewhere; perhaps few people are waiting for the subway, and all of them are preoccupied with news-papers, magazines, or their own thoughts. It is during such mo-ments that the token workers are vulnerable to attack, and it was with such moments that the two scenes were concerned.

The script, and then the movie, called for robbers to attack a high-security train that travels the subway line, picking up the day's receipts from the token booths. To make the story more visually exciting, there were two scenes in which a pyromaniac sprays a flammable liquid through the holes used for exchanging tokens and money. Then the bad guy lights the liquid, setting off explosions.

The visual is meant to be exciting, and there is "redeeming social value" in the fact that the token workers escape serious injury. More important, the real token booths have an extremely effective fire-suppression system, though it can be disabled by the booth worker acting against regulations so that he or she can smoke.

The problem came when people who saw the movie may have decided to duplicate the action.[33] Four days after the film opened in December, a Brooklyn subway token booth worker was torched in the same way. His fire suppression system had been turned off, and the man, Harry P. Kaufman, died on Sunday, December 10. There would be other, less serious attacks, including one in which a person simply tried to throw a match into the booth.

It can be argued that people will apply anything they experience to their lives, and that emotionally disturbed people may try to duplicate that which society finds reprehensible. Studies of one-time rapists have frequently found that the man was an avid viewer of pornography. However, in many instances their actions do not seem to be the result of their being corrupted by what they witnessed. Instead, they were loners, men living without normal social interaction. They had no experience with women, little or no experience dating, and had turned to men's lifestyle magazines and X-rated videos to learn appropriate behavior.

Much of the material they studied was meant to satisfy a man's fantasies. This meant that the man could do whatever he wanted and ultimately the woman would enjoy it. In the extreme, this might include what, in real life, would be torture. But such extremely sadistic videos and books were usually not what these men were studying. Instead they viewed stories in which the man was rebuffed by the woman until he became more aggressive. This might involve surprising her alone in the office when she is working late, then kissing her to stifle her startled outcry, and taking off her blouse while she is expressing anger over the intrusion. Soon she is helping, stripping both herself and the man, perhaps having sex on the desktop, the couch, or the floor.

Or the man in the story might be on a real date, then try to have sex with the woman when they return to her apartment. She says no, but becomes excited when he persists. The more forceful he is, short of striking her or otherwise abusing her, the more erotically charged the incident. Soon her "no's" are spoken only in jest as she becomes intensely passionate, finally turning to "yes! yes! yes!" and cries of ecstasy.

The message is clear: A woman who says no to a man actually wants him to make love to her. Resistance is to be met with forcefulness. Objection is actually part of normal foreplay and does not mean that the woman truly does not want him.

The men who learn their social skills in these ways go on dates, applying what they have learned. By the time they realize that a woman's no truly means "NO!" it is too late. They have committed an assault at best, rape at worst. They are shocked when she is hysterical or violent. They are shocked when they are arrested. And they are horrified to learn that behavior they thought was correct destroyed what may have been a chance to achieve real intimacy.

Such men can be rehabilitated because they are not rapists in the sense of those who act out their anger through violently aggressive acts of sex. They are as devastated as the women they dated. And many are never able to forgive themselves, living the rest of their lives alone, afraid to trust themselves in any relationship again.

There are killers who are devout readers of the Bible or whichever holy book is appropriate for their religion. They respect the Ten

Commandments or their equivalent. They want to do right, and they spend their free time in study and contemplation. The holy book "speaks to them."

Unfortunately, while many Christians and Jews say that when they read the Bible the book "speaks to them," there are those who mean the statement literally. They are mentally ill and believe that they are receiving orders that must be obeyed, orders that may lead them to kill another person.

In many states the standard for judging insanity is whether or not the person knows the difference between right and wrong. Criminal defense lawyers will tell of individuals who were devout Bible readers, seemingly deeply religious, and insane. They heard the voice of God telling them to kill someone. Naturally, being spiritual, they argued with God. They knew that murder was wrong. They knew the Ten Commandments. And they knew the stories of Abraham called to sacrifice Isaac, of Job being tested, and other examples of God seeing if humans would be obedient. They felt that the call to murder was a test, and so they refused.

But God persisted, according to their confessions. God explained that it was God's choice as to how God's wishes were carried out on earth. The men and women hearing God's voice convinced themselves that they were truly meant to be the vessels for God's retribution. After all, God always chooses the most unlikely vessels so that people witnessing an action know it is God's work. Moses was tongue-tied and needed his brother to speak for him. The prophets routinely cried out that they were unfit to bear the word and that God was placing an unfair burden on them. Yet they were obedient, and so are the killers. They murder a stranger, a loved one, or whoever seems appropriate at the time they are convinced that they must act. The threat of jail does not matter because they are right with their Lord.

Although neither act is common, the number of men and women who kill for God is probably equal to the number of people who take a life in the name of Satan. But critics of the media avoid discussing those who imitate the Bible, for they know that holy books cannot be criticized.

The fact that any and all facets of the media can inspire deranged actions combines with the reality of our First Amendment freedoms to make a strong argument against any kind of censorship. This is the argument used by many television and motion picture producers to justify the most dramatic excesses in their storytelling. But the real issue is responsibility.

Each aspect of each medium of communication is aimed toward a specific audience. The Bible, the Koran, and other holy books are almost exclusively read by people seeking a moral and ethical way to live. They understand that the stories of sex, violence, and perversion are presented as lessons from which to learn. Instead of encouraging emulation of the evil, they teach a better way to live, to think, and to grow. Certainly the stories in holy books can be perverted. They are frequently the justification for holy wars and other forms of international violence. But most people read them with a positive attitude.

It is important to note that while all cultures regard their holy books as moral inspiration, not all cultures react to popular media offerings in the same way. For example, in Japan there is a fascination with illustrated novels—stories told in comic book form but usually hardbound and with more-sophisticated, realistic drawings. Such novels are extremely popular in Latin America, but the Japanese, who have long delighted in erotic art without viewing it as sexually prurient, have given a new twist to the illustrated novels. The new books, enormously popular with young and middle-aged women, feature stories in which women are routinely bound, gagged, chained, or otherwise restrained, sometimes with their spouses or lovers, sometimes alone. Then there is a handsome man who rapes them, with or without mild torture. Always the women love it.

Such material would be considered sick perversion in the United States. No legitimate publisher would want to be connected with it. The presumption would be that "decent women" would boycott the material and be outraged if their spouses looked at it. Yet in Japan it is as popular as romance novels are in America. The women who read it say that they do not want to be raped. They understand that the reality of sexual violence is a nightmare no one wishes to experience. Yet when they look at the novels, they find a sexually arousing, extremely appealing fantasy, which they repeat with each new book. One culture's erotica becomes another culture's hard-core pornography.

No one expects American bookstores to start selling Japanese rape-oriented illustrated novels. The idea would be considered reprehensible, even though the material is protected by the First Amendment. The only places it would be sold would be in adult-oriented bookstores and in stores, also selling to adults, that deal with erotic art in all its forms. However, no such standard of restraint is applied by television and motion picture production companies when they plan how they will release their products. It is as though if offensive material is domestically produced, it should be available anywhere, not just in controlled access theaters or on videotapes routinely separated according to targeted audiences.

Motion pictures are meant as escapism for as many people as possible, from illiterate physical laborers to professionals with advanced college degrees. They must appeal in the manner of Shakespeare's plays, which included in their audiences people known as the groundlings. These were individuals who had no education and worked at menial jobs, but had the price of admission. As a result, if you understand Elizabethan English, which sounds so formal and stilted to contemporary Americans, you will find that Shakespeare includes the Elizabethan equivalent of bathroom jokes. Gross sexual humor is quite common, especially in the comedies, such as *A

Midsummer Night's Dream. There is also highly sophisticated language. But both were necessary to appeal to the broadest possible audience.

Today we have the equivalent in explicit sex, wild car-chase scenes, buildings blowing up, and people being hurt in graphic ways. Special effects may make the story seem even more vivid, of course, but the thought is the same. Everyone can relate to bathroom jokes. Not everyone can relate to sophisticated banter. Woody Allen has long been the primary creator of limited-appeal movies, and they do make money. However, if you combine the profits from the box office take for all the Woody Allen films ever created, it will probably be far less than the money earned for a single hit starring Arnold Schwarzenegger, Sylvester Stallone, or Clint Eastwood. Thus, while there is room for the small, thought-provoking film of sophistication, the vast majority of the films are going to be made by people going for the most money.

The tragedy is that if someone is going to be corrupted by graphic sex and violence, it is going to be someone going to a movie theater or watching television. Everyone uses such entertainment. Thus it is critical for the producers to rethink their responsibility in what they produce. They are responsible for negative influences in society and they do need to have better self-censorship.

Violence does not have to be shown as it takes place. It can be shown in the aftermath, the grieving loved ones, the ambulance or life-flight helicopter racing the victim to the hospital, the anger of those who care, and so forth. Likewise it is possible to be aware that a couple has enjoyed sexual intimacy without the camera crawling under the covers with them. The power of the motion picture's story will not be diminished, the artistic integrity uncompromised.

Made-for-video originals have fewer constraints. This is because the vast majority of video stores are acting responsibly. Films of graphic sex and violence, films that seem to glorify perversion, sadism, and masochism, are all available in stores that also may carry Walt Disney's most innocuous animated features for children. Unlike movie theaters, which give a wink and a nod to the ratings system—especially in multiplex cinemas, where frequently, once you have purchased a ticket, you can go into any of the films—video stores segregate their films. They have special sections for each type of picture, and they are all clearly labeled. There are no surprises for the customers. There is no chance for confusion about what a parent or child might be renting. And most employees are willing to stop someone from renting material that is inappropriate for children.

This is no different from the world of magazines. Publications such as *Hustler* are kept separated from *Family Circle*, *Disney Adventure*, and other magazines. There is no censorship of material. It is all available. But the distribution system is such that everyone is acting responsibly. It is only with the motion picture industry and television that there is no thought to the ethics of what they are producing for a mass audience.

What is the answer? First, the public must demand that the owners of area movie theaters always have a range of films for viewing. There is nothing wrong with having an adult feature in the same multiplex as a G-rated movie. But there is a problem when a parent must face a choice of PG-13—a rating that usually means violence and foul language but no sex—R, and NC-17. A movie rated G, or at least PG, must always be available even when it is not first-run. A boycott of a theater that shows only films inappropriate for preteens, coupled with the encouragement of friends and family to use the theater as a source of entertainment when the owner complies with the request, will almost always succeed. In addition, a request should be made to have different tickets for different shows, even if this means printing on consistently different colored paper stock (pink for G, blue for PG, and so forth) so that the ushers can match tickets with movies. This will prevent children from attending inappropriate films being shown within the same multiplex.

Television programming must be rethought. This is a more difficult task, but it is very important. The nature of cable broadcasting is such that parents will have to exercise better judgment and constraint when it comes to pay viewing. But free television, the networks and independent stations shown on VHF and UHF, must police itself. This means that programmers must genuinely reconsider their schedules so that programs that do not have sex and violence are on during the 7 P.M. to 9 P.M. time slot. This includes the quasi-news programs such as *Hard Copy* and *Entertainment Tonight*, which regularly feature material potentially harmful to children in the guise of "news."

Parents can force the change by contacting the sponsors of the shows. Complaints about the programming by adults who have taken the trouble to learn the addresses of the sponsors (found in the standard business reference directories available in most public libraries), then write to them, do get heeded. And be certain to write a letter, not create a computer form, use electronic mail, or fax. Companies feel that people who write letters have thought about what they are doing, are not part of an organized campaign that might have a handful of people sending hundreds of copies electronically, and are serious about wanting change. They are heeded, as is happening at this writing with the television talk shows. Many of these are looking to change their approach because advertisers are rethinking their commitments in light of the mail they are receiving from disgruntled viewers.

It is also important, where possible, to limit a child's access to inappropriate material. This can be difficult in a world where there are many single parents as well as families where both parents must work during periods when their children are home alone. If nothing else, you can begin to make a difference by making full utilization of the public library in your community. There are books, of course, but if you haven't been to the library lately, you will probably be surprised by the volume of multimedia items available. Videotapes, audiocassettes, and CDs are increasingly available. While such material is meant for adults as well as children, and thus may include items that are inappropriate for the very young, children are in the forefront of the librarians' thinking when items are ordered. And because such items can be used for free, there is little financial burden from having appropriate forms of entertainment always available.

It is also critical that you talk with your children concerning why you feel that some shows are inappropriate. Share books with them. Listen to music together. Become involved with their evening and weekend activities as much as possible. This may be a hardship when you are tired and have been working all day, but no matter what ethical issues the media must face, ultimately you have a personal responsibility to your children whenever you are in a position to take it. Even in the throes of adolescent rebellion, children want to know what values their parents have, they want to know limits. They undoubtedly will test those limits, yet even when they do, they are comparing what they are seeing, reading, and hearing with what you have discussed.

In a society as rich with information and entertainment alternatives as the United States has become and is continuing to become, there will always be inappropriate media offerings. Under the best of circumstances, children and young adults will have to make choices. Certainly, you can have some impact on the type of programming that is mass-marketed, but talking about the ethics of the men and women who run the media can be futile. There is more greed than social concern in the majority of corporations, and the most violent, most sexually explicit books, films, and magazines will always be available, and they will always be a matter of public concern.

At the same time, a child who is taught values—who is shown why some things are inappropriate, why they do not reflect life as it is lived, any why they do not reflect the reality of minorities, the elderly, women, and others too often shown in stereotypes—will turn out emotionally and spiritually healthy.

There is no question that the media can be a corrupting force, an uplifting force, or a waste of time, depending on the choices that are made. There is much that can be controlled only by those creating and distributing the product, whether it is news, entertainment, commentary, or something similar. However, there are also instances where the media are able to corrupt because parents abdicate their role as ethical teachers and advisers. The media do not represent an unstoppable, insidious force that must be controlled through censorship and governmental legislation. They simply represent another choice, and among the options are those that can inform, uplift, and entertain in a positive way. We just need to learn this reality for our own lives, then pass the information on to our children. Such action will not be a panacea, but it will better guide them as they face choices with which the adults cannot be involved.

Ethical issues involving the media are clear in many instances, a gray area in others. But neither schools, nor parents, nor purveyors of entertainment product in all its forms can ignore their responsibilities. We cannot expect morality to be legislated. We also cannot expect to see ethical standards established within each medium that will be honored by all parties involved. However, we can change the way we use the media, setting appropriate parameters for our families and teaching a better way to utilize the information explosion through our own example.

What does all this mean? First, the media are diverse. Each medium has its strengths and weaknesses when used to entertain, inform, and communicate. The expectations we bring and the value we can obtain must all be determined by an understanding of those limitations.

Second, the media are comprised of businesses. Most are operated for profit. Those that are nonprofit expect to break even. So long as advertisers—or, in the case of public broadcasting, a combination of public contributors and corporate sponsors—will support a program, it will be aired.

Large sums of money are spent to create most television programs. Even larger sums are spent to create motion pictures. In order to earn that money back, films are planned to ensure that the greatest possible number of people will want to view the work. Since audiences are ever changing and movies are most popular with young adults, adding a little shock value—graphic sex, graphic violence—is an easy way to ensure viewers. The pictures will not be memorable. They probably will have a fairly brief history even in rental. But they will draw enough of an audience to make a profit. Television programming is the same, especially in the early evening hours. There is little incentive to vary the content from whatever works, regardless of quality.

The few changes that are planned are not meaningful responses. First there is the development of the "V-chip," a computer chip to be installed in television sets so that parents can use a device to lock out an offensive program. A child will not be able to watch a particular station at a particular hour if a violent program is being shown. There is also a rating system much like that used by the motion picture industry. This will forewarn parents concerning the type of program and its suitability for different ages.

The problem with all this is that it is unrealistic as a cure. Television news shows will not be rated, nor will a V-chip be used. Yet consider that during ratings periods, most newscasts run special features on such important segments of the community as young women who work in strip clubs and massage parlors. Or they show the local SWAT team in action. And without pandering, there is the real-world violence and suffering of countries at war. Snipers in Bosnia killing children, the elderly, and others. Rape as an act of war. Armies assaulting one another. All of these are a part of our present and our future history as a people. They all have a legitimate place, yet may be unsuitable for children.

There is also the question of what will be rated. Violence is appropriate in a film such as *Schindler's List* because the story is about Nazi excesses and a man who saved people from those sufferings. Violence is inappropriate in a rerun of a Rambo movie because violence is the focus for the film.

More importantly, if television follows the rating system of the film industry, there will be serious questions about what is deemed appropriate. A movie is more likely to receive a rating that strongly limits the audience if it shows a married couple getting into the same bed and kissing before the camera cuts away than it is if it shows two people beating each other to a bloody pulp. And the beating is more acceptable if the good guy wins. Ratings favor violence over love, though they still favor love over graphic sex. Although the "experts" say that the V-chip and the rating system will embarrass the networks and production companies into changing their ways, it certainly has not happened with the film industry. It also does not absolve parents from needing to find alternatives.

Another reality is that there is a very low standard of morality among many of the industry leaders in Hollywood. Affairs are so common that one executive at ABC was fired because he was unfaithful to the woman who loved him. The woman was not his wife—he was expected to cheat on her! In fact, at one point he was in charge of a popular television show that regularly gave walk-on and small speaking parts to beautiful women who provided background "scenery" for the story. The women who were cast in these roles changed each week. They were paid well compared with other work they were doing at the time—usually waitressing while going to auditions. And they were highly visible, albeit briefly, usually dressed in bikinis or form-fitting gowns. Thus most of them willingly went to bed with the man in exchange for the part. Yet none of this troubled the man's employers. But he took a mistress when he already had one of long duration. He lost his job for cheating on that first mistress.

The story, while it has an odd twist, is repeated daily. The desire for power leads many studios to steal from writers, a situation that was exemplified by humorist Art Buchwald, whose idea for a screenplay was proven in court to have been stolen by a major studio and a well-known comedian. In the East, Buchwald is a high-profile, well-connected, well-paid, frequently feted political satirist. In Hollywood, he was a lamb ready for fleecing, only his high income enabling him to get an attorney skilled enough to help him prove his case.

Newspaper reporters are so eager for a scoop that many will produce a story before all the facts are in. They claim the problem is deadline pressure, but often the truth is that they know today's headlines, even if wrong, have an impact, and so long as they issue a correction tomorrow, their careers will not be endangered.

Many of the users of the Internet and other online services are so devoted to free speech that they fight any ethical standards calling for limiting the type of language, graphics, and other material made available. They violate copyright laws through their dissemination of protected material. And some put out material deliberately to shock others, just because they know they can get away with it, like an adolescent using a can of spray paint against the wall in a dark alley.

Should there be changes in the law to counter some of the problems? The idea of tampering with the First Amendment is much too dangerous, as has been proven in every country that has had laws regulating the press. In Germany, for example, a young leader named Adolf Hitler helped restore the nation's economy after it was shattered following World War I. Prior to his coming to power, runaway inflation was so bad that at one point it took a wheelbarrow filled with German paper money to buy a single loaf of bread. Likewise, though Germany had been disarmed, he convinced the other European countries that Germans should be allowed to hold defensive weapons. It was not full rearmament, but the people felt a sense of self-respect they had lost when they lost the war.

Are you happy with the government? Hitler asked. Is there anything you wish to criticize? And in the euphoria of the post–World War I changes, the people told him they were delighted. Jews and Gentiles, Aryans, Gypsies, and all the others who were living there approved the changes.

In that case, if there are no objections, I will make it against the law for any newspaper to criticize the government, he told them. Laughing at the absurdity of the idea that such a change could matter, the people agreed. No matter what the government did, no matter to what illegal excesses any of Hitler's followers would go, there was no way to report it. What should have been national news and a warning of horrors to come was relegated to whispered gossip in the communities where it was happening.

Hitler is an extreme example, but all censorship is a problem. America Online, in an effort to end sexually explicit chat rooms, banned the word "breast" from use. Before the ruling was reversed, this meant that a bulletin board and chat room devoted to women helping other women and their spouses or lovers deal with breast cancer had to be ended. Yet the information and support were often critical for the women, the censorship affecting not only pornography but serious medical concerns.

And what should be censored? There are religious groups that feel they have the "one, true understanding" of God. They consider approaches other than their own misguided at best, blasphemous at worst. Each would want to censor others, whether their thinking is mainstream or on the fringe.

A study of family oriented video rental stores that have an adults-only section of soft-core, X-rated videos has determined that the major renters of X-rated videos are married Catholic couples.

In other studies of human sexuality it has been found that Catholic couples also have sex with greater frequency than members of other religious groups. Presumably some Catholic couples are using the X-rated videos as foreplay or to jump-start their sex lives. They are monogamous. They are consenting adults. Should they be denied such material if they want it?

Another concern is with newspaper reporters who lie, write in a biased manner, or are so incompetent that they fail to produce a factual story. There have been occasional efforts to license reporters, to try to make them meet standards of education and proficiency, perhaps having them take some sort of oath along the lines of the Hippocratic oath taken by doctors. The trouble is that the skills needed to be a journalist are often found in people who are outside the mainstream. They have to be curious about everything and everyone, determined to learn everything they can about a subject, cynical enough to see if there are more sides to a story than the obvious, intelligent enough to comprehend what they are experiencing, and skilled enough to communicate it effectively. Many of these traits cannot be taught in college, and most journalists find college of less value than working in the field when it comes to getting an education. In fact, it is not unusual for someone with a high-school education and extensive freelance experience with national magazines to be hired by a major newspaper over someone with top grades who graduated from a college journalism program. And an oath is only as good as the integrity of the individual taking it.

What can be done is to penalize each specific medium broadcasting or printing material that is inaccurate or knowingly one-sided. This would go beyond the present libel laws, which penalize someone for deliberately printing or broadcasting a statement about someone that he or she knows or could have easily learned was not true. It would affect publishers who use their newspapers to run false reports on real estate development issues that affect the community but in which the publisher or the publisher's friends have a financial stake. It would affect editors who encourage biased reporting of news so that the crime rate in one community is stressed and an equally bad crime rate in a more desirable community (e.g., one providing the paper with advertising revenue) is downplayed.

Yet the tragic reality is that ultimately each person must make an effort to separate fact from fiction, to flesh out incomplete reporting, to complain about programs that are offensive and encourage those they find of value. The more we limit our access to news and information—either by staying with too few publications and/or special interest broadcasts or by not questioning what we read, hear, and view—the less we can be certain we know. The more we let children determine how they will use the media, the more likely they are to be influenced by misleading advertising, violent action, foul language, and reprehensible topics.

The more we look upon a reporter, anchor, or medium of communication as a "god" to be believed at all costs, the more dangerously lacking we become. A degree of skepticism coupled with a desire to learn more from additional sources is important. There is no great national conspiracy by the media, as is sometimes alleged by paranoid extremist groups. But there is incompetence, laziness, self-centeredness, bias, and bigotry, usually unnoticed by the person(s) who have these traits. And if such persons are popular enough with the public or their bosses have the same characteristics, they can color what we experience.

Finally, there is the fact that we do get what we desire from the media. If a show is offensive, turn it off and write letters of complaint to the networks, the station, the producer, and the advertisers. If you enjoy something, praise it in writing. And if you find yourself drawn occasionally to the deliberately titillating, don't mask this human trait by complaining about the very thing you enjoy.

When there is misrepresentation of facts or avoidance of certain types of stories by members of the news media, you cannot be certain of the truth. But explicit violence, sex, disrespect for others, religious extremism, and the like cannot be disguised. Shows stay on the air and movies receive large box office grosses only by pleasing a massive number of people, including yourself. In a free society, anyone may print or broadcast anything he or she desires, though there may be penalties after the fact, such as with child pornography, libel, and extortion. But likewise in a free society, no one is forcing you to choose one medium of entertainment over another, one broadcast channel or movie over another. You can force more ethical standards in the media in part by what you let your dollars and listening/viewing/reading time support.

You cannot legislate morality, but you can be a more discerning user of the media, eliminating what is ethically wrong by the choices you make. Motion picture producers, television producers, radio program directors, Internet users, book, magazine, and newspaper publishers are not going to suddenly adopt a working code of ethics. But you can create an environment by the entertainment/information/news choices you make and the products you buy in which higher ethics becomes the only recourse of members of the media.

Notes

1. 2 Samuel 11:1–26, 13:1–33.

2. Because this book is not meant to provide a theological analysis of the Bible, the issue of whether or not the Bible is the divine work of God will not be discussed. It is clear that the Bible can be contradictory at times. (See, for example, Genesis 1:27–28 and Genesis 2:7–25. As with many other Bible stories, mixed messages are often taken out of context according to the bias of the reader. For example, everyone reading this book knows the story of Jesus' birth, and yet a reading of Matthew is radically different from the birth story of Luke, and Mark was so unimpressed with Jesus' birth that he omitted the story entirely.) If the Bible is looked upon as divinely inspired, the human errors and contradictions make sense. It would also seem logical that the inspiration would not end with a book that was first assembled at the end of the first century following the birth of Jesus. Thus other media presentations, perhaps including one or more films, documentaries, or television specials, could represent the word of God as expressed through the words and works of human beings.

3. Ben Bradlee, *A Good Life: Newspapering and Other Adventures* (New York: Simon & Schuster, 1995).

4. Ernest Angley, *Faith in God Heals the Sick* (Akron, Ohio: Winston Press, 1983), 62–63.

5. Ibid., 62.

6. It is important to note that this chapter is not meant either to support or to criticize faith healing. Some doctors have discussed spontaneous healings. Some attribute such healings to God, whereas others say that they simply show how far we need to go to fully understand the nature of illness. But the fact that spontaneous healings can and do occur, sometimes after prayer, or the laying on of hands, is not questioned.

The July 1988 issue of the *Southern Medical Journal*, the publication of the Alabama-based Southern Medical Association, published a paper by San Francisco physician Randolph C. Byrd, M.D. This paper, reporting on a ten-month study of 393 patients in a coronary care unit, was titled "Positive Therapeutic Effects of Intercessory Prayer in a Coronary Care Unit Population." All the patients had similar health problems, and they were randomly divided into two groups, one of 192 patients and the other of 201 patients. The larger of the two groups was considered the control group, with no one known to be praying for them.

The study was carefully planned. A computer randomly selected the members of the two groups, and although Dr. Byrd and his staff knew the numbers, they did not know the names.

Next, people were selected to pray for the 192 patients in the experimental group. These intercessors had to meet strict criteria:

> They were "born again" Christians with an active Christian life as manifested by daily devotional prayer and active Christian membership with a local church. Members of several Protestant churches and the Roman Catholic Church were represented among the intercessors. Patients and intercessors were not matched by religion or denomination. After randomization, each patient was assigned to three to seven intercessors. The patient's first name, diagnosis, and general condition were given to the intercessors. The intercessory prayer was done outside the hospital daily until the patient was discharged from the hospital. Under the direction of a coordinator, each intercessor was asked to pray daily for a rapid recovery and for prevention of complications and death, in addition to other areas of prayer they believed to be beneficial to the patient.

Dr. Byrd said, "It was assumed that some of the patients in both groups would be prayed for by people not associated with the study; this was not controlled for. Thus some of the patients in the control group would be prayed for, whereas all of the patients in the prayer group would be (i.e., by both nonassociated people and by the designated intercessors of the study)."

Dr. Byrd also explained: "Several points concerning the present study should be mentioned. First, prayer by and for the control group (by persons not in conjunction with this study) could not be accounted for. Nor was there any attempt to limit prayer among the controls. Such action would certainly be unethical and probably impossible to achieve. Therefore, 'pure' groups were not attained in this study—all of one group and part of the other had access to the intervention under study. They may have resulted in smaller differences observed between the two groups. How God acted in this situation is unknown; i.e., were the groups treated by God as a whole or were individual prayers alone answered? Second, whether patients prayed for themselves and to what degree they held religious convictions was not determined. Because many of the patients were seriously ill, it was not possible to obtain an interview extensive enough to answer these two questions. Furthermore, it was thought that discussions concerning the patients' relationship to God might be emotionally disturbing to a significant number of patients at the time of admission to the coronary care unit, though it was generally noted that almost all patients in the study expressed the belief that prayer probably helped and certainly could not hurt."

The results of the study were dramatic. The patients being prayed for healed much faster than those who did not receive prayer. All the patients had the same prognosis at the start. All the patients were expected to recover in about the same time and in about the same way. Thus the finding of radical differences in the speed of healing seems to have been related to the prayers.

Since that time, other studies have been done, with similar results. Thus there is no question that faith healing occurs in some form. The issue is the person who uses religious television programming to solicit contributions to support the programming.

7. The interview with Christine Lee was originally conducted for, and appeared in, my book *When the Devil Comes to Visit* (London: Arrow Books Division of Random House, U.K, Ltd., 1995).

8. The *National Enquirer* should not be confused with other supermarket tabloids, though it is often used by the public as a generic symbol for the worst excesses in this field. Ironically, the publisher also owns the *Weekly World News*, which is primarily a fantasy paper. The latter publication told the story of Elvis Presley, alive, well, and re-

cently married. It showed that John Kennedy had never died but was in a nursing home, where he was photographed with a camera equipped with an extremely long-range telephoto lens. And it followed the story of the space aliens (complete with pictures) who met with then President George Bush at Camp David. Later the aliens apparently decided to support the Democrats, because they were shown with Bill Clinton, and a subsequent story told how they had given Clinton a ride in their spaceship so he could get a unique perspective of Washington.

The *National Enquirer* was once a fantasy tabloid that reported such stories as that of a baby being born with an ax in his hand and killing its mother after the birth. It was a fantasy freak show before being changed into its present form—a publication that features celebrity news, gossip (frequently planted by the star or the star's publicist), and features concerning health, consumer news, and other family-oriented topics. The features are not unlike many that run in more respected papers such as *USA Today*.

I have frequently been told by book publishers to look to the *National Enquirer* for topics that might warrant a book-length study. They explained that the readers of the *Enquirer* are avid book buyers. Mostly women, they encounter this periodical at the worst possible time, when they have shopping carts loaded with groceries, and paying for these purchases will wipe out almost all the money in their purses. Still they pick up the tabloid because they are readers, not television addicts. I have successfully followed this reasoning over the years, and I have also found that, with only one exception, every book I have written, coauthored, or "ghosted" that became a best-seller was excerpted in the *National Enquirer*. Only Phil Donahue's show was ever able to match this image, although the *Oprah Winfrey* show came close prior to the explosion of talk show competition.

9. The interviews with the Barr family were originally conducted for the book *My Sister Roseanne*, by Geraldine Barr with Ted Schwarz (New York: Birch Lane Press, 1994).

10. I am one of the pioneering writers in the field of extreme hysteric dissociation, commonly called multiple personality disorder. I have coauthored such works as *Minds in Many Pieces: The Making of a Very Special Doctor* (with Ralph Allison, M.D.), *The Five of Me* (with

Henry Hawksworth), and *Tell Me Who I Am before I Die* (with Christina Peters). Although a lay expert, not a professional, I was asked to present a paper on post-integration hysteric dissociation to the Second Pacific Congress on Psychiatry in Manila, the Philippines. My questioning of Roseanne's statements was confirmed by experts in the field, including the pioneering Dr. Ralph Allison. Although none could rule out the truth of what she claimed, they all stated that the details did not seem to be what one would expect for a well-understood problem. And though Roseanne never revealed the name of her doctor, reports indicated that, if she was being treated for the problem, it was by a doctor who had been trained in part by Dr. Allison and who would never have made the statements Roseanne claimed he made concerning her treatment and prognosis.

11. Roseanne Arnold, *My Lives* (New York: Ballantine Books, 1994), 177.

12. From *Sally Jessy Raphael*, Transcript #872 (R-#808), for the program aired January 8, 1992.

13. I conducted interviews with Roseanne's youngest sister when I was working on Geraldine's book. She was not happy with my mentioning her name in that volume, though she understood Geraldine's need for her involvement. Because she did not agree to go on record for this book, I have chosen not to mention her name or where she is living.

14. Excerpt from an interview conducted with Mr. Barr by the author for *My Sister Roseanne*.

15. The incident involving the mental institution did occur. Her family feels that her attitude toward it was another aspect of what Geraldine calls Roseanne's "drama queen" personality. When Roseanne was interviewed for the February 1994 cover story of *Vanity Fair*, she allegedly told writer Kevin Sessums that "her parents . . . put her away for almost a year in a state hospital. To this day she refuses to go into details about her life there."

That alleged refusal, one that had been made public and was readily verifiable by any of the talk show staff members who might have cared about accuracy, balance, and fairness, was nonsense. In her first book, *My Life as a Woman*, a 1990 *New York Times* best-seller for four months, which eventually sold approximately 425,000 copies, she spent ten pages talking about being in the hospital in Provo, Utah. It was also in that book that Roseanne admitted she had lied about being a drug addict in order to join other addicted teens who went to area schools to discuss their problems. She just wanted to get out of the hospital and considered the experience an early evidence of her theatrical nature.

But the important point is that she was not "trapped" in the mental institution. Her parents were against her going, and her father made weekly trips (150 miles of driving) to bring Roseanne home for the weekends. More important, given the nature of her circumstances, she had to admit herself to the hospital and could check herself out whenever she desired. She was not somehow held against her will or at the request of her family.

16. Report provided by the Barrs to the author for *My Sister Roseanne*.

17. Attorney Melvin Belli has been quoted several times as saying that he advised the Barrs not to sue their daughter. The issue was not whether they would win or lose the lawsuit. He apparently was confident that they would be successful. The issue was reconciliation, for he was convinced that if there was any chance for reconciliation, it would be destroyed by such an action.

18. It is not unusual for talk show guests to take such an approach. By criticizing sleazy television, tabloid television, those "other" shows, or using images to that effect, they raise the image of the show on which they are appearing. And since neither the studio audience nor the viewing audience wants to admit to being associated with sleazy programming, their decision to attend or watch that show is reinforced. Yet the fact is that Roseanne, by referring to the other shows as "jive," was working the media in the same manner she accused her parents of doing.

19. From *Sally Jessy Raphael*, Transcript #872 (R-#808), for the program aired January 8, 1992.

20. The full story of the Thorpe appearance was first reported in Tom O'Neill's article "Welcome to the Jungle," which appeared in the February 1994 issue of *US* magazine, pp. 78–81 and 90–91. Other details can be found in *Tuning In Trouble*, by Jeanne Albronda Heaton and Nona Leigh Wilson (San Francisco: Jossey-Bass, 1995).

21. Excerpt from telephone interview conducted by author for this book. The interviewee asked not to be identified.

22. Almost immediately after the rape allegations, I was one of a number of people invited to appear on *Sally Jessy Raphael*. I was in the process of writing a book on the third generation of the Kennedys, a generation that included William Kennedy Smith. I was collaborating with Barbara Gibson, the woman who had been Rose Kennedy's assistant for the decade that preceded Mrs. Kennedy's debilitating stroke. The booker wanted us both, knowing that Barbara was the expert and I was the writer making commercial sense of the story. But the booker did not realize that Barbara had previously been exposed to the media both extensively and successfully. I was asked to appear on the off chance that if the show dragged, I could add something from my research, and because of my media experience, I could be expected to talk as extensively or as briefly as the time required.

Cassone dressed in shorts and a fairly form-fitting top. Someone apparently not connected with the show arranged for newspeople to be present to interview her before the program. They were not alerted to the fact that a representative of Patty Bowman was present, as was Barbara.

23. This and subsequent quotes from Dr. McGrath are from phone interviews conducted by the author on July 6 and July 12, 1995.

24. *Journal of Popular Culture* 28, no. 1 (1994).

25. Quotations and sales information concerning Those Characters From Cleveland are from material supplied by Derrill Dalby, Director of Licensing for the corporation. As explained in their promotions:

> In a world where licensing is commonplace, Those Characters From Cleveland is unique. With a history of creating record-setting programs such as Holly Hobbie, Strawberry Shortcake, Care Bears and Popples, the Cleveland-headquartered company continues to take a leading role in an industry it helped pioneer. With a substantial full-time staff, coupled with the talents of many freelance artists and the creative resources of its parent company, American Greetings, TCFC has grown to be the largest and most broadly based company dedicated exclusively to creating, developing and marketing licensed brand and character programs.

The literature adds that "behind the worldwide success of toys and related brand products lies an inherent consumer appeal that's built into the products right from the start. This is accomplished by building *play value* [emphasis in the original] into the products and giving the brand or character family a real reason for being. These qualities are so apparent that the parent and child can see the same benefits."

The company explains to potential customers that "Strawberry Shortcake was developed out of research that showed strawberries to be a popular design motif with women. TCFC took that insight and created licensing history with its creation of the first full-character program. Teddy bears have been a traditional children's favorite, but not until TCFC created Care Bears did teddy bears come in colors (pastels), each with a personality of its own and with the capacity to help children better understand their own feelings. And Popples, another successful concept, gave children a chance for the first time to do more with the always-popular plush toys than just squeeze them or put them on a bed."

26. The information concerning Time Warner was developed through an analysis of the events described and interviews with present and former staff members. Representatives of *Time* magazine, Little, Brown publishing, and other corporate and division executives refused to be quoted. Most denied requests for interviews because, as the company was also under fire for the lyrics of some of the songs its music division was releasing, talking on or off the record was something many top personnel were refusing to do.

27. It is important to note that there are critics of author appearances on any show because such appearances are arranged by the publicity departments of the book companies. The author's work may be genuine news, such as a politician's memoirs about an important event in history that he or she alone knows intimately, they may be celebrity gossip of a type that is of strong public interest, or they may simply be amusing, making the host look good.

Over the years I have made approximately 250 media appearances promoting my books. Always the goal is to entertain the viewing and listening audience while helping the star of the show, who seldom has read the book, look knowledgeable.

Is there an ethical issue here? That depends on the show, and if there is an ethical problem, it is usually with the author. For example, when I spent three weeks appearing on shows to promote my book *The Hillside Strangler*, the hosts either had read the book or let me tell the story. One of the issues that arose was children in crisis and the need for adults to intervene in their lives. This was a serious concern, separate from the murders, and had a strong impact in some communities. I was later told that the information had helped both church groups and social organizations better focus on home intervention on behalf of children in crisis. The situation even affected my own life, because a dozen years later, in part because I had kept reminding myself of what I had learned, my wife and I adopted the first of our four children. All came from physically and/or emotionally abusive environments.

By contrast, the most blatant example of playing the game occurred during promotion of my book *Satanism: Is Your Family Safe?* Despite the rather extreme title, the book was actually a reasoned account of why some people choose to worship evil. It was considered the most objective book on the subject by some of the major booksellers, and the stories were carefully researched. Still, the title made it exploitive, which is the reason the publisher chose it.

I was scheduled to be interviewed on Pat Robertson's show, *The 700 Club*. At first the interview was to be conducted by the female co-host, a former British rock singer. She read the book the night before the interview and was prepared to discuss its specifics.

On the day of the interview, according to the staff member who briefed me on what to expect, it was decided that I would talk with Pat Robertson himself. He was making a move into the political arena, looking to a possible run for the presidency. He was trying to solidify support from the Christian right wing of the Republican Party, and denouncing Satanism was a good way to boost his popularity. This apparently was why he chose to interview me at the last minute without having any idea what my book was about.

As I sat next to Robertson on the set, he rarely looked at me, instead focusing his eyes on the camera so that he would be looking at the viewers. Then he asked several very general questions, the answers to some of which would have made him look like a fool had I responded with the thoroughness he would have liked. Instead of showing him to be unprepared and naive, as I felt him to be, I worked with him, making him look good for the viewing audience.

Thus the show was not an honest one. Did Pat Robertson act unethically? Perhaps. Did I? Most certainly. I had a book to sell and that was my overriding concern at the moment, probably a not uncommon attitude among writers who are promoting their books.

28. *Ms.*, July/August 1990, 19.

29. This and subsequent quotations from Gail Featheringham and Peter Harter are from a telephone interview conducted by the author on June 23, 1995.

30. As I mention later, a study of video stores offering a selection of adult material along with the broad range of family entertainment reports that married Catholic couples are most likely to rent their X-rated material. These are also likely to have the most frequent sex, according to their response to surveys, the average couple within the studies having sex a minimum of 2.2 times per week. How accurate the studies might be is always subject to question. However, it is certain by the number of cable sex channel renewals versus sensually oriented video rentals (soft-core vs. hard-core, as the industry would describe such material) that the preferred source for X-rated material is video. It is cheaper, allows choice to be made based on the mood of the moment, and is readily obtainable in the form most people desire who use such material for entertainment or sensual stimulation.

31. This and subsequent quotations from Dr. John Kappas are from interviews conducted by the author for *Satanism: Is Your Family Safe?*, by Ted Schwarz with Duane Empey (Grand Rapids, Mich.: Zondervan, 1988).

32. This quotation is from an interview conducted by the author.

33. The connection has not been positively made. One of the perpetrators may *not* have seen the movie. At this writing, the other person's knowledge is unknown. If he definitely saw the picture, the fears are reinforced. If he did not, there are still questions about what seeing such violence might trigger in someone else. And as for "art," how graphic does a scene have to be to get a point across? Often what is not shown can be more dramatic than what is shown.

Index

DATE DUE

DEC 17 1998	
DEC 16 1999	
APR 30 2002	